CRUSADER
FOR
JUSTICE

WAYNE STATE UNIVERSITY PRESS *Detroit, Michigan*

CRUSADER FOR JUSTICE

FEDERAL JUDGE
DAMON J. KEITH

Compiled, written, and edited
by PETER J. HAMMER
and TREVOR W. COLEMAN
Foreword by MITCH ALBOM

18   17   16   15   14   6   5   4   3   2

Library of Congress Control Number: 2013948123
ISBN: 978-0-8143-3845-2 (jacketed cloth);
ISBN: 978-0-8143-3846-9 (ebook)

∞

Assistance provided by the Detroit Metropolitan Bar Foundation
and the Detroit Metropolitan Bar Foundation Book Committee.

Designed and typeset by Charlie Sharp, Sharp Des!gns, Lansing, MI
Composed in Monotype Bell

Rarely do you find someone who has no parallel. Such a person was my wife of fifty-three years, Dr. Rachel Boone Keith.

Her unique blend of beauty, brilliance, goodness, and a servant's heart put her in a class by herself. Without her support, I would not be a federal judge today. And without her love, I would not have known happiness all of our years together.

The proverbs speak of the blessing I found in Rachel:

"A wife of noble character who can find? She is worth far more than rubies. Her husband has full confidence in her and lacks nothing of value. She brings him good, not harm, all the days of her life (Proverbs 31:10–12).

"Charm is deceptive, and beauty is fleeting; but a woman who fears the Lord is to be praised. Honor her for all that her hands have done, and let her works bring her praise at the city gate" (Proverbs 31: 30–31).

By dedicating this book to my precious bride, I hope to give her the credit, recognition, and love reward she richly deserves.

Damon J. Keith

J udge Damon J. Keith is a giant. Every chapter of his life—as an active citizen, a prominent lawyer, a celebrated judge, a profound thinker, and a bold leader— is an eloquent testament to his passion for equality and for his willingness to commit that passion to action. Always a fierce and courageous advocate for civil rights, Judge Keith built a legacy as a fair and tenacious jurist unwilling to compromise on our country's most precious ideal—liberty and justice for *all* people. Through great courage and tireless effort, he helped turn the principles embodied in our Declaration of Independence into a reality, and for that we are forever in his debt. This book brings to life the story of this man, whom we are honored to call an alumnus of Wayne State University.

ALLAN D. GILMOUR

Former President, Wayne State University

CONTENTS

FOREWORD

The first time I met Damon Keith, he was waiting by the doors of the Theodore Levin U.S. Courthouse, peering out through the glass like a grandfather waiting for the kids' station wagon to pull up. He was by himself. No interns. No clerks. He shook my hand and escorted me though the lobby, making small talk, laughing at my jokes. You would never have known who he was, what he'd accomplished—the sheer *largesse* of this eighty-nine-year-old, white-haired judge—unless perhaps, just before the elevator door closed, you caught his name on a plaque on the wall, commemorating the Bill of Rights.

As if we all have one of those.

Rudyard Kipling once celebrated a man's ability to "walk with kings, nor lose the common touch." It is Damon Keith's special gift. He has walked with the best and brightest—presidents, prime ministers, Supreme Court justices, titans of industry—but his shoes have never lost the soil of his poor and humbler upbringing.

He will wait for you in the lobby.

And then lead you into chambers that are a virtual law history of the second half of the twentieth century.

•   •   •

In Greek mythology, Damon is a loyal friend to Pythias. When Pythias is sentenced to die, he is given time to get his affairs in order—but only because Damon vows to sit in prison, holding his place. If Pythias doesn't return, Damon will die instead.

That's a big dice roll. But Damon waited. And in the end, Pythias returned—just as Damon knew he would. The king was so impressed by their friendship, he spared them both.

Well, Damon Keith isn't quite as old as his Greek namesake. But they do share a certain trait: fierce patience. An unshakable belief that what is right will prevail, no matter how many voices whisper, "It will never come."

Just as the mythological Damon waited on his friend, the real life Damon waited on the world to get right. Fierce patience. He endured a segregated society, racial slurs, the cruelty of lowered expectations. He wasn't allowed to be part of certain high school teams, attend school dances, or join clubs—all because of the color of his skin. He had to change trains to sit in the "colored" compartment on his way to college. He fought for his country in a segregated army. He mopped floors in the *Detroit News* bathrooms while studying for the bar exam.

Fierce patience. Damon Keith endured. He would not let the words "born into" be equated with "dies unchanged."

•   •   •

His accomplishments in our judicial system would take all day to list— and the pages of this book will chronicle them beautifully—but suffice it to say when people needed a champion, he was there, when principle

needed a champion, he was there, when the rights of free society clashed with the power lust of certain politicians, he was there.

And when his hometown needed help, he was there. Detroit was desperate for calm and reason after the turmoil of the late '60s, so Judge Keith opened his home on Thanksgiving for an unusual turkey summit of leaders, black and white. He built a coalition. He made the best peace.

He never let ego rule him. Nor anger. Not even when, shortly after being appointed by the president to the Commission on the Bicentennial of the United States Constitution, he was mistaken for a hotel porter, called "boy," and told to go park a car.

He could have let rage take over. He did not. He lived—and lives—by the oft-quoted line, "The higher you build your barrier, the taller I become."

Fierce patience.

• • •

Have you ever seen the walls of Judge Keith's office? They are like a memorabilia shop of the twentieth century. You could take all the famous delis in New York City and still not have as many photos on the walls as he has on his. Presidents, world leaders, celebrities, athletes. The last time I was in there, I thought about sneaking my photo up, so I wouldn't be the only person on earth *not* hanging on his hooks.

But those people are there for a reason. They are proud to know this man. They are proud to be his friend. That tells you something. He has wonderful children and grandchildren. And—as you will learn in the coming pages—he had the greatest blessing a man could ask for in life, a loving wife whom he adored from the moment he met her in a lab at Detroit Receiving Hospital. He was not going in for a procedure, but he might as well have had a transplant—because the second he laid eyes on Rachel Boone, he was sharing his heart with another soul.

By the way, it is worth noting that Damon and Rachel's first date was a Detroit Lions game at which Damon refused to cheer for the home team because they didn't have any black players. For the next sixty years, there were many other reasons not to cheer for the Lions, most of them having to do with the score.

But live long enough and look at where we are: Damon Keith, once told a black man could never be a lawyer, is now one of the most respected judges in America—with a beautiful new civil rights center named after him—and the Lions made the playoffs last season.

I don't know which is more stunning progress.

I do know this. The Greek Damon was loyal to something special—friendship. This Damon has been loyal to something equally special—human rights, civil rights, justice. He defined these things, he stood up for them, he ruled on them, and ultimately helped shape them.

"Is life fair?" he once told me. "No. And yet I am in the fairness business. If you have the power to make it fair, you should do it."

He has done it again and again, with grace, intelligence, thoughtfulness, and courage. His opinions were not always popular—particularly one famous ruling during the Nixon administration. But they have stood the test of time. That's the true barometer of justice, isn't it?

•　　•　　•

There's an old proverb in which a dying man asks an angel to show him heaven and hell. First the angel takes him down. He shows him a long banquet table. It is filled with the finest meats, cheeses, desserts—but all the people have their arms locked out in front of them, unable to move or to ever partake of the bounty.

"This is tragic," the man tells the angel. "Please, show me heaven." The angel takes him up to another place. It looks remarkably like the first one, an endless banquet table, filled with the most exquisite food.

And all around, the people sitting with their arms locked out in front of them.

The only difference is, in heaven, they are feeding the person across from them.

You inherit the world you are born into. And you can do nothing, or you can give, feed, and nourish those around you. Damon Keith was born into a country that treated his grandparents as slaves, but he will not die in a country like that. He has helped shape it, helped change it, helped make it more fair. He has reached across the table and fed the legacy of our society.

He has lived up to his Greek namesake, clinging to what he knew to be true, waiting—with fierce patience—for what he knew had to come, because it was too strong a feeling in his heart not to be real.

Pythias proved that Damon was not wrong to trust in the best part of us, and time has shown that Damon Keith was not wrong to trust in the best part of himself, the part that saw justice, humanity, and equal rights as friends of mankind.

It is a special thrill to have a man of such accomplishment standing at a glass door, waiting for your arrival—but he would do this for anyone, really. Give you a hug. Show you around.

He stands before you now, in the pages of this book, ready to do so again, open and candid and funny and so significant, a cohort to kings who has never lost the common touch. Such an honor, this is, to introduce him on paper. His story, like the man himself, will transport you.

MITCH ALBOM
Author of Tuesdays with Morrie

A CRUSADER
FOR JUSTICE

U pon conferring an honorary doctor of laws to Judge Damon J.
Keith in 1981, Yale University president A. Bartlett Giamatti
said: "In your long career as a civic leader, lawyer, and judge in your
beloved Detroit, you have come to stand not only for the rule of law but
for common sense in its application. You were a pioneer in fashioning
the central role of the courts in ensuring equal justice, and you had the
courage to face and resolve as a judge the most divisive issues of our
time. You have championed the causes of Black Americans, of working
people, of dissenters, and the poor."

• • •

Damon J. Keith may be the greatest American jurist never to have sat
on the Supreme Court, and certainly the staunchest on behalf of civil
rights for all and on government conducted in the open, to be seen by all.

From one landmark case to another over the last forty-plus years,
Judge Keith has exhibited rare judicial courage.

In *Davis v. School District of City of Pontiac* (1970) Keith was the first judge to address racial segregation in the North and to apply remedies so all children had access to quality education. He did so in the face of public outcry from many white parents, threats against his life, and sabotage of school buses by the Ku Klux Klan.

In *Garrett v. City of Hamtramck* (1971), Keith identified as *negro removal* what city officials had touted as *urban renewal*—a benign term used in the name of discriminatory practices that forced many black people from their homes.

In *United States v. U.S. District Court* (also 1971) Keith found himself in the middle of a case filed by the government on behalf of then-president Richard Nixon. The Nixon administration had been conducting wiretaps on American citizens without court approval. Keith ruled that the Fourth Amendment required that even the president must obtain a judicial warrant before engaging in wiretapping. The Supreme Court ultimately upheld his decision, 8-0. The case has gone down in history—and is taught in law schools—as "The Keith Case."

And in *Detroit Free Press v. Ashcroft*, Keith once again defied a president, when, after the terrorist attacks of September 11, 2001, President George W. Bush's Justice Department sought to close deportation hearings to the public and the press. Keith disagreed and claimed the government's actions were unconstitutional. His opinion offered the now oft-quoted sentence: "Democracies die behind closed doors."

A grandson of slaves, Damon J. Keith, born on the Fourth of July, has spent decades upholding the U.S. Constitution, defending civil rights, and crusading for justice. His career has inspired countless lawyers, judges, and lovers of freedom, and inspired these words from Attorney General Eric Holder: "Time and again, he has proven his allegiance to the most sacred principles of the American justice system as well as his unwavering commitment to the four words etched upon the building where the highest court convenes: 'Equal Justice Under Law.'"

Acknowledgments

A s in most things in life, this book is not the result of the efforts
of a single hand. The writing, editing, and compiling of this
book has been a labor of love by a large number of people. Special
thanks should go to Mitch Albom, who authored the foreword, but
whose spirit, wisdom, and inspiration have helped shape every aspect
of the project.

The support of major institutions has also been critical. Gratitude
is owed the Detroit Metropolitan Bar Foundation and the members
of the Detroit Metropolitan Bar Foundation Book Committee: the
Honorable Eric L. Clay, Professor Spencer Overton, Alex L. Parrish,
and Gary Spicer; as well as Wayne State University (including its
former presidents Irvin D. Reid and Allan D. Gilmour), the Damon J.
Keith Center for Civil Rights, and the Damon J. Keith Law Collection
of African-American History (including its former director India
Geronimo) at Wayne State University Law School. Additional thanks
must be extended to Jade Craig, Adhana Davis, Jonathan Grey, Justin

Hanford, Mitra Jafary-Hariri, Kimberly Kendrick, Jennifer Lane, Praveen Madhiraju, Mallory Tomaro, and Erika Washington.

• • •

Trevor W. Coleman additionally thanks the memory of his late mother Mary C. Coleman and grandfather Austin L. Carr, as well as Karla Thornhill Coleman and his children, Sydnie and Trevor, for their patience, love, sacrifice, and unwavering support.

CRUSADER
FOR
JUSTICE

HUMBLE ROOTS
THE LAWYER AND THE JANITOR

I f it is true, as Martin Luther King once suggested, that the measure of a man is not where he stands in moments of comfort but where he stands in times of challenge, then let us begin the story of Damon Jerome Keith as he stands in an old brick bathroom in the *Detroit News* building, holding a mop and a bucket.

It is 1949. Damon is a law school graduate.

And a janitor.

He hates the job. Hates the sound of flushing toilets. Hates the smell. Every time he sniffs the stale, fetid air, he asks himself the same question:

What the hell am I doing here?

Earlier in the day, he had taken his lunch in a quiet hallway, hoping to sneak in a few minutes of study. Leaning against a wall, he nibbled on a sandwich while propping a *Ballentine's Law Dictionary* in his arms. He softly recited the legal terms to himself.

"What are you reading?"

He snapped to attention, almost dropping his sandwich. An older white man, a grizzled news reporter whom Damon had seen around the building, was peering at him as if watching a zoo animal do a trick.

"Just a law dictionary, sir," the young man said.

The newsman stared.

"Law dictionary?"

"I'm studying for the bar exam."

"What for?"

"I'm going to be a lawyer."

The newsman paused. He eyed Damon up and down.

"A black lawyer?" He laughed. "You better keep mopping."

And he walked away.

Now, hours later, alone in the bathroom, Damon Keith feels that comment in the depths of his soul. *You better keep mopping.* He grips the wooden handle tight enough to choke it, then smacks it back in the bucket and yanks it out, spilling water everywhere. Ten years he has been gone from Detroit. Ten years. He's earned a bachelor's degree. He's fought in World War II. He's graduated from Howard University School of Law, a bastion of civil rights education. The parchment bears his name: *Damon J. Keith.*

Yet every moment cleaning that foul bathroom reminds him that he has come so far, yet hardly gone anywhere. *You better keep mopping.* He closes his eyes and sees himself back in moot court at Howard Law listening with rapt attention as his law professor, Thurgood Marshall, challenges students.

"The white man wrote the words 'Equal Justice Under Law' before the Supreme Court in marble," Marshall would bellow. "Let's make him live up to those words—'Equal Justice Under Law!'"

Ten years.

He is a janitor.

He knows he is better educated, more talented, and more traveled than many white men working in this building. He knows no young white lawyer with the same credentials would ever have to start off where he is. But it is 1949 in Detroit, Michigan, and if you are black, even with a law degree, your options are limited. He knows there are others like him, doing nights at the post office or the loading docks, trying to eke out a law career during the day. He reminds himself of this during breaks at work, sitting in a corner with his thick law books splayed out in front of him. When the other janitors huddle around a radio, or play cards, or shoot dice, he studies. When they implore him to join them, he smiles and waves them off. They are good men. But they seem too *satisfied* with their lot. He expects more.

Ten years.

As he sweeps the office floors, he recites the Bill of Rights. Ten years. As he wipes down sinks, he makes mental notes of precedent-setting cases. Ten years. Sometimes, working in that bathroom, he catches his reflection staring back at him through the mirror, and what he sees is his future self, dressed in an expensive suit, carrying a briefcase like those black lawyers he sees going in and out of the Tobin Building on his way to work. He fantasizes about parking an expensive car next to his office and walking through the elegant double glass doors, as the doorman greets him with a "Good morning, sir!"

The sound of a flushing toilet disabuses him of such fancy thoughts. The lawyer in the mirror gives way to the janitor, the expensive suit to a drab blue uniform, the briefcase to a mop and bucket. That is the future. This is the hard, cold present. *You better keep mopping.*

How do you measure a man? Not in moments of comfort, but moments of challenge—not by where he is, but where he has come from.

This is the story of Damon Jerome Keith.

It begins with his father.

•　　•　　•

Like thousands of other black men from the South, Perry Keith migrated to Detroit after hearing of Henry Ford's promise of five-dollar-a-day wages for both blacks and whites. Unlike many of his associates, however, neither Perry nor his wife, Annie, had come from the sharecropper fields, although both were children of slaves. Annie was from an affluent Atlanta family and had been a schoolteacher before her marriage. Perry had been a businessman, operating a hotel and a barbershop, but bad debts and bad loans had driven him to bankruptcy.

And so, in 1915, leaving his wife and five kids behind, he came north.

The world he found there was nothing like what he'd known in Atlanta. Life in the auto factories was not only grueling—physically and mentally—but black workers had to be constantly on guard against their white workmates sabotaging their machines, breaking their tools, even taking a swing at them when they were not looking. The white supervisors could make life miserable. And when they went home at night, living conditions for black migrants like Perry were appalling. Overcrowded. Excessive rents. Bathrooms that seemed unfit for human use.

Even worse was the treatment they received from the "native" black population. Many black Detroiters not only considered the migrants inferior but resented their presence, believing that they disturbed the social order of the city and made life harder for them.

Despite this, blacks from the South continued to arrive in Detroit in droves. Between 1910 and 1920, the black population of Detroit increased seven-fold from 5,741 to 40,838. Perry Keith was in that group, but he was not typical. When he arrived at age forty, he was already at least ten years older than the average black migrant.

Nonetheless, in time, Perry found a spot at Ford, as a machinist. In 1917, two years after leaving the South, he sent for Annie and the kids. Five years later, in 1922, he scraped together enough wages to purchase his own home, on Hudson Street in Detroit.

And he and Annie welcomed their sixth and last child.

They named him Damon Jerome Keith.

Born on the Fourth of July.

• • •

From his earliest memory, Damon recalled his father as an important man. That's because, despite shouldering Atlas-like burdens—supporting six children, plus a granddaughter, an elderly sister, and a sister-in-law—Perry Keith never lost his entrepreneurial spirit. Even while working at Ford, he saved enough to open his own real-estate and loan business, P. A. Keith & Sons Realty, Inc. His eldest son, Luther, assisted him despite being plagued with medical problems since birth. The business was run out of a small office in his house.

Over time, his hard work, sense of honor, and personal dignity made Perry one of the most respected men in the neighborhood. They called him "Mr. Keith." Berry Gordy Sr., a prominent businessman and father of the legendary Motown founder Berry Gordy Jr., was among those who would seek him out for advice.

But for Damon, the most important thing about his father was the time they spent together. They would hold hands walking to Detroit's Eastern Market, or to the local barbershop. They would visit Northwestern High School when the black baseball teams came to town. Later, when Damon was a budding teenager, there were trips to Olympia Stadium to see the great boxer Joe Louis, who was fighting in his prime.

Sons learn from their fathers simply by watching them. And what Damon saw over the years was a relentlessly dedicated family man who took heavy responsibility without complaint. Perry would leave the house early in the morning in the most inclement weather to catch the trolley to the Ford foundry. Heavy snow. Sleet. Didn't matter. Even fighting illness, Perry walked to that trolley, snowflakes gathering on his face and mustache. At that time, Ford was not unionized, and there was no sick leave or pension. You worked from paycheck to paycheck, and you had to show up.

When Perry came back at night, there was no rest. He would check on his wife, who was never well physically, then start dinner. After the meal, he would go out in the street, where the coal man had made a delivery, and load coal in a wheelbarrow to bring to the basement furnace. Their household was crowded, as evidenced by data in the 1930 U.S. census. Along with his wife, Annie, Perry Keith's domicile included two adult sons, his oldest, Luther, who was twenty-five years old and worked as an insurance agent, and Perry Jr., who was a twenty-one-year-old chauffeur for a wealthy family. Also in the house were Napoleon, now seventeen; daughter Annie, fifteen; and young Damon, who was seven at that time. The eldest daughter, Marie, twenty, was married, seven months pregnant, and at the time still living in the house with her husband, Harold Irving Harris. Lula Pearson, Perry's sixty-one-year-old older sister, lived in an apartment he built for her in the back of the house. Nellie Williams, Annie's twenty-nine-year-old younger sister, stayed intermittently. Each family member had a role to play. Each had to pull his or her own weight. And while the older siblings lived independent lives, everyone was expected to come together for Sunday dinner.

Although Damon was much too young to hang out with his big brothers, he had fond memories of them playing with him as a child. Impressions of Perry Jr. were more poignant; he was bright and talented, but deeply troubled and, by Damon's memory, drank so much that he was regularly taken to Detroit Receiving Hospital. His drunkenness constantly led to drama in the household. He came home late, woozy, and cursing and making a mess. He suffered repeated brushes with the law, which put enormous stress on his parents. When a crime was reported in the neighborhood, the police would invariably come to the house looking for Perry Jr. and take him down to the police station.

His troubled life would be brief. In 1946, at the age of thirty-eight, Perry Jr. would die from alcoholism. But he would leave one small yet important legacy. Because of the damage Perry Jr. displayed, his kid brother, Damon, swore he would never start drinking.

Despite the family troubles, by 1930, Perry Sr. had built himself up. He was promoted to inspector at the Ford plant. At one point, the Keith home was valued at eight thousand dollars—tied for the third most expensive home on the block.

And then came the Great Depression. Black unemployment in Detroit reached seventy-five percent. All of Perry's hard efforts could not spare him from the economic tidal wave, and he, too, was out of work much of the decade. This meant the family had to rely on relief during those tough times to make ends meet, yet another blow for the proud, soft-spoken patriarch. Life had now repeatedly taken away what he had built.

Still, family members never heard him complain. But Perry Keith did stress repeatedly to his wife and to Damon that he never, ever wanted his youngest son to have to work in the factories of Detroit. "Son," he said, "I don't want you to go through what I have gone through. I want you to get an education."

Damon would honor that desire—beyond his father's or anyone else's projections. He would later refer to Perry Keith as "the finest man I have ever known." And everything he did, he did to make his father proud.

THE EARLY EDUCATION
OF DAMON J. KEITH

———————————————————

It wasn't the first time he heard the word. But it still stings, nearly seventy-five years later.

"Hey, nigger!"

Damon Keith was fifteen years old, standing inside the Fisher YMCA in Detroit, just across from his high school. He gazed at the white kids using the fine gym equipment, unencumbered, having fun. He was not permitted to use the facilities. They were off-limits to blacks.

"Hey, nigger!" one of the white teens yelled again.

Not surprisingly, Damon yelled something back. One insult led to another. The situation escalated. "I'll meet you outside, if you want to settle this!" Damon hollered.

In the perfect story, he would avenge the insult, win the fight, then help the white teen up and forge a friendship. But that's in the perfect story. In the 1930s, there wasn't much perfect about black-white relations in America.

As Keith now recalls it, "The kid came outside, and we started fighting.

I started to pull off my jacket, and my arms got stuck in my sleeves; as I was trying to untangle them, he came up and sucker-punched me."

Not exactly Hollywood. No enlightenment. No new friendship. But as he straggled home that day, scraped, bitter, hurt, and angry, Damon Keith was more intent than ever on changing the world around him.

Effecting such change, however, would require education.

A product of Columbian Elementary School and McMichael Intermediate, Damon was a popular student at Northwestern High School in Detroit. He ran track, played trombone for the band, and was the first black member of the N Club, a prestigious Northwestern varsity club for students who lettered in sports. Given what he would one day accomplish, it might seem strange that his teenage ambitions were modest at best.

But then, who would he model himself after? From first grade until high school graduation, Damon never had a single black teacher or instructor. He could not recall any black kids on his block going on to college. Other than his father and his minister, he never saw a black man in a position of authority. Every day at high school, the message of limited opportunities was as consistent as the school bell. Blacks at Northwestern, although studying side by side with whites, were not permitted to participate in many sports, were not permitted to attend the school dances, were not permitted to join many of the academic clubs, or sit on student council, or take part in theatrical plays. Other than being able to go to school in an integrated fashion, Damon's student experience was as rigidly segregated as if he'd gone to class in the South.

This dehumanization began to eat away at a teenaged Damon. His parents became concerned about increasingly confrontational behavior. Once, when his mother was reading him the story of Christ and the crucifixion, he scrunched his face in disappointment.

"Oh, Mom," he said. "I thought God could fight."

•   •   •

One afternoon, Damon was playing baseball in the neighborhood when he heard his mother yelling for him to come home. Her yelling was common. The tone of her voice was not.

"What's the matter?" he said when he entered the house.

"Your father wants to talk to you," she said. "He's in the bedroom. He's very sick, Damon."

Very sick? His dad? Although he'd become accustomed to such news about his mother, hearing it about his strong role-model father left Damon stunned.

He entered the bedroom with his heart pounding.

The mentholated smell of Vicks rubbing cream hung in the air as his father lay weak in bed, a victim of double pneumonia. A hot blanket was draped across his chest.

"Son," the old man croaked, "I'm really sorry that I'm so sick. I just wish to God that I could see you graduate from college, because none of your brothers and sisters have gone."

Damon was stunned, frightened, and at a loss for words. He was sixteen years old, ill equipped, perhaps, for such a moment. He mumbled something in response, urged his father not to talk like that, and assured him he would get well soon.

As it turned out, Damon was correct. Perry Keith would slowly recover from that health scare and live a few more years. But the covenant he'd apparently made with God weighed heavily on young Damon's mind.

College? Was he really going to college?

•   •   •

A year later, as Damon's high school graduation approached, higher education remained a dream. College cost money. And in 1939, the Keith family, like many American families, was still struggling to make

13

ends meet. Perry Keith had insisted his son not work in the factories. He wanted something better for Damon, who shared his desire, but, realizing there were no funds available, kept his wishes quiet. He didn't even tell his parents that he'd applied to—and been accepted by—Wayne State University. Why break their hearts? There was no way he could afford to go.

One afternoon, everything changed. It was late August, and Damon was hanging outside with his neighborhood pals—Delbert, Calvin, Wilbur, and Dempsey—doing what young men do when the summer day loses its heat; talking sports, talking girls, shadowboxing like their favorite fighter—Joe Louis, "The Brown Bomber," who had just defeated Tony "Two Ton" Galento. Damon knew that in a few weeks, college semesters would start up, and he would be left behind to melt into the masses, just another young black man looking for work.

That afternoon, his mother's cousin Ethel McGee Davis made an unexpected visit. Damon, still shooting the breeze with his friends, saw her get out of the car. He recognized the expensive clothing and the proper manner with which she carried herself. Ethel was the "rich" relative in the family, and her elegance was obvious—even from across the street.

She was married to Dr. John Warren Davis, the highly esteemed president of West Virginia State College—a historically black college fifteen miles east of Charleston. Damon always thought her a bit eccentric (she named her kids "Dit," "Dot," and "Dash"). But she was family. And, besides, his mother had made a big meal of fried chicken, so it was unlikely Ethel was going anywhere before enjoying some.

Damon wandered home to play the dutiful son. He made small talk with his aunt and smiled when she remarked on how tall he had grown.

Then Ethel asked him a question that would change his life forever.

"Damon, where do you plan on going to college?"

"Um . . . ," Damon began.

He stumbled over his words. He knew how late in the summer it was. He knew college kids would be heading back any day. He knew he should have had his own plans set. Worst of all, he knew Ethel knew all these things—and was staring at him expecting an answer. Damon glanced at his parents, who also were silent with embarrassment.

"Damon," Ethel repeated, "where do you plan on going to college?"

"Well, you see . . ."

Ethel turned to Annie Keith. "Damon just finished high school. Where is he going to college, Annie?"

Embarrassed, Annie and Perry confessed, "We don't know if he can go to college, Ethel. We are still trying to raise the money."

Ethel set her chicken down. She daintily wiped her mouth with a napkin. Then she folded her hands in her lap. She took a long look at Damon. He wondered who was going to get the lecture—his parents or him?

Instead, Ethel simply said, "Why don't you send him down to West Virginia State College? You don't have to worry about money, because you don't have any. It's OK. We'll take care of it. Damon can get a job down there and work some of it off."

Annie and Perry Keith literally jumped from their seats. "That's great! He'll go! Thank you!" they gushed.

Damon watched in disbelief. His future, in that instant, had just been decided. *West Virginia?* As he watched his parents hugging his aunt, he realized—not for the last time—that life turns on the smallest things. A chance visit. An innocent comment. A plate of fried chicken on a summer afternoon. After worrying for more than a year, Damon had an answer to his college question.

He was going south.

He had two weeks to pack.

of that journey changed. It became a lesson. Damon Keith arrived at college with a new sense of purpose.

He was going to learn things.

So he could change them.

•   •   •

"Is that all you have on? Take this sweater. You'll catch pneumonia!"

Cousin Ethel was there to greet him at the train station, handing him a green sweater and taking charge of this new stage of life. She loaded up the car—noticing but making no comment on his feminine luggage bag and pillowcase—and drove him to West Virginia State College. As they pulled onto campus, Damon felt as if a chariot were pulling into a new kingdom. He had never been to a college campus before. He saw the classroom buildings, the dormitories, the students bustling up and down the paths—all black students at that! Decades later, he would reflect on his emotions: "I suddenly felt . . . important. As if I were part of something that I had been excluded from before. I felt—to be honest—at home."

He entered room 314 of Prillerman Hall and met his new roommate, a 6'6" freshman named Stanley Wallerstein Kemp, from Macon, Georgia. He unpacked his bags. There were two beds and two desks and the walls were barren. Unlike kids today, who personalize their dorm rooms the moment they arrive, Damon had nothing to hang up. He took a photograph from his wallet of a girl he had been dating in Detroit, but Cousin Ethel saw it and laughed. "Damon, why would you bring that picture down here? We have lots of beautiful girls on this campus!"

He put the photo away.

Although Ethel would consistently watch over him—and be instrumental in his new world—Damon's most important relationship would actually be with her husband, Dr. John Warren Davis, the president of West Virginia State College. Born on February 11, 1888, in Milledgeville,

Georgia, Davis graduated Morehouse College in 1911. Eight years later, when he was just thirty-one years old, he was named the second president of WVSC, and he set about raising academic standards, faculty pay, and benefits.

By the time Damon arrived on his campus, President Davis had built the institution up into one of the premiere black colleges in the nation. He took an immediate liking to his young cousin, helped mentor him, and opened his eyes to people and possibilities he had never considered. He spoke with Damon about the burning issues of the day and personally introduced him to some of the nation's most highly esteemed black leaders. He encouraged Damon to think beyond his immediate surroundings and about the larger struggle for racial justice taking place all across the country.

Being at WVSC was a revelation for Damon; for the first time in his life, he saw and mingled with black professionals, PhDs, even a black college president. Most importantly, he saw and listened to the great black leaders of the day, who visited the college to speak to students, including Mordecai Johnson, Dr. Benjamin Mays, Adam Clayton Powell Jr., Dr. Channing H. Tobias, and Mary McLeod Bethune. Damon's exposure to black intellectualism and civic activism was transcendent.

"It was as if I had awakened from a deep sleep," he would recall. "As if someone had lifted cataracts off my eyes."

Damon was a popular student and had many friends, including a high school buddy from Northwestern, James "Scoop" Parker ("Scoop" because "he knew everybody's business," Keith would laughingly explain) and Stanley Kemp, his roommate. Those two found a kinship in their humble roots and their need to work to pay their way through college. Damon helped clean the campus, drove the president from time to time, even waited on tables—making good on his promise to Cousin Ethel to earn his keep in exchange for an education.

Damon also developed a social life, going to parties and learning to dance. He was not very familiar with Greek organizations, but he noticed that fraternities and sororities were at the center of student life and leadership. All of the original black Greek organizations, including the Alpha Phi Alpha fraternity, Alpha Kappa Alpha sorority, Kappa Alpha Psi fraternity, Omega Psi Phi fraternity, Delta Sigma Theta sorority, Phi Beta Sigma fraternity, Zeta Phi Beta sorority, and Sigma Gamma Rho sorority, were represented on WVSC's campus. He was most impressed, however, by the men of the Alpha Zeta chapter of Alpha Phi Alpha. They were very serious and very studious. Their national membership boasted a roster of some of the most prominent and influential black Americans in the nation, many of whom Damon identified with as role models. They included Dr. W. E. B. DuBois, Dr. Channing H. Tobias, Paul Robeson, Adam Clayton Powell Jr., Thurgood Marshall, Charles Hamilton Houston, Duke Ellington, Countee Cullen, and Jesse Owens.

So, in November of his freshman year, Damon, along with Scoop, Stanley, and several other friends, decided to pledge. It was a nearly month-long period that he—and his rear end—would never forget.

At that time, fraternities routinely engaged in extreme hazing patterned after the physical rigors of military boot camp. The process included physically intimidating the young pledges through excessive exercise, verbal abuse, and, frequently, corporal punishment with a wooden paddle. Every day during pledge period, the Alpha Zeta wannabes had to walk around campus in tuxedos; every night they took a beating with the paddle.

"The wood—is good—for the hood!" the brothers would chant—referring to the fraternity hood—as they whacked away at the young pledges. "The wood—is good—for the hood!"

It was not all teasing and physical intimidation, however. The fraternity stressed scholarship and love for all mankind, and the pledges were also required to rigorously study both their schoolwork and fraternity history, and to memorize the words to the poems "Invictus" by William Ernest Henley and "If" by Rudyard Kipling. To this day, Judge Keith can recite the verses from memory. The end of the Kipling poem seems fitting to his pledge process:

> *If you can fill the unforgiving minute,*
> *with sixty seconds' worth of distance run—*
> *Yours is the Earth and everything that's in it,*
> *And—which is more—you'll be a Man, my son!*

After nearly a month of daily testing, Damon and his pledge brothers—their distance run—were initiated into Alpha Phi Alpha fraternity. They swore an oath. The process was often referred to as "crossing the burning sands," which, as Keith would later recall, meant "your butt was on fire. I am glad they got rid of the physical hazing. I never liked it."

But as tests of character go, that would prove a minor one. Two years later, on December 7, 1941, Damon and a friend would be sitting in his dorm room, listening to the radio say the Japanese had just bombed Pearl Harbor.

"We're at war, Damon," his friend would whisper.

"No, no," Damon would insist. "Congress has to declare war."

His friend looked straight at him.

"I think it's just been declared."

4.

"THE FINEST MAN
I'VE EVER KNOWN"

U ntil his college graduation, most of Damon's life had been about
saying hello—to new experiences, new classmates, new mentors,
new horizons.

But 1943 would be about saying goodbye.

The first farewell would be to college itself, a bittersweet parting,
because Damon had excelled there. He'd majored in political science
and sociology, lettered in track, was a popular student on campus, and
became one of the college president's favorites. Now, at twenty years
old, he was receiving his bachelor's degree. Such a long way from that
first lonely train ride, carrying his bags to where the "colored people"
rode and greeting his cousin Ethel, who handed him a sweater.

Here he was, four years later, awaiting a cap and gown, the first
child in his family to earn a degree. He knew how meaningful this was
to his family. His mother, Annie, was immensely proud, although once
again too ill to make the journey from Detroit. His father, Perry, and
his sister, Marie, traveled to WVSC for the ceremony.

As Damon walked around campus with his father, he could barely contain his inner sunburst of adulthood. His dad had so wanted him to attend college. Well, he'd done it. He'd made it. He pointed excitedly to various buildings and sites of his favorite memories. He waved at a few friends. His mind drifted to the parties he would attend that evening.

Then his father said something that snapped him back.

"Damon." He sighed wearily. "God let me live long enough to see you finish college. Now I'm ready to die."

The somber words shook Damon to his core. What? *Ready to die?*

"Oh, Dad, there's nothing to that," he said quickly. "You'll be here a long time."

Perry looked at his son with pride and melancholy. Nothing more was said. Later that evening, when the ceremonies were complete, Perry and Marie caught the train back to Detroit. Damon stayed on campus for a few more days to see off some of his friends who, like him, were bound for the army. When he returned to Detroit, he entered the house with his bags in hand. He hugged his mother, who told him how proud she was. He hugged his father, privately glad that his own prediction—*"You'll be here a long time"*—seemed to be more accurate than his old man's.

They sat at the dinner table and talked and laughed, one of those rite-of-passage meals where the parents beam as the child they sent away returns a young man, with big plans and unbridled dreams.

After dinner, Damon went to change. There was a party for Clarence Camp, a neighborhood friend, and he was itching to go.

"I'll be back in an hour or so," he told his parents.

"All right," his father said.

That would be their final conversation.

The second farewell of 1943 was coming.

• • •

The next day, Damon awoke to the sound of his mother's voice, shaky and scared.

"Your dad had a stroke," she said. "He can't speak. The doctor is coming."

A million thoughts ran through young Damon's head. A stroke? What did that mean? Could he recover? Would he speak again? He wasn't dead, right? His dire prediction had not come true. There was still hope, right?

Had this happened today, Perry Keith would have been rushed to the hospital, monitored, scoped, his blood pressure controlled. But this was 1943. The doctor, upon arrival, told Damon to fetch some medicine from the drug store, and Damon raced off with his older brother, Perry, who was drunk, as usual.

Damon was livid. "Perry, you got to straighten out," he implored. "Dad's sick. Mom's all worried. You've got to stop this drinking now and be the man of the house."

But even as he said it, Damon knew it wouldn't happen. His brother's demons manipulated him like a puppeteer, and no amount of real-world trauma would shake him loose. Damon was trying to pass the torch of "man of the house" to the rightful sibling. But he somehow knew it would fall back on his shoulders.

The next day, Perry Keith died, in his bed, in the house.

He was sixty-eight.

Annie told her son. "Dad's passed." Damon fell into a chair in the kitchen. He felt as if he'd been kicked in the gut. He tried to deny it. He railed against it. But deep inside, he saw his father's acceptance all over it. He thought back to just a few days earlier, when they'd been walking in West Virginia. *"I'm ready to die."* That's what he'd said. He had struck a deal with the Lord. Let him live long enough to see his son graduate college. Then, as was his custom, Perry Keith kept his end of the bargain.

"The finest man I ever knew." That's the phrase Damon would use in the years that followed—a phrase that so many would use in the packed funeral ceremony, at Macedonia Baptist Church, where Perry Keith had been a deacon.

But that spring morning, as Damon sat in the kitchen, remembering his father, there were no lofty words. Just the tears he felt streaming down his cheeks.

Dad was gone.

The second farewell of 1943 was the most heartbreaking.

5

1943

WAR IN THE STREETS /
WAR OVERSEAS

D amon's third farewell of 1943 would be a farewell to innocence—
courtesy of one of the worst race riots this country had ever seen.

It began on a muggy summer Saturday evening, June 20—just two weeks after Damon's father passed away—at a Detroit park known as Belle Isle. Attached to the city via a bridge on the Detroit River, Belle Isle was a popular gathering spot for all Detroiters—black and white—to fight the summer heat. That evening, the place was packed with young people. Reportedly, a fight broke out when a white sailor's girlfriend was insulted by a young black man. Confrontations spread. On the bridge, another fight escalated between several hundred African Americans and white sailors. Before long, an angry crowd of white residents, thousands strong, had assembled at the base of the bridge, ready to attack any blacks trying to cross.

The violence quickly spread into the city itself, where two rumors about what happened at Belle Isle turned the night explosive. One began at a predominantly black Detroit nightclub, where a man calling himself a police sergeant told patrons that whites had thrown a black woman and her baby off the bridge. Furious, the crowd spilled into the streets, looting and destroying white-owned stores and attacking white residents.

The second rumor, spreading through the white community, claimed a black man had raped and murdered a white woman on that same Belle Isle bridge. Enraged whites descended on a downtown theater called the Roxy, around 4 A.M., attacking black patrons as they exited. As the rumors grew more horrific, so did the violence. Whites targeted streetcars transporting black laborers to work. Vehicles were overturned and set on fire.

By Sunday morning, the situation was out of hand, with the streets at the mercy of seething gangs of both races. Black leaders implored Mayor Edward J. Jeffries Jr. to call President Franklin Roosevelt and bring in federal troops. But it was not until that evening, when white mobs invaded Paradise Valley, one of the oldest and poorest neighborhoods in Detroit, that Jeffries sought the outside help. Six thousand U.S. Army troops were eventually brought in and stationed throughout the city—despite the fact that the nation was at war overseas.

Detroit settled into an eerie, uneasy silence.

It was one of the most traumatic events in Damon's Keith's young life. And all he could do was watch.

"Mom, I'm getting ready to go in the army," he'd told Annie as the fighting raged outside. "I could die over there protecting our country. But if I have to die here protecting our family, I will."

His mother shook her head. "Please, Damon. Just stay inside. Stay inside. Don't go out there."

This, remember, was just weeks after his father's death. Damon's brother Napoleon was already in the army. His brother Luther had a disability. His brother Perry was a drunk. Damon was, by his mother's and his own definition, "the man of the house." If she wanted him to stay inside, he would stay inside.

By the time all the riots ended, twenty-five black residents and nine white residents were dead. Seventeen of the black victims had been killed by white policemen. The number of people injured, including police, approached seven hundred. The property damage—from looting, burning, and destruction—was estimated at two million dollars.

Damon was rocked by the violence. His hometown was smoldering. His exposure to racial strife had just springboarded from insults and attitudes to something far more dangerous. He wanted desperately to speak to his father about it all, but his father was gone. In the solitude of his room, he was overwhelmed with loneliness and grief.

His mind drifted back to a cold December morning when he was seven years old, holding his father's hand as they walked down the street. Young Damon spoke excitedly about "Santa bringing us Christmas presents."

But Perry Keith, with the nation reeling from the 1929 stock market crash, had been laid off. He gently explained that there would be no big presents this year. At the hardware store, he took a dime from his pocket—the last dime he had—and purchased a new wheel for Damon's old green wagon.

"Damon, we as a family should be thankful to God for putting food on our table, a roof over our head, and allowing us to be together for another year without a link in our family chain being broken," he said.

Damon let the words echo in his head. "Without a link in our family chain being broken." He knew he should be thankful. None of his family had been hurt or killed in the riotous violence. But the chain was broken anyhow. Dad was gone. He felt so lost. He began to cry. His city was wounded. His family was in mourning. And a World War was calling him.

He was twenty-one.

●　　●　　●

The final farewell of 1943 took place at a train station. He was about to enter the army. His mother and sister came to see him off. His mother had another paper bag of fried chicken and biscuits, the grease stains already working their way through. Her farewell words—as they had been the day he left for college—were "Be a good boy."

But this time, Damon was not heading to some leafy campus to expand his opportunities. Quite the contrary. The U.S. Army would test every limit of his conscience—and inspire him, once his fighting days were over, to fight more than ever for equality.

The events of December 7, 1941 had inspired Damon Keith's patriotism. When the ROTC was formed on his campus, Damon signed up, which allowed him to graduate college before starting his commitment. Now basic training awaited in Fort Sheridan, Illinois. He rode the train scared of many things—scared of fighting in a foreign land, scared of enemies in foreign uniforms. He didn't think to be scared of the men who wore the same uniform as he did.

That would change.

A Sergeant Hopkins was his first senior officer, an African American who dressed him down with a typical "You're in the goddamned army now, soldier." As the weeks went by, it was demeaning but tolerable.

"I can handle this," Damon thought.

What he'd encounter next—in Cheyenne, Wyoming—would turn that all around. "Mean to the core," is how Damon recalls his commanding officer there, a harsh, unyielding Alabama man named Thomas E. Powell. There were four platoons. Over two hundred black soldiers. And four officers to command them all.

Four white officers.

Powell was the man in charge, and he ran his platoons with an iron hand. His demeanor was aloof, gruff, belligerent, and racially abusive. Damon recalls him constantly referring to the black soldiers as niggers. The atmosphere sank. Morale was low. Tension boiled. And, as if racist treatment weren't enough, Cheyenne, Wyoming—specifically Fort Francis E. Warren—was freezing, desolate, and about as foreign to a young man from Detroit as any place in America could be.

Damon endured those weeks feeling as if he'd been shipped to the tundra, his lungs burning with the cold, the screaming of white officers echoing in his ears. His fellow black solders were tough, many were from the streets or the Deep South—"hard cats" as Damon remembers them—and they cursed every other word and refused to let the white officers make them feel small.

Sadly, what the officers didn't do, the army did itself. Because it refused to use black soldiers for any real fighting, men like Damon went through all the brutal training only to be relegated to menial tasks, like baking bread.

Which was Damon's job in Wyoming. Baking bread. He couldn't believe it! Was this why his country called him? By the time Christmas came around, he wasn't even bothered that his orders called for him to ship overseas. Baking bread? How much worse could it get?

•   •   •

On Christmas Eve, 1943, Damon was sitting in the lower cabins of the USAT *George Washington*. He was about to leave America for the first time in his life. There were no phone calls home. No holiday wishes for his mother or siblings. Patrol boats would replace caroling neighbors, escorting the *George Washington* in case of enemy submarines. Damon and hundreds of other black soldiers had the lowest-level bunks, in the bowels of the ship. It was called "serving your country," but it felt like plain old serving.

The boat pushed forward.

Damon and his fellow soldiers were truly "off to war."

Yet, because the army was still rigidly segregated, he was part of an all-black unit that was assigned to the Quartermaster Corps, providing supplies to the infantry and fighting men. No fighting. Not on the front lines. Though several hundred thousand blacks served overseas during World War II, nearly eighty percent of them held menial positions in areas such as the quartermaster, engineer, and transportation corps.

Nonetheless, Damon, who spent time in South Wales, Scotland, France, and Belgium, discovered that the horrors of a war front can find you, even in the back. His duties required him, among other things, to transport wounded white soldiers to ambulances or medical facilities. He drove the truck. Once, after a particularly bloody winter battle, his lieutenant screamed from the back "Stop! We got two dead soldiers back here! We gotta get them off and bury them."

So Damon stopped the truck. And there, in the middle of an obscure, empty Belgian field, coated in snow, he dug two graves and laid two white solders' bodies inside them.

As he later recalled it, "I didn't say a prayer. We got pretty hard-nosed after a while." But he often found himself thinking about those soldiers, their families, the fact that those families would never be able to visit the graves. Damon found himself repeating the old phrase, "There, but for the grace of God, go I."

It was one of the few moments he was glad to be in the quartermaster corps.

Finally, in 1945, Damon was stationed in France, with orders coming down to ship him to Japan. There were rumors of the war coming to an end. He and his fellow black soldiers tempered their enthusiasm, not wanting to be disappointed. But when word came and peace was declared, nothing could quell their happiness.

"We're done! We're going back!" they yelled to one another. Beer flowed. French wine. Songs were sung. Damon had never been so relieved. He looked around the barracks and took in the smiling faces. But as the night went on, his mind was already on a boat, and his heart was heading home. He had seen a great deal of injustice during the war—on the battlefield and in the armed forces themselves. And while his fighting was limited on foreign soil, he privately vowed to never stop fighting injustice back home.

6

HOWARD UNIVERSITY SCHOOL OF LAW

THE WEST POINT OF CIVIL RIGHTS

The laughter and music of those final days in France echoed in Damon's head as his ship reached home shores. *America.* He was back. He owed the army a few more weeks in several southern states before going home, and he figured he would be spending that time walking tall in his staff sergeant uniform, enjoying slaps on the back from a grateful nation.

It didn't happen. Despite his military sacrifice—and that of his fellow black soldiers—Damon saw the same "Whites" and "Coloreds" signs in the towns to which he was assigned. Even worse, he witnessed captured German soldiers, escorted by white American officers, being led into restaurants where Damon was forbidden to eat. They rode up front on buses that relegated Damon to the back.

It soured his taste of victory, so much so that in his final military days, when a sergeant tried to convince him to join the reserves—"You know there won't be another war for a long time, Damon!" he said, "Just sign up! You'll get paid as well!"—Damon tersely replied, "I am never signing anything for the army again. I'm through with this. I'm going home."

Once again, a train brought him to Detroit. Once again, he was greeted by family members at the station. Once again, his mother set a big table in the house on Hudson Street, and with the spirit of his departed father hovering in the room, she fêted him with a big meal, a rump roast, fried chicken, rolls, and her special chocolate cake.

But seared in Damon's mind was a recent conversation with a fellow black soldier named Tommie Newsome, who hailed from Inkster, Michigan, just outside of Detroit. They'd discussed the biting racism each had discovered upon returning to the U.S.

"Well, Damon," Tommie said, "I'm going back to law school. I suggest you go to law school, too. And maybe we can do something about this."

To that point, Damon Keith had been thinking about social work. He'd majored in history and sociology at college and had considered getting an advanced degree, perhaps working for a social service agency in Detroit.

The army changed all that. He knew America's racial inequities would not be shaken loose by one more social worker. He had to get to the very stain in the fabric, to identify places where the Constitution was quoted but not adhered to, and to change them. There was one best way to do that.

Damon Keith hung his army uniform in the bedroom closet.

And went into law.

•   •   •

His good grades—and the funds provided by the G.I. Bill—got Damon admitted to both Wayne State University and the University of Detroit's law schools. But once again, the Cousin Ethel connection would alter his path. John Davis, Ethel's husband and the president of West Virginia State College, told his young alum, "Listen, Damon, if you really want to make a difference, you should go to Howard University School of Law. That's where the legal machinery is churning to eliminate racism."

Damon was thrilled at the notion of such a program. But it was late in the summer, nearly August. All his paperwork was already done. Davis said not to worry, he would make a call. Transcripts were rushed. Letters exchanged. And sure enough, come September, Damon arrived in the nation's capital, Washington, D.C., as a first-year law student at a school that would change his life forever.

Not that the place was much to look at.

In 1946, Howard University School of Law was confined to the basement of the historic Founders Library. Classes were conducted there. Lectures. Study groups. Damon learned the law in mostly windowless rooms.

It might have been symbolically odd—going underground to change the world above. But a basement school of free ideas was much preferred to skyscrapers governed by "separate but equal." There was a sense of serious purpose at Howard that rendered classroom location or lack of windows moot.

Besides, the building itself was beautiful. And the history of Howard University—and its people—gave off its own luminescence. Howard's founder and namesake, General Oliver Otis Howard, served on the Union side during the Civil War. He fought in Bull Run, Fredericksburg, and Gettysburg, to name a few. A staunch opponent of slavery, Howard was appointed by President Andrew Johnson, after the war ended, to be commissioner of something called the Freedmen's Bureau. Charged with helping former slaves in areas of education, medicine, and labor, he ultimately founded the university that bears his name and served as its president for several years.

Many others carried the mantle after his death in 1909, including, most notably, Charles Hamilton Houston. Like Judge Keith, Houston was forced to endure extreme forms of American racism when he served his country—only this was during the *first* World War, not the second.

After returning from the army in 1919, Houston applied to and was accepted by Harvard Law School. An exceptional student, he soon became the first African-American editor of the *Harvard Law Review*. Armed with his law degrees and a burning passion for racial and social justice, Houston returned to Washington, D.C., for the sole purpose of training black lawyers.

By 1929, he was the vice dean of Howard Law. He had two goals: to turn the school into "a West Point of Negro leadership" and a place "that Negroes could gain equality by fighting segregation in the courts." He infused his students with what became known as his "Houstonian theory of jurisprudence"—the view that lawyers and judges should purposefully effect social change through the fervent pursuit of full equality between the races. By the time Damon arrived there, Howard Law had trained a huge percentage of the African-American lawyers in the country. "Charlie" Houston's enormous efforts had paid off. He'd created a vibrant, thriving, intellectual haven and was still on staff when Damon entered for the first day of classes.

"I was scared to death," Keith would recall of those opening minutes. One professor told the nervous students to look around, left and right. Because a year from now, "someone you see won't be here. They'll have flunked out."

Damon vowed it would not be him.

•　　•　　•

It was during his time at Howard that Damon first met Thurgood Marshall, a Howard Law graduate and then chief counsel to the NAACP. "Thurgood's here!" the whisper would spread. "Thurgood's down the hall!" Although intimidated by the tall, handsome, and already legendary Marshall, at first sight of him, Damon went right up to shake his hand.

He admired him that much. Over the coming months, he would observe Marshall, learn from Marshall, listen to Marshall hone his arguments in Howard Law's moot court, arguments that would later be made before the Supreme Court itself. During Damon's time in law school, Marshall argued and won the famous *Shelley v. Kraemer* case, which held that courts could not enforce covenants that would keep a person from buying real estate based on race or color. It was one of numerous civil rights victories that would fill Marshall's file.

Damon and his classmates actually got to see such cases argued at the Supreme Court. They went as a group, sitting in the public chairs. To witness such eloquent justice, and then to walk the streets of Washington, D.C., where certain restaurants and clubs remained off-limits to people with his skin color, both angered and inspired Damon to push forward in his law studies. It was clear there was so much to do, and even clearer the law was the way to do it.

He lived in a rooming house. He ate at cafeterias or in nearby restaurants. He was popular, joined fraternities and the moot court, even served as business manager for the yearbook. But he was there to work. "I sensed it was my last chance," he would recall. "Most of the men in my class were GI's. We had been through a war. We wanted to make something of ourselves. It was serious business.

"I felt I could make a difference if I just got out of law school. They indoctrinated us. Use the law as a means for social change."

Elsewhere in America, reports of violence against returning black soldiers were disturbing. A black veteran was attacked and blinded by policemen in South Carolina. Two black veterans—and their wives—were taken from their car and shot to death by a white mob in Georgia. A dozen more black southern veterans met violent deaths over a four-week stretch. Some suggested a deep-seated fear that black soldiers, having fought for their country, would now expect more from it.

Against this backdrop, Damon Keith dove headfirst into the law, because he did expect more from it. In 1949, he graduated with the praise of his venerable instructors. It was the proudest moment of his academic life. For decades to come, Keith celebrated Howard Law as integral to his development as a legal mind.

Many years later, a phone call would come to his Detroit office, a young man identifying himself as the grandson of Charles Hamilton Houston, the former dean of Howard Law. He said he had applied to be a clerk under Judge Keith but hadn't heard anything back.

"Hold on a moment," Damon said.

He walked down the hall and asked his staff if this was true. They confirmed the still unread paperwork.

"Let me have it," he said.

He walked back to the phone and told the young man to come on up, he could start as soon as he wanted.

"Really?"

"What your grandfather did for me," Damon said, "I could never repay."

Sadly, in 1949, with his law degree in hand, there was no such open door for Keith. He would begin his working life by scraping for employment. But the lingering distaste from his return to the U.S. had faded. He'd seen what was possible when courageous men fought for equality.

And he was on fire to do it himself.

LEAPING THE BAR

With a law degree in hand and a support group of professors, friends, and loved ones urging him on, Damon Keith began his professional life . . . by cutting down trees.

Jobs were hard to come by in 1949 Detroit, and being a black man with a law degree often meant little more than being a black man looking for work. Any work. The forestry department hired Damon to trim branches and pull up dead trees around the city. That's what he did.

Meanwhile, he prepared for the bar exam. It was offered twice a year, and he was determined to pass the autumn test. He spent his spare hours studying in his bedroom or in the local library. On occasion, he would travel to Ann Arbor—home of the University of Michigan, where the test would be administered. Damon would study with other young hopefuls there, including several white Michigan law school graduates. When they asked him where he'd gone to law school, he said, "Howard." This evoked one of two responses:

"Where?"

Or, "*You* went to *Harvard?*"

(Decades later, when honored at galas and banquets, Judge Keith would encounter similar mistakes, people introducing him as "a graduate of Harvard Law School." Each time he took the microphone, he would thank them for the honor, then smile and make the gentle correction: "It's Howard University, not Harvard University.")

In 1949, he did not see humor in it. In fact, Damon felt intimidated. These future lawyers who'd attended elite schools believed that Howard was no match for their superior training, and that Damon, as a Howard graduate, and as a black man, was somehow lesser legal clay. Although he generally ignored such insults or used them to make himself stronger, the day Damon took the bar exam, he felt stung by a sensation of unworthiness. As they administered the test, he looked around and counted fewer than a half dozen black faces in the room, versus several hundred whites. He flashed back to his army regiment (four white leaders, two hundred black soldiers) and the train ride down to West Virginia—any and all examples of his kind being outnumbered or considered inferior. It hung over him like a cloud as he proceeded.

"How did you do?" his mother asked when he returned home.

"I think I did OK," he said, hiding his concern.

The next day he went back to work—cutting down trees. No one on the crew asked where he had been. Few of his fellow workers even knew what the bar exam was, let alone thought he would be taking it.

As he awaited his results, Damon and his family received a reminder of just how far America's actual civil rights remained from the idealistic ones his Howard professors implanted in his dreams. Annie, Damon's mother, went looking for another house. It was time to move, she felt. She saw a two-story brick duplex she liked on a street called Virginia Park in Detroit, less than a mile from where, a decade later, a young man named Berry Gordy would form Motown Records.

The house had a FOR SALE sign out front, but when Annie went to look at it, she was told, "You can't buy this house," because the owner had a covenant that restricted it from being sold to blacks, Jews, or other minorities.

Ultimately, two friends of the Keith family, Robert and Jean Harbour, purchased the house for them. They, too, were African American. Their advantage?

They looked white.

And they never told the sellers otherwise.

The Harbours immediately quitclaim deeded the house to the Keiths, who moved into the upper flat and rented out the bottom. Annie had her new home. But such were the twists and turns needed to skirt racism embedded in the laws—laws Damon hoped to address once he was a licensed practitioner.

Which, he soon learned, would take him a little longer.

"Damon," his mother said when he came home from work one December afternoon. He could tell from her face the news was bad. In those days, people who passed the bar exam were listed in the newspaper.

The newspaper was on the kitchen table.

Damon's name was not in it.

"I'm sorry," his mother said.

"It happens," Damon replied. "I'll just have to do better."

But inside, he was crushed. Christmas was approaching. The tree-cutting work was seasonal, and he'd been forced to take a new job—as a custodian for the *Detroit News*.

The 1940s were ending. A new decade was rising. Damon Keith, the graduate of a four-year university, and a three-year graduate school, with a three-year stint in the army, was twenty-eight years old and pushing a mop across dirty floors. He felt like a clenched fist of potential, still powerless to hit back.

But that was about to change.

• • •

His second attempt at the bar exam was successful—he felt it the day he took the test—and it was confirmed a few months later with a surprising phone call. Damon's mother had read the newspaper that morning, and she called down to the *Detroit News* (where it had been printed the previous night) and somehow found her son.

"Damon, you passed!" she exclaimed.

"Really?"

"Yes! Your name's in the paper!"

He felt as if he'd grown ten feet high. He went to his fellow custodial workers and said, "Fellas, I passed the bar exam. Ballgame's over! I'm gone!"

"Good luck, DK!" they said, slapping him on the arm. "Way to go!"

"Congratulations!"

He left that very afternoon. His janitor days were finished. He never again encountered the man who scoffed at him in the bathroom and derided him with, *"A black lawyer? Better keep mopping."* He didn't care. His eyes were on the future, not the past.

But becoming a black attorney in those days was one thing; finding employment as one was another. Damon Keith was sworn in to the State Bar of Michigan in 1950 by Charles W. Jones, a senior partner at the law firm of Loomis, Jones, Piper & Colden, located at 1308 Broadway Street in downtown Detroit. Damon knew Jones's daughter, a connection that helped him land his first job in that firm. He worked mainly as a clerk—filing papers, conducting research, and performing other essential clerical duties.

As for actual lawyer work? Like his fellow young black peers, Damon was responsible for finding it on his own. White clients would not hire black attorneys. Black clients also hesitated, believing their chances in court were bad enough, why invite prejudice with a black attorney?

Consequently, young black lawyers in Detroit were left chasing legal table scraps. They often spent their days hanging around Recorder's Court, which handled traffic and ordinance matters and felonies committed in the city. Sitting in empty jury boxes or pacing the hallways, they waited, hoping a judge might assign them a stray indigent case. This could take hours, while the judge was at lunch or socializing. Finally, the moment might arrive when a defendant came before the court without a lawyer and wanted to plead guilty.

"Well," the judge might say, "I won't accept the plea, but I'll ask Attorney Keith to come up and talk to you and then come back, and if he thinks it's worthy, you can plead guilty; I'll accept the plea. But you're entitled to counsel."

In fact, that's exactly how Damon Keith got his first case. The defendant pleaded guilty, and Keith was paid thirty-five dollars. He stared proudly at the payment voucher from the court: his first paycheck as a lawyer. That evening, he rushed home, excited to share the news with his mother: "Mom, I made thirty-five dollars today; that's more than I made in a week at the *Detroit News*."

She smiled and said with a quiet pride, "Well, that's good, Damon."

But once the giddy excitement passed, Damon began to realize the serious consequences of black defendants' reluctance to hire black lawyers. It deeply concerned him. Justice was not blind, he was discovering, and the fundamental lack of black judges was a huge problem. Ensuring fair treatment for black clients—or their black attorneys—was difficult.

"Many of the white judges simply were not nice to us," Keith would later recall. "They didn't treat us as they did other lawyers, with dignity and respect. Some were actually outright mean, nasty, and belittling in their dealings with black attorneys.

"Clients saw how poorly black lawyers were treated in court. Many of the black citizens in Detroit came from the South. They knew, firsthand, about racism in the legal system and how it could determine the outcome of their cases. Judges, as much as anything, caused many black clients to shun black lawyers."

Those early court experiences made Keith ever mindful of how powerful and influential a judge can be—and shaped the type of judge he someday would become. He was determined to one day show all lawyers the dignity and respect they deserved as officers of the court. He would end up spending more than four decades on the bench—and he would never hold a lawyer in contempt.

8.

RACHEL

By the fall of 1952, Damon had scrambled several rungs up the legal ladder. He'd been hired as the first black attorney in Wayne County's Friend of the Court office, which dealt with child support and alimony. It was steady work—no more chasing what fell loose in Recorder's Court—and his reputation grew steadily in the Detroit community. He had become heavily involved in various civic groups, and his rising influence and visibility made him an extremely eligible bachelor. His nice looks and pleasant demeanor didn't hurt, and he was never lacking for dates. Friends would often try to set him up, thinking they had found the perfect future Mrs. Keith.

But even approaching his thirtieth birthday, Damon was highly ambitious and not ready to settle down.

Or so he thought.

One afternoon, Dr. Malcolm West, a Howard University classmate completing his residency at Detroit Receiving Hospital, approached Damon with news of a woman he had befriended, Rachel Boone, a stunningly pretty young physician from Virginia who was also in the middle of a two-year residency in internal medicine. He thought she'd be a perfect match for Damon.

"Do you have a problem with professional black women?" Malcolm asked.

Startled by the question, Damon replied, "Heck no! Why would you ask me something like that?"

"Because, man, if I were single, I'd marry this one, if she'd have me," he said, laughing. "You want to meet her?"

"Sure," Keith said, intrigued.

An encounter was set for later that week at the Herman Kiefer Health Complex, where Rachel was working on an assignment. Damon thought about Malcolm's enthusiasm: "This Rachel must really be something special if she's got him acting like that." He wore his best suit to work at the Friend of the Court office that day, and at the close of business, he hurried over to the health complex. Meeting him at the entrance, Malcolm smiled and led him down a long hallway to a lab. Just before entering, he gripped Damon's elbow and whispered, "Just be cool, man. Don't blow it."

Before Damon could respond, the lab door swung open. Standing before him was Dr. Rachel Boone, beautiful, petite, with a demure smile that left Damon short of breath. Even in a white lab coat, she looked more like a college co-ed. "I bet she doesn't weigh a hundred pounds," Damon thought. But when she said hello, everything about her simply floored him, like a hundred-pound hammer to the heart.

To this day, Judge Keith will say that, other than Malcolm, he cannot recall if there was another person in the lab. It was love at first sight. Beyond that. It was a soulful connection that left him dizzy. He stared. They made small talk. But Damon had already determined, in the first skipped beat of his usually practical heart, that he would not "blow it," not with this small miracle in front of him.

As Damon reflects on his life, nearly sixty years later, he remembers this as the greatest thing that ever happened to him. He knew from the moment he met her that Rachel Boone would one day be his wife.

The feeling was apparently mutual, because after the small talk, Damon asked Rachel out, and she immediately said yes. Their first date was not a fancy dinner. Instead, they went to see the Detroit Lions play the Los Angeles Dons in professional football. They met for breakfast at Kinsel Drug Store on Michigan Avenue. From there, they walked ten blocks to Briggs Stadium.

It was Rachel's first time at a Lions game. Every time the Lions would score a touchdown, she would cheer loudly, thinking that by rooting for Damon's hometown team, she was scoring points with him. But Damon kept his cheers muted. The Lions, like the Detroit baseball and hockey teams of that era, were still segregated and did not have any black players. By contrast, the Los Angeles Dons had a few black players.

Bemused by her enthusiasm, Damon finally explained to his date, "I'm not pulling for the Lions, because they don't have any blacks on their team. Until they get some, I won't cheer. But the LA team has three or four. I'll cheer for them." Rachel was not political at the time. She took a long look at her date and smiled. Then she placed her hands in her lap and did not cheer for the rest of the game.

Moments like that separated Rachel from all the other women Damon had dated. He found he could speak to her about anything and that their kindred spirits went beyond the basic things they had in common. True, he didn't smoke, and she didn't smoke. He didn't drink, and she didn't drink. He went to a Baptist church; she went to a Baptist church. But they shared so much more, including early struggles and family grief, and the principles that drove him drove her as well.

Rachel Boone was the daughter of missionaries; her father, Dr. Clinton C. Boone, was a physician who, along with her mother, Rachel Tharps

Boone, left the United States in 1922 for Monrovia, Liberia, to spread the gospel and bring medical relief to struggling people. Rachel was born in Liberia, on May 30, 1924, two years after her parents arrived.

She was, quite literally, born into public service.

Her parents returned with her and her brother to Richmond, Virginia. The South was segregated, and one can imagine the difficulties even a professional black family faced. But from an early age, Rachel set herself apart. She graduated from Armstrong High School in 1938 at the age of thirteen. She was valedictorian of her class.

Tragically, within a two-year period, Rachel lost both her mother and her father and was forced to move in with an aunt in Rhode Island. She made a vow to become a doctor one day and help those in need, as her parents had. In the fall of 1939, when she was just fourteen years old, Rachel enrolled at Houghton College, a small Christian school in upstate New York—where she was the only African-American student.

Four years later, she graduated magna cum laude and second in her class. She completed her postgraduate studies in biology at Brown University and attained her medical degree from Boston University School of Medicine in 1949.

She was twenty-five.

Only her courtship with Damon was more rapid than her academic career. They saw each other as often as work would allow. And within several months, it was apparent they belonged together. Damon's mother, Annie, thought highly of this small, impressive woman—she told her son as much—and Rachel would say, with no self-consciousness, "Mrs. Keith, I'll make a good wife for your son."

Four months after their date at the football game, Damon went to the first jewelry store he'd ever been to, on Broadway in Detroit, and, with some help from the owner, picked out a ring for Rachel. He put down a deposit. Earning little money at the time, he had to pay it off in installments. But six weeks later, when the ring was his, he put it in his pocket, borrowed a car, and, on Rachel's twenty-eighth birthday, drove her to dinner and later to Belle Isle.

"Darling," he said, using the word he would reserve for her forever, "I have something I want to give you for your birthday."

"You do?"

He took out the ring. He presented it to her. And then, surprisingly—for a lawyer and future judge whose legacy would be recorded by the words he chose—he said nothing else. Damon never formally popped the question. But she knew. He knew. And they kissed and hugged and kissed some more.

At some point, gathering his emotions, he did say to her, "Now, sweetheart, remember, I'm a young lawyer, just starting out. I believe in long engagements, OK?"

Rachel smiled. She didn't say a word. A few days later, they met for dinner. And she made an announcement.

"Darling," she said, "the wedding is October the eighteenth, in Richmond, Virginia."

Keith was flabbergasted. October? Five months away?

"I thought I told you that I believed in long engagements," he protested.

"Yes, you did, Damon," Rachel softly replied. "And that's long enough."

•   •   •

At the time of their engagement, Damon had not yet met any of Rachel's relatives. She'd arranged for them to be married at a Richmond church and have the reception at "the family farm." Damon came home one night and told his mother. He didn't know what to make of that.

"A farm?" he said. He envisioned a bunch of people standing around an old barn, waiting to use an outhouse.

"You chose the right woman," Annie told him. "And you committed to this marriage. Don't worry. Everything will be fine."

Still, Damon warned his friends that this might not be a typical wedding. As the date approached, Rachel—who would go down to Virginia early to prepare—gave Damon driving directions. He and his brother Napoleon, along with Wilbur Hughes, Damon's best man and childhood pal, filled the car with gas and made the ten-hour haul from Detroit to Richmond. They followed the directions to Creighton Road.

"Don't expect too much," Damon warned his fellow passengers, recalling the things he'd seen in college and the army. "This is the South, remember."

The directions ended at "the farm," which apparently belonged to Rachel's uncle, Fred D. Tharps. As the car edged up a long road, the three men looked out the window and saw a beautiful home high on a hill. Obviously, they were lost.

"Wilbur," Napoleon said, "according to Rachel's instructions, this is where the Tharps live. But ain't no black folks having a home like this down here. Let's drive up to the farm and ask somebody."

The car continued to the top of the hill, passing cows, chickens, horses, pigs—and fields of soybean and corn. It was a sweeping landscape. Hundreds of unspoiled acres. "Quite beautiful," Damon thought. He wondered how badly they were lost. They finally saw a farmhouse and parked the car. Damon stepped out, his eyes searching. He spotted a small black man who appeared to be working there, so he walked over and put on a smile.

"Excuse me, sir, can you tell me where I can find the farm of a Fred D. Tharps?"

The man stared at him. "I am Fred D. Tharps," he said. "And this is my farm."

Damon was stunned.

"Um . . . I'm Damon Keith," he said sheepishly, "Rachel's fiancé."

"Maude!" the man yelled to his wife, who looked out from a kitchen window. "This is the city slicker attorney from Detroit that Rachel's going to marry."

Maude came outside, looked at Damon, and smiled. "Freddie, if Rachel selected him, he's all right. You be nice to him."

From that point on, Damon refused to be surprised by anything. Instead he just enjoyed it. The ceremony was held on a hot and sunny Saturday morning at the First African Baptist Church of Richmond. It was led by Rachel's brother, the Reverend C. C. Boone. The bride, in a long-sleeved, flowing white gown and veil, and the groom, in a dark tuxedo coat with a formal white vest, said "I do" and "I do," and they were wed. They kissed and held hands as Rachel carried a bouquet up the aisle.

The reception, sure enough, was held on Uncle Fred's farm—his sprawling six-hundred-acre farm. *Six hundred acres!* Damon still couldn't believe it. The guests ate homemade food and wandered in the sunshine, some of them even rode horses. It was a fabulous celebration of two people clearly in love.

As the afternoon waned, Damon and Rachel changed clothes and, to the cheers of the many guests, got in a car and headed to the Richmond airport for a flight to New York and the start of their honeymoon. In the car, still beaming from the day, Damon slapped his pants pocket and, suddenly panicking, yelled to Wilbur, who was driving, "Hey, I left my money back at the farm! I left it in my other pants! I don't have any money!"

"Don't worry," Wilbur said, reaching in his pocket, "take what I got. You'll pay me back in Detroit."

Rachel didn't say a word—something he would always be grateful for. An hour later, they were lifting into the air. Damon held his young wife's hand and smiled. With borrowed money in his pocket and the prettiest woman in the world beside him, he looked out the airplane window and felt he couldn't possibly get any higher.

9

TAKING A CHANCE
LIFE AS A YOUNG LAWYER

The problem with goals is that once you attain one, your eyes settle on another. Damon Keith wanted to be a lawyer; he'd done it. He wanted steady work; he'd found it. He wanted a decent paycheck; he'd achieved it—although his government job paid him every *other* week, so he made an arrangement with the owner of a nearby gas station to regularly advance him a week's pay in exchange for a post-dated check. This way, Damon brought home the money to Rachel every seven days, a weekly paycheck, another goal he associated with being a good husband.

Still, in his heart he dreamed of making a difference—a serious difference. Working every day for the Friend of the Court left him tired, sometimes miserable, but rarely confronting the stirring challenges of his old Howard University professors. *Change the world. Break down the walls. Heal the injustices.*

Instead, he was spending one day each week presenting alimony and child support recommendations to a judge and one day each week visiting the residences of divorcing parents, observing the fitness of the home for children. He witnessed every type of child-rearing setting during that time: rich and sprawling homes; tiny, cramped apartments; houses that looked like a party had just taken place; houses that looked as if a party were still going on. He was harangued constantly by angry husbands and wives alike, each blaming the other for the failed marriage, each insisting that the children would be better off away from the other one.

"My God," Damon found himself thinking "I hope my marriage never turns out like this." He would come home at night to the lower-level flat on Euclid Street in Detroit that he and Rachel called home. He would tell her of the things he'd seen. On occasion, he would even take Rachel with him, just to witness some of the broken family lives firsthand.

It was Damon's job to make recommendations based on what he'd observed—not only on where the children should live but also on the division of marital assets, based on the ledgers of what the husband and wife possessed. A judge would then make the final decision. As Damon had witnessed in Recorder's Court, it was the men in the robes who held the real power. Lower-level government attorneys could influence lives, and his work was not without purpose. But it felt small. America was still reeling from racial inequity. And what exactly was he doing to change that?

A year after the wedding, Damon and Rachel returned to Fred Tharps' farm for a visit—something that would become an annual summer tradition. Damon sat with his new "Uncle Fred" outside the farmhouse, overlooking the hundreds of acres of crops.

"So, what's happening with you in Detroit?" Fred asked.

Damon told him of his job and its limitations. He told him he'd been thinking about leaving but that his family—including his mother and his siblings—had warned him about a bird in the hand.

"Black lawyers are lucky to find work," they'd said. "They're working at the post office—or scrubbing floors like you did at the *Detroit News*. You don't walk away from a steady paycheck."

Fred listened. He nodded. Then he said something that would remain with Damon for decades.

"You see those fields? I planted them all. Soybeans. Corn. I knew there'd be a demand for it. I'm a self-made man. I do my own work. But when I harvest that crop, I can't take it up to Richmond to sell it. Nuh-uh. I have to give it to my neighbor who's white, and he takes it up there and sells it for me.

"You know why? Because if they see me, they'll give me the black man's price, not the white man's price."

He looked Damon square in the eye. "Did you go to law school?"

"Yes."

"And you graduated and became a lawyer?"

"Yes."

"Did you do that so you could just work all day for someone else? Have to ask someone else for a day off? Have to ask someone else when you could have your vacation? Get out on your own, Damon. Don't let anyone else control you. Otherwise, you'll wake up one day and they'll be giving you a watch when you're sixty-five, and you'll never have known what it was to work for yourself and live your own life."

Damon was stirred by this small, powerful man. He returned to Detroit, where, shortly thereafter, despite protests from his family, he told people at the Friend of the Court Office he would soon be leaving.

It was a bold move. And a risky one. During the first year of their marriage, Rachel had gotten pregnant. But she'd suffered a miscarriage between her third and fourth month. Both Rachel and Damon were crestfallen. Their doctor insisted it was not uncommon and they should try again. Still, Damon thought realistically about the responsibilities of a child. He thought about the responsibilities of more than one, which is what he and his wife wanted. Through his job, he'd seen firsthand how households could collapse—often because of financial strain. Giving up a steady paycheck while trying to start a family was almost haughty in light of his position.

But he also knew the lessons he wanted to teach his children once they arrived. He knew these lessons should come not merely from words but from example.

So he took a new job with his original firm, Loomis, Jones, Piper & Colden, and set a new compass in his mind.

Paycheck or not, be your own man.

And start making a difference.

10

A Room on the Second Floor

Rebuilding Detroit's NAACP

A lthough his paid work as a lawyer was often less than fulfilling, Damon Keith, in the early 1950s, did find a home for his civil rights passion: above a Detroit storefront on the second floor of a rickety building on Vernor Highway. These were the offices of the Detroit branch of the NAACP. It was there that the fledgling attorney—"all revved up with the stuff Thurgood Marshall and Charlie Houston had taught me"—met a man named Dr. Arthur L. Johnson and said to him, "If you need a lawyer, I can be your man."

Johnson, a former classmate of Dr. Martin Luther King Jr., had just come up from Georgia to be the executive secretary of Detroit's NAACP office. Founded in 1912, it was the organization's largest branch. And with five thousand members, it proved influential in many local lawsuits and public demonstrations. It also played a crucial role in national civil rights cases, including the Ossian Sweet case in 1925, where an African-American physician was forced out of his home by a mob of whites who refused to allow blacks to move into their neighborhood, and *McGhee*

v. Sipes, the companion case to *Shelley v. Kraemer* in 1948, in which the Supreme Court ruled that restrictive covenants in real estate violated the Fourteenth Amendment.

Yet, despite its legal successes and growing reputation, the branch was a financial mess. There wasn't enough money to pay the operating expenses or the staff. Even keeping the lights on was a struggle. Fighting for civil rights was a noble endeavor, but not a profitable one. The national NAACP was under severe financial strain and had nothing to offer its Detroit operation.

Keith and Johnson worked hard to keep things going. They made an ambitious pair, but neither had any funds to invest.

Enter a man named Johnny White. In many ways, he was like a character out of a Damon Runyan story. He "looked white," as Keith remembers, and he moved in all the right circles as the owner of the Gotham Hotel, one of the finest hotels in America to serve black patrons. In the 1950s, blacks were still shut out of all major hotels in downtown Detroit. But Johnny White made sure his place had the best accommodations. With legendary entertainers such as Sarah Vaughan, Harry Belafonte, Erroll Garner, Billie Holiday, and Josephine Baker performing around town at some of the city's hottest clubs, the Gotham became the hotel of choice for African-American celebrities and dignitaries—as well as all the professional black organizations that periodically met in the city. The hotel's Ebony Room, a magnificent restaurant with a first-rate chef, was a spot of choice and a place where White could entertain his famous guests, many of whose pictures hung on the hotel's Wall of Fame.

In addition to his legitimate work with the hotel, Johnny White ran a major numbers racket. There was big money in it. Fortunately for the NAACP, White had as much passion for equal rights as he did for the gambling business. Employing a touch of urban Robin Hood, White and his business partner, Eddie Cummings, would come by the

NAACP offices at Vernor Highway every Friday and give Keith and Johnson enough money to pay the salaries, utilities, and any other bills.

"He did that in cash," Keith would recall. "Johnny White may have looked white, but he was a man totally committed to the struggle and the emancipation of black people. He literally kept the branch together, because times were tough.

"He was the wind under the wings of the NAACP."

•   •   •

Still, even with White's generosity, both Keith and Johnson knew the branch could not rely on him indefinitely. And raising money from the outside was not easy. White businessmen—even those sympathetic to the cause—were hesitant with their donations. They were so intimidated by racism in the region they would tell Keith, "Don't put our names in the book"—even as he took their money. They didn't want anyone to know.

Keith and Art Johnson realized this was no way to grow an office. They had to develop a meaningful plan. The most effective first step would be to increase paid membership. Keith was appointed chair of the Membership Committee, where his ties to the community and gregarious nature were natural advantages. He was already president of the Cotillion Club, a local social club for prominent blacks that advocated for equality; he encouraged those members to buy memberships in the NAACP branch. He even started a contest with rewards for the most memberships collected. Keith connected the NAACP to his fraternity, Alpha Phi Alpha, and other black Greek organizations. He urged local churches to encourage congregants to join.

"That's how we built the NAACP," he would recall. Pretty soon, a lifetime membership was a badge of honor among the black middle class of Detroit. Recruited members chased new recruits. If a member went to a black doctor's office and did not see a NAACP card, he would ask the physician why not—and offer a membership on the spot.

Keith and Johnson also used the power of the press. Detroit's black-owned newspaper, the *Michigan Chronicle*, published the names of everyone who had purchased lifetime NAACP memberships or was a member of the Detroit branch. This put black businesses and professionals under subtle pressure to join, while also providing free advertising.

And then came a big idea.

• • •

In 1955, Dr. Channing H. Tobias, the national chairman of the NAACP, called for a one-million-dollar "Fight for Freedom" fund. Each branch was asked to create a new fundraising concept.

Johnson and Keith decided upon a dinner event. Targeting educated, middle-class, and professional blacks, they felt confident that an elegant sit-down affair—featuring a prominent keynote speaker—would succeed.

Johnson was particularly keen on the idea, because two years earlier, in 1953, he had called upon his friend, the glamorous singer and actress Josephine Baker, to host a small private fundraiser at the Gotham Hotel. The event drew many black professionals who wanted to meet her, including such luminaries as Nat King Cole. Baker made a passionate appeal to support the work of the NAACP and donated the first hundred dollars to the fund. Within minutes, every man in the room had followed suit.

Keith and Johnson decided to call their event the Freedom Fund Dinner. Their goal? Create a spectacular night that would leave a lasting impression on the guests—and the community.

The key to their inaugural effort would be Thurgood Marshall, Damon's hero from his Howard University days. Still basking in the glow of his historic victory in *Brown v. Board of Education* two years earlier, Marshall, as chief counsel to the NAACP, had reached rock-star status within the African-American and legal communities. At the time, he was arguably the most well known black man in America, outside of the sports and entertainment business. He also fondly remembered Keith from Howard. And to everyone's delight, Marshall agreed to deliver the keynote address in Detroit. Suddenly, the event, set for April 1956, had a prestige and sense of purpose that no other public figure short of the president could have provided.

Not that Keith and Johnson had any more money. They still scrambled to get everything done. They even went to a printer themselves and promised to pay him for the programs *after* the dinner, if he would just print them up beforehand.

Two months prior to the event, a brutal killing had taken place in Georgia. A black doctor named Thomas Brewer was shot to death in a store by its white owner. Brewer was a prominent civil rights activist, a NAACP chapter founder who had fought to register black voters and integrate the schools in Georgia. He'd often had his life threatened by the Ku Klux Klan. His violent death—and a suspicious claim by the store owner that he'd shot Brewer in self-defense—prompted many black Detroiters to surge toward the NAACP. The Freedom Fund dinner list grew exponentially.

The day of the event, Keith and Johnson walked around the ballroom of Detroit's Latin Quarter, an elegant banquet facility, and placed the programs on every seat themselves. There were some four hundred place settings. It took a while.

Then Damon drove off to pick up Thurgood Marshall at the airport. He stood nervously waiting on his law school hero, hoping he'd be on time, hoping he'd be enthusiastic, hoping the night would come off with no hiccups.

He was worrying for naught. The dinner was a huge success. Marshall was eloquent and inspiring. And the event brought in nearly thirty thousand dollars. It would prove to be the start of an annual tradition that now raises millions and hosts up to ten thousand attendees per event. It has offered a stage to everyone from Barbara Jordan and

Chief Justice Earl Warren, to General Colin Powell, Lee Iacocca, Sammy Davis Jr., Aretha Franklin, Anita Baker, then-senator Barack Obama, and President Bill Clinton.

It is well known as a highly celebrated and star-studded affair. But back in 1956, it was strictly do-it-yourself.

"That's why it means so much to me," Keith recalls. "We threw ourselves into it. We created it. And we can never take it for granted."

•　　•　　•

While 1956 would provide Damon a milestone in his professional life, it also marked one of his greatest personal joys: the birth of his and Rachel's first child, Cecile.

The Keiths were still living on Euclid Street in Detroit, in the first-floor apartment. As the due date approached, it looked like it might fall on Damon's birthday and the national holiday, Independence Day, the Fourth of July.

"Wouldn't that be great?" Damon said to Rachel. "Then the baby and I could always have the same birthday."

She smiled. But she was also cautious. By this point, Rachel had suffered two miscarriages. Each had left husband and wife devastated. She didn't care about dates or timing. She only wanted a healthy baby—whenever it arrived.

But sure enough, on July 4, 1956, Damon's thirty-fourth birthday, Rachel felt her first labor pains. She turned to her husband and said calmly, "Darling, I think the baby is coming."

And the reaction from the brave young lawyer, who was taking on discrimination, prejudice, and a racially unbalanced American legal system?

He started to have pains, too.

"Ow, Rachel, this really hurts," he said. He was in agony—all over his body. His stomach. His sides. It would prove to be an early example of what is now called Couvade syndrome—or a "sympathetic pregnancy"—but at the time, all Damon could think was, "What the heck is the matter with me? My wife is pregnant, and I'm doubled up with pain. This is *embarrassing!*"

Of course, having a doctor for a wife has its advantages. Instead of a pregnant woman dragging her agonized husband into the hospital, Rachel retrieved her medical bag, took out a vial and syringe, and gave Damon a shot of something—right in his rear end.

Not long after—as her pains were increasing—his subsided. They drove to Crittenton Hospital together, smiling, keeping that little incident between themselves.

Once there, Damon hoped to see the child come on his birthday. But his doctor had other plans. Reached on a golf course, where he was celebrating the holiday with eighteen holes, the doctor replied that the delivery could wait until tomorrow, when he would do a C-section.

With no alternative, the expectant couple waited in the hospital room—which is how the rest of Damon's birthday was spent. Holding his wife's hand, he fell asleep in a chair next to her. And for the last time in their lives, Damon and Rachel Keith spent the night together as a couple.

The next day they became a family.

Cecile Louise Keith came into the world on July 5, 1956. Damon waited, as was common in those days, until the waiting-room nurse called his name.

"Mr. Keith? You have a baby girl."

The words hit him in a way no judge or jury's words ever would. He was a father. *He was a father.* He raced to the room where Rachel was holding the baby. She was healthy. Their little girl was healthy. Damon kissed them both. He smiled until his face hurt. In a year full of milestones for the future judge, the biggest one had just taken place.

11

"GET OUT ON YOUR OWN"
HOW DAMON KEITH BECAME HIS
OWN START-UP

By 1957, Damon Keith no longer had to imagine himself wearing a suit and tie. He wore them. He no longer had to imagine himself carrying a briefcase. He carried one. He no longer had to imagine himself entering the Tobin Building with other black lawyers, or having secretaries, or entering courtrooms, or addressing judges, or speaking with high-ranking political officials, or hearing the respectful greetings of everyone from the elevator operators to the bailiffs.

He had achieved so many of those youthful dreams that kept him going during his mop-pushing days at the *Detroit News*. And yet, as is often the case with accomplishments, having more led to wanting more. The civil rights movement was in full swing, and the Detroit branch of the NAACP was considered one of the most robust chapters in the country. Keith, working with Loomis, Jones, Piper & Colden, was considered one of the most influential black lawyers in the city, if not the entire state. He had a growing family. An excellent reputation.

He decided it was time to take the next step, to act on the advice that Uncle Fred had given him that day on the farm.

Start his own law firm.

"It's so risky," Rachel said. "We have a family now."

"I know, darling," he said. "But I think I can make it. I want to try and put this together."

One night, over dinner, Keith and fellow up-and-coming black lawyers Herman Anderson, Nathan Conyers, Myron Wahls, and Joseph Brown agreed to strike out on their own. The firm would be called Keith, Conyers, Anderson, Brown & Wahls. It opened in 1957 in the Tobin Building—just one floor below where Keith had been working at Loomis, Jones, Piper & Colden. It was a little odd—and a bit nerve-wracking—coming to the same building but exiting the elevator at a different floor, needing now to make it on his own. But Keith parted on good terms with his former employers (there may have even been a few there who wanted to join him), and, very quickly, his fledgling firm began to flourish.

Each man had a role. Nathan Conyers, a former special assistant to the Michigan attorney general and brother of longtime Michigan congressman John Conyers Jr., mostly handled business clients and civil trials. Herman Anderson did probate. Myron Wahls did criminal law. Joseph Brown handled hundreds of domestic relations cases every year.

And Keith? He brought in the business. They nicknamed him "The Rainmaker." His rising profile and engaging personality kept people coming through the doors. His name on the firm was perhaps the single most important element of its success.

Years later, Keith would recall those early years fondly. "I was doing a lot of community work with the NAACP, United Negro College Fund, with the churches, and so my name was being bandied around. People were coming in to see me, and after I'd interview them, I would introduce them to Nate or Herman as clients."

These included several prominent black funeral parlors, including the House of Diggs and Stinson Funeral Home. Once again, Keith's social connections—he was friends with both Charlie Diggs and Sonny Stinson—would prove profitable. Although white lawyers dominated in so many areas, black families traditionally went to black-owned funeral parlors, and when they expressed a need for help on probate issues, the people at Diggs or Stinson would recommend Keith's firm. It was the rare area in which black lawyers held an upper hand over their white counterparts, and it brought funds to Keith's firm in the early days, when they were most needed.

The first case Keith took, as his own boss, was assigned to him by a judge. It came out of Dearborn, then a city with a notorious reputation for racism. In 1925, Dearborn hosted one of the largest Ku Klux Klan rallies Michigan had ever seen. Years later the residents would elect Orville Hubbard as their mayor, buoyed by slogans like "Keep Dearborn Clean," with "clean" meaning "white." Hubbard once told the *New York Times* that integration would lead to a mongrel race.

Keith was assigned the case of a black man accused of robbing a Dearborn gas station; in truth the man had merely stopped there to use the restroom. But at that time, as Keith would recall, "Dearborn was off limits to blacks. Orville Hubbard had complete control." This emboldened the owner of the gas station to tell the black man, "You know we don't allow any niggers here. Get out."

The allegation that a crime was committed was not supported by a shred of evidence. Still, Keith was worried going into the case. The jury was all white. He braced for inequity to rear its ugly head.

Fortunately, the jury gave his client a fair hearing. They presumed innocence. And in the absence of any real evidence of wrongdoing, the man was acquitted without ever having to take the stand.

Keith marveled at the justice system working like it was supposed to work.

And he'd just won his first case at his own firm.

•   •   •

The following year, 1958, brought another milestone to the Keith family. Rachel gave birth to a second daughter. Damon suffered no sympathetic pains this time, and no needles in the rear end were required. The trip to the hospital was uneventful, and the birth went smoothly.

At the time, Damon was still president of the Cotillion Club, and the day the child was born, May 2, was the night of its biggest event, the Debutante Ball, held at the famed Latin Quarter.

In the hospital, an ebullient Keith, sitting next to Rachel, held his baby girl. He was beyond happy. He thought about his obligation that night. And he said to his wife, "Darling, I have an idea. . . ."

That night, at the ball, Damon stepped to the microphone and announced to the crowd that he and Rachel had just become proud parents once more, and that their new daughter's name, apropos to the Debutante Ball, was . . . Debbie.

Meanwhile, Daddy's business was booming. Although Damon had initially worried about how much work his young firm would attract, the clients and cases grew so fast that it was soon time to consider larger offices—and another location. The options were limited. Detroit's racial climate kept most black professionals in the Tobin Building on the edge of downtown. This was where black lawyers worked; this was where black clients came to find them. But the Tobin Building posed problems. For one thing, it was closed on Sundays, and there were times when the attorneys needed to meet their clients on that day. When Keith informed the building's manager, he was told, "We understand, but we can't just open the whole building for your firm."

Around this time, Keith ran into a friend named Bob Fenton, a white lawyer who had an office in the Guardian Building, a forty-story art deco skyscraper in the heart of downtown. "If the Tobin Building was ninety-nine percent black occupied, then the Guardian was ninety-eight percent white," Keith would recall. Nonetheless, Fenton told Keith, "You should come over here. You should be the first black law firm in the building."

Fenton introduced Keith to the manager, who was willing to offer space, but Keith's law partners were not so sure about the move. Black clients had always gone to the Tobin Building. "Do you think they could find our offices?" the partners said. "We can't afford to lose any clients." While acknowledging these concerns, Keith felt confident that their business would follow them.

Besides, this was part of the reason he got into law in the first place, wasn't it? To break down the barriers—including the spatial ones? His mother being told she could not live in a certain neighborhood because of her color still stung. His family had fought that prejudice. He would fight this one.

Two years after opening his firm, he moved it. And he never looked back.

Oh, there were a few hiccups. It was impractical to move the old furniture from the Tobin Building into the new space, and starting anew left no money for luxuries. The Guardian Building housed a branch of the Michigan Bank Corporation. Keith approached the branch officer, Bud Stratton, to inquire about getting a loan. Again, he was cautious. A black law firm in a white building, and they wanted to borrow money right away?

"Sir, if you would advance us enough so that we can get all of our office supplies and chairs and tables, we will pay you back weekly," Keith promised.

To his surprise and delight, Stratton replied, "Sure, I'll be happy to do it." With the loan, Keith, Conyers, Anderson, Brown & Wahls was able to open its offices right away, with new furniture and equipment. It lost no clients in the transition. Keith remained forever grateful to Stratton for taking the chance on his young business—and for bucking the status quo.

Not every barrier would be so easily hurdled. One bizarre probate issue illuminated the depths to which race had become a dividing line between citizens and even social classes.

The case involved a black doctor who was passing as white. One day, Keith received a call from Richard E. Fields, an old classmate and fraternity brother from his college and law school days. Fields now was living in Charleston, South Carolina. He was the lawyer for the estate of a black physician and was seeking to distribute the estate to the man's heirs. He asked for Keith's help in locating the son, who reportedly lived in Grosse Pointe, an affluent Detroit suburb.

Keith, who by then was deeply involved in the social scene of black professionals, told Fields he must be mistaken. No blacks lived in Grosse Pointe. Fields, however, insisted that the son lived in Grosse Pointe and that he was black. So Keith looked into the matter. He eventually found the man, who was a doctor, and called to introduce himself. When the doctor confirmed he was indeed the son, Keith told him about his inheritance and asked to meet with him to sign the paperwork.

To Keith's utter shock and dismay, the doctor, who was very light-complexioned and married to a white woman with whom he had children, insisted that Keith stay away. He'd been passing for white and didn't want that disturbed.

"Attorney Keith, I don't want anything to do with the estate. Don't come out here. Send the money back."

Send the money back? Keith was stunned. The doctor's absolute fear of being exposed as a black man was so palpable that Keith said no more. But for years he struggled to make sense of it all, the legacy of a racism so strong and so destructive that it could lead a man to refuse his inheritance and deny his own identity.

•   •   •

Such incidents only made Keith more determined to fight for equality. In the late 1950s, it remained a bruising battle. In more cases than he cared to remember, Keith sought justice for a black client before a judge who was blatantly racist. It reminded him that despite his flourishing practice, and all his work with the NAACP, an attorney could only do so much in a system still infected with prejudice.

In one particularly poignant case, Keith represented a young black man who was home for Christmas from a historically black college. A supermarket had been robbed on West Grand Boulevard right near Damon's old high school, Northwestern, and the young man was arrested. He told Keith, "I didn't rob this store," and Keith was convinced that he hadn't. But the young man had taken and failed a lie detector test.

The young man's father worked as a probation officer in the juvenile court under Judge Nathan Kaufman, who recommended that the accused man be placed on bond. When Keith took his client before Judge John Ricca to set that bond, he was momentarily encouraged; a white lawyer had a client, a young white man, about the same age, charged with basically the same offense. Judge Ricca placed the white man on personal bond. Keith had reason to hope for a similar outcome.

However, as he later recalled: "I approached the bench. I said, 'Your Honor, this young man is just home from college with his family. His father is a probation officer over in juvenile court, and Judge Kaufman has recommended that he be placed on personal bond. I recommend that you do that. He's had no prior record; he's in college.'"

The judge listened—then totally ignored the recommendation. He placed the young black man on a twenty-five-thousand-dollar bond.

Keith could barely hold his tongue. He pointed out the inequity between the two cases—just minutes apart.

"Your Honor," Keith said, "Why did you treat this man differently?"

Images of the army, his father's struggles, the fights in school all came rushing back. He knew he should keep quiet, but the fire inside him would not allow it.

"I have a wife and children to support, Judge Ricca. And for you to mistreat me and mistreat my client, based solely on the fact that he's black, is something I cannot understand. And I don't like it."

The judge glared at him.

"Mr. Keith, you can go now," he said.

"Thank you, Your Honor," Damon seethed.

He left the court with his heart pounding and his anger boiling. His client was taken to jail. Keith agonized over the case—until a month or so later, when he got a call from the judge's office.

"Bring your client over here to court," Keith was told. "We have a man they picked up for robbery, and we went through a string of other robberies, and he confessed that he robbed that store on West Grand Boulevard. We're going to let your client go."

When Keith arrived with his client—who had been behind bars all this time—he was struck by the close physical resemblance between the actual culprit and the young man. This only made him feel worse.

"What a miscarriage of justice," he thought. "If we had gone to trial, it would have been hard to get an acquittal. The two men look so alike. He could have been one more innocent man in jail."

Keith left that courtroom shaking his head. He thought this case was over. But years later, when he was being considered for a federal judgeship, the FBI came by his office.

"Can we speak with you?" they asked.

"Yes. What's wrong?"

"Mr. Keith," one of the agents said. "In going through your file, we discovered that you were accused of disrespecting a judge."

"What?" Damon replied. "That's simply not true, I never disrespected any judge."

"Well, there was something in your file, a complaint that goes back years, from a Judge Ricca. He reported you. Said you were disrespectful to him in his court."

Damon squeezed his eyes closed. Some things never stop haunting you. "I was not disrespectful," he explained, searching for patience. "I was simply responding appropriately for my client."

They wrote it all down. And in the end, nothing came of the FBI visit. The judgeship went forward, and that story fell back into the shadows. But Keith never forgot the rot of racism and how a judge could forever shape the futures of those who came before him. To this day, that case compels Keith to seek fair, polite, and respectful treatment of attorneys in his courtroom.

"I never want any attorney to feel the way I had to feel on that day," he would say.

•   •   •

Time passed. The firm continued to blossom. And in 1960, Damon and Rachel had one more moment of parental bliss. Gilda, their third daughter, would help them welcome in the new decade. It was Rachel's third C-section birth.

"It's probably too risky for us to have any more," she told Damon.

"That's fine, darling," he said. "You've given me three beautiful daughters, and I am so very happy."

They beamed over their new addition. The Keith family unit was intact. Mother, father, three young girls. It was a portrait of domestic bliss.

But the 1960s were upon them.

And peace and quiet would not last long.

Damon J. Keith as a child with his family.

Judge Damon J. Keith's parents, Annie L. and Perry A. Keith, 1941.

Private Damon J. Keith serving in a segregated army during WWII (*circled*) in the 3004th Quartermaster Bakery Company, Fort Francis E. Warren, Wyoming, 1943.

ABOVE: *(Front row)* Arthur L. Johnson, Damon J. Keith *(back row, left to right)*, Judge Theodore Bohn, Governor G. Mennen Williams, William Matney Jr., Judge Wade H. McCree Jr., and Judge Elvin L. Davenport, outside of Detroit Housing Commission, Detroit, Michigan, 1950s.

OPPOSITE, TOP: Northwestern High School classmates Damon J. Keith, Calvin V. Porter, and Wilbur B. Hughes in Detroit, Michigan, 1945.

OPPOSITE, BOTTOM: Dr. Rachel Boone and Damon J. Keith on their wedding day in Richmond, Virginia, October 18, 1953.

ABOVE: Brooklyn Dodger Jackie Robinson, Attorney Damon J. Keith, Detroit's Gotham Hotel, 1957.

OPPOSITE, TOP: Willie Horton, William Ellmann, Judge Ira Kaufman, and Attorney Damon J. Keith at the signing of Willie Horton to the Detroit Tigers, 1961.

OPPOSITE, BOTTOM: President John F. Kennedy, Attorney Damon J. Keith, and Dr. Rachel Boone Keith at the White House Emancipation Day, Washington, D.C., February 22, 1963.

ABOVE: Governor George W. Romney swearing in Damon J. Keith and John Feikens as co-chairs to the Michigan Civil Rights Commission, 1963.

OPPOSITE: Joe Coles, Arthur L. Johnson, Damon J. Keith, Attorney General Robert Kennedy, Richard Marks, Senator David Holmes, and Vice President Lyndon B. Johnson at a civil rights meeting, Washington, D.C., 1963.

ABOVE: Sammy Davis Jr., Dr. Rachel Boone Keith, and Judge Damon J. Keith at a dinner party at the Keiths' home in Detroit, Michigan, November 20, 1969.

OPPOSITE, TOP: Myron Wahls, Nathan Conyers, Joseph Brown, Herman Anderson, and Damon J. Keith at the Law Firm of Keith, Conyers, Anderson, Brown & Wahls in Detroit, Michigan, 1964.

OPPOSITE, BOTTOM: Michigan Supreme Court Justice Otis M. Smith, Damon J. Keith, Dr. Martin Luther King Jr. and Michigan Secretary of State Richard Austin, 1965.

Damon J. Keith and Muhammad Ali, 1969.

Judge Damon J. Keith and Supreme Court Justice Thurgood Marshall.

Judge Damon J. Keith being presented with the NAACP Spingarn Medal by Congressman Charles C. Diggs Jr. in New Orleans, July 2, 1974.

ABOVE: NAACP Spingarn Medal recipients Judge Damon J. Keith and Justice Thurgood Marshall with Chief Justice Earl Warren *(center)*.

OPPOSITE, TOP: Judge Damon J. Keith and President Gerald R. Ford, May 1975.

OPPOSITE, BOTTOM: Dr. Frederick Patterson, founder of the United Negro College Fund, Henry Ford II, and Judge Damon J. Keith at a UNCF meeting.

Damon J. Keith, Rachel Boone Keith, and their young daughters, Debbie, Gilda, and Cecile.

12

A Leader Emerges

From Jack Kennedy to Willie Horton

I n politics, Damon Keith was becoming a true rarity, a man who could move in almost any circle. He compiled an impressive track record as a campaign manager, successfully helping to elect William T. Patrick Jr., the first black member of the Detroit City Council, and Wade McCree, who won a seat on the Wayne County Circuit Court. Keith helped white candidates as well, like Governor John B. Swainson and Michigan Supreme Court Justice John D. Voelker. Keith's engaging personality and growing community influence were sought after by politicians and eventually drew the attention of a Massachusetts senator who had his eye on the White House.

His name was John F. Kennedy.

Kennedy was deciding whether to run for president in 1960. He was having difficulty garnering support among black voters. His team made a call to then Michigan governor G. Mennen (Soapy) Williams, who arranged for a group of Michigan's most prominent black leaders to meet the young senator in his Georgetown home for a roundtable discussion.

Keith was among them.

Kennedy sent his private jet to collect the group. To that point, Damon Keith had not been on many airplanes—and certainly never a private one. So when the twin engine Corvair 240 (dubbed "Caroline" after Kennedy's baby daughter) arrived in Detroit to transport the contingent, Keith was stunned. A sixteen-seat aircraft with a desk, a map of the United States, and special meals served by a friendly, designated hostess was almost beyond his imagination. Then again, that kind of privilege was part of the reason men like Keith were being summoned. John F. Kennedy did not move in their world—any more than they moved in his. If he wanted to be president, he needed to improve on that.

Upon landing, the group was picked up from the airport in a limousine and treated to lunch at Kennedy's home in Georgetown. Jacqueline, Kennedy's wife, was there as well. After the meal, a discussion ensued, and Senator Kennedy admitted he didn't know many black Americans, and thus was fairly ignorant of their concerns.

Keith, never shy, quickly threw down a challenge. Here is how he would recall it years later:

> Senator Kennedy had just returned from a campaign event in West Virginia. So I asked if he favored the sit-in demonstrations that were going on in the South, where young black people were protesting at lunch counters and restaurants that would not serve black customers. The senator said that he was for the sit-in demonstrations "as long as Negroes conducted themselves orderly." I reminded him that Senator Hubert Humphrey, his chief competitor in the presidential primary, had said that he unequivocally approved of the sit-ins. I suggested to Senator Kennedy that he was either for them or against them.

When Kennedy objected, Keith kept going.

"Senator, you say, 'As long as they conduct themselves orderly.' Do you assume we, as blacks, are going to be disorderly?"

"No, I don't assume that," Kennedy said.

"Then why would you warn us not to be?"

Now, most houseguests do not get in the face of their hosts—especially not a popular U.S. senator who had just flown them five hundred miles in a private jet. But Keith felt strongly about the issue, and he figured if Kennedy wanted to get to know black people's opinions, he ought to actually hear one. The tension at the table was palpable. Finally, Governor Williams intervened, saying, "Jack, what Damon is saying is this: If I invite you to my house for dinner, I don't tell you to wash your hands."

To Kennedy's credit, he answered, "Soapy, I've got it." The tension subsided, and the rest of the afternoon went well. Keith left impressed with the Massachusetts senator and told colleagues at the NAACP convention a short time later that he would be happy if Kennedy made it to the White House.

Three years later, when Kennedy was president, Keith was invited to the White House as part of a small group of lawyers asked to discuss civil rights issues. Kennedy greeted him with a knowing smile. "I still remember our talk at the table in the Georgetown house," he said. Keith was so impressed with the new president that he asked if might bring his three daughters to Washington to meet him.

"We can do that, Damon," Kennedy said. "Just get it set up."

They never got the chance. Several months later, Kennedy was assassinated.

The day it happened, November 22, 1963, Keith was in his office at the Guardian Building. Someone told him the news. Keith shut the door and slumped in a chair. He wondered what was happening to this country.

•　　•　　•

As his career and influence continued to grow, Damon was careful not to forget where he came from. He kept tabs on old friends and old neighborhoods. So when he got a call from a man named Sam Bishop, he was quick to respond. Bishop had coached Keith in track and field back at Northwestern High School and was currently the baseball coach there. He told Damon there was a player at his alma mater who, with the right influence, "could be a big star." Would Damon go to his house and meet him and his parents?

Keith agreed and soon found himself shaking hands with a beefy teenager named Willie Horton, the youngest of twenty-one children born to Clinton and Lillian Horton. At school they were already calling the kid "Willie the Wonder," and Keith found him to be polite and deferential. Yet there was something more, some sort of personal connection that Keith felt instantly, not unlike the moment he met Rachel Boone for the first time. He somehow knew this would turn into an important relationship.

Mr. and Mrs. Horton must have felt it, too, because in their home, before the meeting was over, they asked Keith to be Willie's legal guardian. They were worried about the attention Willie was getting, the potential trouble awaiting him on the streets, and the fact that they had so many other children to watch over. Major league teams were already swarming around their son, talking about contracts, filling his head with ideas.

"I was flabbergasted," Keith would recall. "Legal guardian meant I would be responsible for him in every way. I couldn't believe they were asking me that. But they said, 'Mr. Keith, we believe you can take care of our son. We trust you to watch out for his best interests.'"

Keith said he would do it, but he needed to speak with his wife. After he left, according to Horton, the teenager sat on the porch with his father, and, fighting tears, said, "You ain't giving me away, are you, Daddy?"

"No," his father told him. "But this man, Keith, ought to be the first black president of the United States, and I want him to guide you."

Meanwhile, Damon went home to Rachel and told her what had happened. He knew accepting this role would essentially mean they had taken on a sixteen-year-old son.

"What do you think?" he asked.

"Darling, if Coach Bishop asked you, then it must be important. I trust your judgment. If we can help this young man, we should do it."

That would mark the start of a loving, nurturing, and often raucous relationship that spanned the end of high school all the way through and beyond a seventeen-year all-star baseball career. In the early days, Willie would frequently stay with the Keiths, particularly if he got in trouble. The local police knew about the relationship, and, as Keith would recall it, "If Willie got into a scrape, they would call me and say, 'Mr. Keith, come on down, we have Willie here, and you need to take him home.' I'd drive down, pick him up, and he'd come stay at the house until morning."

One time, Horton's parents were concerned that Willie was driving without a license. Keith confronted the young athlete.

"Willie, your mother tells me you've been driving a car without a driver's license."

"No, Mr. Keith. I've got licenses. Here they are."

He pulled out several drivers' licenses, none of them his. Keith couldn't believe it.

"Willie, you can't just use anyone's driver's license! You have to get your own! You could go to jail for doing this!"

He made a call, put Willie in the car, and took him to get his license. It was one of countless episodes where Keith yanked Horton out of the fire. And one of countless reasons that Horton cherished the relationship in the fifty-plus years that followed.

Of course, when he wasn't bailing Horton out of trouble, Keith, as his legal guardian and representative, was often steering his financial career. Horton's baseball talent was extraordinary—his batting average was over .400 during high school. After leading Northwestern to a city championship in 1959, he piqued the interest of numerous major league teams, including the Detroit Tigers—even though he was just a teenager. In those days, teams frequently came to the home and brokered a fast—and often cheap—contract with a player's parents, who were only too happy to have their son sign a big league deal. But with Keith as Willie's guardian, the Tigers were forced to meet with a highly competent lawyer.

To sign a player who was still in high school, hardship needed to be proven. Clinton Horton was on disability, unable to work, and the Hortons' financial situation, especially with so many children, certainly qualified them as a hardship case. Keith heard from multiple teams, including the New York Yankees and the Boston Red Sox. But he knew it would be best if Willie could play close to home, where Keith could keep an eye on him. He and the Tigers officials carved out a deal, but not without some haggling.

"We'd like to see him stay in Detroit," the Tigers said.

"Yes," Keith said, "but, you know, Boston is interested in him, too."

"How much will it take?"

Eventually, Keith negotiated a contract that included a $50,000 signing bonus. At the time, it was an extraordinary amount for a high school prospect. In fact, it was three times the annual salary that Keith was earning. But he was gratified to help the Horton family and to keep his all-but-adopted son in the area. In August of 1961, Damon, Willie, and Willie's father drove to Tiger Stadium and walked down a hallway to the office of Tigers General Manager Rick Ferrell. With cameras flashing, Willie signed the deal.

He still had a year left in high school.

An Associated Press story from that day began this way:

If physical resemblance means anything, the Detroit Tigers can expect real dividends from the estimated $50,000 they shelled out Monday to 18 year-old Willie Horton.

With a neck like a tree trunk and a spectacular set of muscles, the newest Tiger acquisition looks enough like Roy Campanella to be his twin.

"And that's not all," said one of Willie's former coaches who watched while Tiger officials presented Horton, a Negro, to the press. "He also hits like Campanella."

The fact that Horton was identified, in an AP story, as a "Negro" speaks to the time. But Horton would become an important figure in Detroit's history. He had a stellar rookie season with the Tigers and would go on to garner seven All-Star selections and become a household name.

But on a fateful night in 1967, he stood on the roof of a car in the middle of Detroit's burning streets, still wearing his Tigers uniform, imploring the citizens of his hometown to stop the violence. It was a defining, iconic stance, in a riot that would resonate harshly with blacks and whites alike.

A riot that would affect Damon Keith forever.

13.

DETROIT 1967

THE FIRE THIS TIME

In 1963, upon the one hundredth anniversary of the signing of the Emancipation Proclamation, the writer James Baldwin expounded on racial atrocities of the past and present and warned that America, without change, would face "The Fire Next Time." Next time was not far away. Trouble in Detroit was about to begin.

It was early Sunday afternoon on July 23, 1967, and Damon and his wife, Rachel, were packing their suitcases for Hawaii. There was a judicial conference there, and they planned to combine that with a long-overdue vacation in the islands. By this point, Keith's prominence in Detroit was matched only by his superhuman workload. He was an integral part of the first Michigan Civil Rights Commission, appointed by Governor George Romney. He was president of the Detroit Housing Commission, ensuring the discrimination his mother went through trying to buy her house didn't happen to others. His fundraising was prolific, as was his networking and pro bono work for the Detroit NAACP, along with his tireless work for the Democratic Party. And of course, his "day job" as

a lawyer and the face of Keith, Conyers, Anderson, Brown & Wahls, which had risen to one of the most influential minority law firms in the nation. It was a hugely impressive body of work. And it was about to be tested in his own back yard.

The phone rang. Keith moved away from his suitcase to pick it up. On the other end was his close friend Joe Coles. He sounded worried.

"There's trouble in the city, Damon," he said. "You need to turn on the TV."

Keith did so. His jaw dropped. There, on the screen, were images of roaming crowds of angry black men and women of all ages. They were smashing store windows, tossing rocks and other projectiles, defiantly—and dangerously—ignoring police demands to disperse.

For a brief moment, Keith was frozen. He knew what he was witnessing. Over the past two summers, he had seen similar scenes play out in cities across the nation, most vividly in the Watts neighborhood of Los Angeles in 1965 and in Newark, New Jersey, the following year—two communities exploding in rage after years of pent-up frustration by urban residents.

Keith knew if riots were breaking out in cities similar to Detroit, it was just a matter of time before one hit home. He had been warning of this danger for years.

Now, apparently, it had arrived.

As Damon and Rachel watched the violence escalate, calls began to come in reporting that it had spread to the old Virginia Park neighborhood where Damon once lived, and where his older sister Marie and niece Sweetie and her two boys, Keith and Kenny, now resided. Damon flashed back to the 1943 riots that held the city captive for three days before federal troops came in. He remembered wanting to go outside and fight and his mother pleading with him, "Please, Damon, don't go out there." Back then he was a son. Now he was a father. He felt the

anguish and frustration all parents feel knowing the streets are suddenly unsafe for their children.

He turned to his wife. "Darling, we're going to have to cancel this vacation. We can't leave with the city like this."

"I understand," she said, softly, seeing the violence on the screen. "Go do what you can do."

The first thing Damon attempted to do was use his connections with the media. He had grown friendly with many newspaper and radio people. He phoned Martin S. Hayden, editor of the *Detroit News*, and Jim Quello, general manager of Detroit powerhouse radio station WJR 760 AM and a fellow Detroit Housing Commission member.

"I asked them if they would hold off publicizing the violence until we could get a better hold on what was going on," Judge Keith would recall. "I didn't want the news going out all across the country. I knew once the media started streaming in, the situation would just get worse."

Both men were sympathetic. In the interest of not sparking copycat violence, they agreed to restrain coverage until they were better able to determine the facts.

But just hours later, Keith received phone calls from both of them.

"The national news is on it," they said. "We have no choice."

Keith knew what that meant. The storm was about to rage out of control.

•　　•　　•

What he did not know, as he sat staring at the chaos on his television screen, was how this all started. But he knew the raging anger that created it and the oppressive circumstances that set off the fury. For many years in Detroit, black frustrations roiled just underneath the city's surface: poverty, rampant discrimination, overcrowded and inadequate housing, terrible schools, and an overall sense of hopelessness.

White flight from Detroit in the 1950s and 1960s had accelerated the problem of black unemployment, as businesses started to follow white consumers to the suburbs. At the same time, factories were becoming more automated. Entry-level jobs that might have been available to young black men were becoming less available. With the downsizing of the auto industry, those with the least seniority were the first to be laid off. These, invariably, were black employees.

Meanwhile, the burgeoning Civil Rights Movement in the South began to capture the attention of blacks everywhere, including Detroit. Local churches, labor unions, and black civic organizations actively supported civil rights efforts. Black Detroiters took a closer look at the racial dynamics in their own community and did not like what they saw, particularly in the Detroit police force and the violent—even criminal—behavior it often engaged in against black citizens. That became tinder for the dry and brittle twigs of frustration and injustice. Once lit, it was like a Molotov cocktail.

And the city would burn.

"The police had a 'stop-and-frisk' policy," Judge Keith would recall. It was a euphemism for harassing anyone the police felt like harassing. As a black man, it was hard to escape it; Keith himself had endured the practice several times.

"Even when I was already a lawyer, I was walking down the street and a police car rolled by. They saw me, they stopped, and they got out of the car. They asked, 'Who are you? What are you doing?' I told them my name. Told them I was a lawyer. They patted me down anyhow. It was humiliating."

That incident was mild. Keith's fellow Detroiters could recall far less pleasant experiences with police officers. If you appeared nervous, you were in trouble. If you forgot your license, you were in trouble. If you didn't have an acceptable explanation for where you were going, you were in trouble. Arrests were rampant. Harassment was constant. This may seem incredible in the telling. But in Detroit, in 1967, it was simply understood that blacks had no rights that the police would respect.

The unwarranted stop-and-frisk incidents were not the individual acts of a few bad apples, but rather snapshots of an agency that formalized racist practices. Burton Levy served as the head of the Community Relations Division of the Michigan Civil Rights Commission, the same commission to which Keith was appointed by Governor Romney. In 1968, Levy wrote that the Detroit Police Department "recruits a significant number of bigots, reinforces the bigotry through the department's value system and socialization with older officers, and then takes the worst of the officers and puts them on duty in the ghetto."

By 1967 only a small fraction of the force was non-white, and there were many instances of police brutality against blacks in Detroit. Far from being a reassuring presence, the Detroit police were often viewed as a menacing, demoralizing, and destabilizing presence in the black community.

One final act of police brutality pushed it over the edge.

·　·　·

The 1967 riots, or "urban rebellion," as many black scholars refer to it, began in the wee hours of that Sunday morning, July 23rd, after police raided an after-hours drinking club in a black neighborhood, at the juncture of Twelfth and Clairmount Streets. In Detroit, such unlicensed clubs were commonly referred to as "blind pigs." This one was located on the second floor above a print shop.

On Saturday night, about eighty people had crammed inside to celebrate the return of two Vietnam War veterans. It was not, by its nature, a combative gathering. But in a typical roughshod and overreactive way, the Detroit police, upon learning of the celebration, decided to detain and arrest everyone in the club. This drew a crowd of onlookers.

As the patrons were being herded into a line of police vehicles, the crowd began to jeer the police. Confrontations ensued. Insults flew back and forth. Shoving and tussling began, and, before long, people began to toss rocks and bottles as the squad cars pulled away.

It wasn't long before someone smashed the windows of the clothing store next door, and from there, vandalism, looting, and arson took root. It began to spread throughout the neighborhood and quickly grew through the entire west side of the city. Blacks throughout Detroit had seemingly had enough of racism and contempt from the overwhelmingly white police force. The flames were fanning out of control.

As the hours passed, the violence grew more intense. Because it was now Sunday morning, reinforcements for the police were slow to arrive, and Twelfth Street in particular was out of control. The first major fire broke out in the afternoon, at a grocery store, and the crowds prevented fire trucks from extinguishing the blaze. More fires were set. The city was going up in smoke.

As the rebellion continued to escalate, Keith's closest friend from the NAACP, Arthur L. Johnson, joined Congressman John Conyers Jr. in going to the epicenter on Twelfth Street. By the time they got there, the crowd had grown so dense that it could no longer move, and the men jumped on the hood of their car with a bullhorn and implored people to stop rioting and go home.

The frustration, however, had gotten out of hand, and they were jeered and cursed by the volatile crowd. As Johnson recalled in his memoir, "John shouted through his bullhorn to the crowd, 'Stay cool, we're with you! But, please! This is not the way to do things!'"

Conyers's call for calm only seemed to agitate things, and soon accusations of being Uncle Toms, police informants, and part of the establishment were hurled as furiously as the curses, rocks, and bottles.

The men hurriedly left the scene for their own safety, with Conyers telling a local news reporter, in a quote that made international news reports, "You try to talk to those people, and they'll knock you into the middle of next year!"

It didn't matter who was urging calm. Even Damon's "adopted" baseball star, Willie Horton, hurried after the game at Tiger Stadium, still in his uniform, and stood on cars screaming for calm. It was a symbolic moment. But it had no effect. This was bigger than any one man or one speech.

Keith watched his beloved city descend into near anarchy. He was torn. Though a black man and sympathetic to the pent-up frustrations of the populace, he was also a successful lawyer, a political operative, and, therefore, in the view of some blacks, part of the establishment. But being that powerful meant he knew what government officials were capable of when they felt order was threatened. And he was deeply aware that there were very few, if any, black people among them to counsel restraint.

This scared him nearly as much as what was happening in the streets.

He called Johnson, who had just returned from Twelfth Street and was still shaken from what he'd seen. "We've got to get down to 1300," Damon said, referring to the Detroit Police headquarters at 1300 Beaubien Street. "These people are making decisions about us right now, and there are no blacks there!"

They drove to the building, uninvited, and announced themselves to the guards there. Fortunately, they were welcomed and ushered inside. When they entered the room, they realized it was a virtual command center of state and city authority: Governor Romney, Mayor Jerome Cavanagh, Detroit Police Commissioner Ray Girardin, and others. The severity of the situation was obvious.

"They were vacillating on whether or not federal troops should be brought in," Keith would recall. "At one point, President Johnson called in from Washington. They put him on speakerphone, and he talked about sending a force in to deal with the violence. That's how bad the situation had gotten."

91

Out on the street, the looting and arson escalated. Over the next twenty-four hours, more than four hundred fires would be set. Shots rang out everywhere, and firefighters attempting to put out the blazes were often targets of gunfire. Hundreds of businesses were looted, many of them black-owned. The rounding up and arresting of citizens was widespread and rampant, resulting in nearly two thousand people being herded to police stations before Monday night, many of them simply for standing and watching.

Perhaps because he was older now, Keith perceived this riot as angrier than the one in 1943. It felt darker, more urgent, more intense. It also ignited similar disturbances elsewhere around the region: Pontiac, Flint, Saginaw, Grand Rapids, and Toledo, Ohio, all experienced unrest.

That night at police headquarters, Keith looked around the room. The issue was whether to support Governor Romney's request for federal troops. Many leaders in Detroit's black community were against it. They feared, for good reason, the idea of black citizens waking up to mostly white soldiers pointing weapons as they tried to go about their daily routines. Congressman Conyers noted that there was plenty of reason to fear an overreaction by the troops. He and Keith were among the many citizens who still had vivid memories of 1943 and the wanton acts of violence committed by the authorities; over half of the African Americans who died during those riots lost their lives at the hands of law enforcement.

Wouldn't the federal troops be mainly white soldiers? Wouldn't that only escalate the violence?

Because of such concerns, Keith was initially opposed to federal intervention. But soon a more persuasive argument emerged. It was made by the son of Keith's close friend and former client, Charles Diggs Jr., who, at that time, was the federal congressman for the thirteenth district, the area most affected by the rioting.

Diggs feared that the damage being inflicted on homes and businesses was so catastrophic that, without an immediate cessation of the violence, the city might never recover. His district, in many ways, was being destroyed.

"That's when I realized we needed outside force," Keith would say.

He and Arthur Johnson stressed to Governor Romney the need to ensure that troops protect the rights of civilians. Romney agreed. But in order to bring in federal authority, Romney would have to declare Detroit in "a state of insurrection." It was then up to President Lyndon Johnson.

The group disbanded for the night. Damon drove home, listening to reports of the violence on the radio. He went inside and hugged his wife.

"Tell me," she said.

"It's out of hand," he said. "We need help."

Late Monday night, President Johnson finally gave the order. By Tuesday, some 8,000 National Guardsmen were deployed. Eventually, nearly 5,000 paratroopers and 360 Michigan State Police would be added to the force. For much of that week, Detroit screamed, smoked, and smoldered. It left Damon Keith heartbroken.

"It still remains one of my ugliest memories," he would say.

•　　•　　•

By Friday, six days after the violence broke out, the federal troops—many of whom were black—began to withdraw from Detroit. They were completely gone by Saturday. It was one week on the calendar. But it felt like a lifetime to Damon and other longtime residents.

When the dust settled, 43 people were dead, 1,189 were injured, over 7,200 arrests had been made, and more than 2,000 buildings had been destroyed. It remains one of the worst riots in American history, and gave Detroit the sad distinction of being the only city that required federal intervention three separate times. The riot received the kind of widespread media attention that plagues a city for decades. Detroit burning was an indelible image—one Keith and other leaders would spend years trying to correct.

Estimates of financial losses ranged from $22 million to $500 million. But statistics do not adequately measure the losses sustained in those hours of turmoil. Most of those arrested had no criminal record; some were held as long as thirty hours on buses. Others were held in underground garages without bathroom facilities. Action by police officers accounted for at least twenty of the forty-three deaths. If poverty, racism, and white flight had weakened Detroit's resources, the riots left it crippled.

The troops were gone and the streets were quiet, but the truce was an uneasy one. Keith worked tirelessly behind the scenes to de-escalate simmering tensions. He became a founding member of a civic group called New Detroit. It was formed just days after the unrest in response to a request from Governor Romney, Mayor Cavanagh, and Joseph L. Hudson Jr., the owner of Hudson's department store at the heart of downtown Detroit. It became the nation's first urban coalition of political, corporate, and community leaders dedicated to critically examining the underlying causes for racial and civil unrest.

As a condition of their participation, Keith and Johnson demanded that participants listen to all segments of the black community. These voices ranged from the traditional civil rights establishment to the young black militants on the street. But even as the new members pledged to work well together, the initial meeting got off to a rocky start after a prominent member of the business community noted all the media attention that black grassroots and Black Nationalist leaders were garnering.

Looking over at Keith and Johnson, the businessman complained, "We've been listening to the wrong Negroes all this time."

The comment deeply offended Keith, who had been dealing with many of these community leaders for years through the NAACP, the

National Lawyers Guild, and the Detroit Housing Commission. He stood up and fired back:

"How can you say that? We've been saying what they're saying for years! We have told you about police brutality! About education! About housing and all the discrimination in this city! We have told you and told you—and it's taken this kind of damage to the city to make you wake up!

"Don't say you've been listening to the wrong Negroes. You just haven't been listening!"

He sat back down. The weight of the riots and the enormous damage to his city weighed heavily on his soul. It would eventually drive him to make the best kind of peace, forging coalitions and bringing unlikely forces together—like his friend, Henry Ford II, the son of Henry Ford, and the Reverend Albert Cleage, a charismatic black preacher who preached racial separatism. Few people besides Keith could have engendered a dialogue between such disparate men. But he knew it would require that kind of bridge-building to raise Detroit from the rubble of July 1967. He set about the difficult task of making it happen.

To this day, he has never been to Hawaii.

APPROACHING THE BENCH
THE LONG AND WINDING POLITICS OF
BECOMING A JUDGE

"The American judiciary and our nation would have been far lesser institutions if Damon Keith had not been appointed a federal judge."

—Judge A. Leon Higginbotham

Langston Hughes's famous poem ponders the fate of a dream deferred and asks if "maybe it sags like a heavy load." As the deferred dreams of racial equality sagged heavily on blacks in the mid-1960s, so, too, did deferred legal dreams weigh heavily on the mind of Damon Keith.

Although more successful than most of his African-American law colleagues, Keith the attorney endured major disappointments before becoming Keith the federal judge. These setbacks would make him question his friendships, his politics, even the lengths to which he could trust people.

And all of them would teach him a lesson.

As early as the mid-1950s, even before he opened his own firm, Keith had public-sector ambitions: at first, he wanted to be a prosecuting attorney. His legal heroes argued cases, they went to trial, and Keith felt he needed to do the same to fully sharpen his skills. He privately hoped—and occasionally jockeyed—for a position as assistant prosecutor in Wayne County. Arguing cases in Recorders Court would provide the battle scars needed to be a top-notch attorney. Or so he thought.

But standing in his way was not the color of his skin this time, but his lack of influence in a small clique of connected black lawyers who seemed to always get the call from the Wayne County prosecutor when positions became available. "For whatever reason," Keith would say, "I couldn't crack into that group. I tried. But I never did it."

Instead, he sharpened his formidable skills as a community organizer, maintained his devotion to civil rights work, and heightened his reputation for steering political efforts in the black community. Simply put, Damon Keith could help get people elected. And he did. In Michigan, where state court judges are voted on rather than appointed, Keith successfully campaigned on behalf of Wade McCree for Wayne County Circuit Court and later for John Voelker and his Michigan Supreme Court seat. He also helped John Swainson get elected governor of Michigan. That relationship would lead to a defining moment in Keith's life.

Swainson was a war hero, a Purple Heart recipient who'd lost both legs in World War II. He'd ascended from state senator to lieutenant governor when Phil Hart left the post to serve in the U.S. Senate. And when Swainson's boss, Governor G. Mennen Williams, announced he would not seek reelection in 1960, Swainson decided to go for the top spot.

Damon was there to help. He organized for Swainson and took him to NAACP gatherings and to the black churches, which were vital in getting African-American support at the polls. Keith and Swainson became quite close—in Keith's mind, they were friends—and Keith celebrated with him when he won a hotly contested election.

Politics is a business of payback—for those who help you and those who do not—so it was reasonable to expect that, during Swainson's term, if a spot opened on the bench, and the desire to appoint an African American was clear—as happened with a Common Pleas Court position—the governor would look Damon's way. In fact, given how Keith helped Swainson, many in the black community expected it. Charlie Diggs Jr., Michigan's first black congressman (and son of Damon's old friend from Diggs's funeral home days) lobbied hard for it, visiting the governor at his mansion to pitch Damon's qualifications.

For several months, it seemed understood. The judgeship was going to Keith. There were no other names bandied about. Damon and Rachel planned for their new life. They tried to control their excitement. It was the culmination of a dream. From high school to college to law school to private practice, Damon had wanted to sit on the bench, where real differences were made. What could be better?

"Darling," Rachel said, "You'll make a good judge."

That would prove to be true.

But it would take longer than they thought.

•   •   •

At the eleventh hour, the spot went to someone else.

Damon was reading the morning newspaper when he did a double take. It said that Governor Swainson had just named Charles Farmer to the Common Pleas Court. Damon felt like he'd been kicked in the gut. He called Rachel over and showed her the news.

"Charlie Farmer?" he asked. Nothing against the man, but what had he done to deserve that spot? Damon had played the game by the rules: help someone politically, do good work, earn your recognition. The first two were within his control, but the final step was in the governor's hands. And, instead of proper payback, the governor had chosen Farmer—the friend of a friend—for Damon's dream position.

"I was heartbroken," Keith would admit. He went to work that day and encountered an office full of headshakes. "Can you believe it, DK?" asked friend and associate Nate Conyers. "As hard as you worked for him?"

Damon bit his lip. He had indeed worked hard—"worked my butt off" he would later recall—to help get Swainson elected. This was his reward? He did not call the governor. In fact, he did not speak with him in any significant way ever again. In 1962, Swainson lost the governorship to George Romney. He would ultimately land on the Michigan Supreme Court, where he remained until 1975, when he was accused of accepting a bribe and found guilty of committing perjury before a grand jury.

By that point, no thanks to Swainson, Keith was a federal district court judge; and the Swainson sentencing was scheduled before him. A call came into Damon's office asking if he could help his old colleague: allow the former governor to begin serving his sentence quickly and in a less-than-severe facility. Damon thought back to the early 1960s, the agony he'd gone through, how the man he considered his friend had let him down, never even bothering to call to discuss the appointment. Payback of a different kind crossed his mind.

But he took the higher road.

"I'll help him to the extent the law permits," Keith told Swainson's attorney. "But I want you to know, if the positions were reversed, I doubt he'd do the same for me."

•   •   •

Years later, Judge Keith would opine, "Be careful what you wish for. God just might give it to you." Had Swainson actually appointed Keith to that judgeship, he would likely never have achieved all he did. In fact, he might be off the bench completely, as the Common Pleas court no longer exists in Michigan. Still, Keith's education in professional disappointment was not finished. Quite the contrary; it was due to repeat itself in even grander fashion.

By June of 1966, Keith was once again deeply involved in community activism and local politics, and he set out on the campaign trail for Michigan's chief justice, Thomas M. Kavanagh, and its supreme court justice, Otis M. Smith. Both were up for reelection. Both were worth fighting for, Keith believed. He had long admired Kavanagh's work, and he was inspired by Smith, who was Michigan's first black supreme court justice, appointed there in 1961 by—of all people—Governor Swainson.

A native of Memphis, Tennessee, Smith had worked his way up from poverty. An Air Force veteran and graduate of the Catholic University of America Law School in 1950, he was appointed chairman of the Michigan Public Service Commission (MPSC) in 1957 and, two years later, auditor general, making him the first African American to hold both posts. Tall, handsome, light-skinned, and soft-spoken, Smith was intensely hardworking, which garnered him the respect and admiration of black and white Michiganders alike.

For black lawyers, and Keith in particular, having an African-American justice on the state's highest court was a psychological breakthrough. No longer would black lawyers have to feel like aliens when, on those rare occasions, they would appear before the justices. Even more significant, Smith could demand that his colleagues and other state judges treat black lawyers with the respect and decency they deserved. It was one of the reasons Keith joined Smith's reelection campaign. He admired him. He respected him. He believed it was important to keep him on the court.

"We gave a dinner in our home to raise funds for Otis and Tom," Keith would recall. "I drove Otis all over the city, from this stop to that stop. I was with him almost every day. I worked like crazy to get him reelected. But I could not get him to go deep into the black community to campaign—especially not in the churches."

Damon knew how critical such support would be. He implored Smith, who could often be reserved and somewhat elitist, not to view campaigning as beneath him. According to Keith, their conversations about campaigning went something like this:

"Otis," Keith would say, "let's go over to this black church. I know the minister."

"Damon, I feel a little uncomfortable going there as a supreme court justice."

"But you're running for office, Otis. We need every vote we can get."

"Damon, let's campaign in another fashion."

Although he would never say it aloud, Damon sensed that Smith felt above such campaign stops and that he didn't need, in his mind, to pander for votes. Others felt that Smith did not want to strongly identify with the black community, for fear of losing white votes. Nate Conyers would recall that Smith didn't even want his photo on campaign posters for that same reason.

Smith's hesitancy to embrace his roots was noticed by many of Detroit's black leaders. It suggested to them a lack of organic connection with the community. Nonetheless, Keith campaigned hard for Smith, whom he considered a friend, personally raising thousands of dollars for his reelection.

But despite Keith's best efforts, the black vote in Detroit was not enough to offset the balloting in other parts of the state, and Smith lost his bid to his opponent, Thomas E. Brennan, by a wide margin.

That same year, Keith had been quietly nursing another judicial dream—his own. He'd worked for a long time with Senator Phil Hart, who admired Damon's tireless efforts at grassroots politics, civil rights, and leadership in the NAACP. One night during campaign season, Keith and Hart huddled in a restaurant in the Book Cadillac building. Keith had heard rumors that Judge McCree (whom Damon had also helped elect) might be leaving his seat in U.S. District Court to take a spot on the Sixth Circuit Court of Appeals. Damon had been a practicing attorney for seventeen years at that point. He was one of the most respected legal voices in the community. He was ready for a new step.

"If Wade leaves, and you think I am worthy, I would really like to be considered for that post," Damon told the senator. He felt comfortable in the request. After all, Keith helped get him reelected in 1964—handholding him through the black community, taking him to the churches and the NAACP gatherings, singing his praises. They shared similar hopes for the future. Hart would tell Keith, "Until we can eliminate the fact that when a white man sees a black man the first thing he feels is suspicion, we will never make the progress we need to make as a nation."

Hart greatly admired Keith's indefatigable work ethic and many contributions to the Democratic Party. At that meeting in the Book Cadillac, he said, "Damon, if you keep working hard for the party and doing all you are doing, I will recommend you to the president as a federal judge."

Keith was beyond thrilled. When he got home that night, he raced in the house, found Rachel, and said, "Darling, Senator Hart told me he would recommend me for a federal judgeship should Judge McCree step down." Once again, she gave him a hug and said, "Darling, you'll make a good judge." But in her heart she remembered what happened the last time, when her husband let a potential bench seat lift him so high, only to drop him like a heavy sack. *The sag of a dream deferred*, as Langston Hughes wrote. She silently prayed for no similar disappointment.

It happened anyhow.

• • •

This time, it wouldn't be a politician who sucker-punched Keith, it would be a colleague: Otis Smith—Michigan Supreme Court Justice Otis Smith—the same man Keith had just worked so hard to try and reelect. When Brennan defeated him, Smith was out of a job.

"I'm sorry, Otis, we did the best we could," Damon said. He never admonished Smith for failing to plunge deeper into the black community. What was done was done.

But Smith wasn't. He let Senator Hart know that a federal bench seat would go a long way toward healing his political wounds. The spot he had in mind? The soon-to-be-open seat on the U.S. District Court for the Eastern District of Michigan—the same seat that Senator Hart had promised Damon Keith.

"I walked the plank for Otis," Keith would later say. But it didn't seem to matter to Smith, who saw the post as compensation for his loyal service to the Democratic Party. After all, he had been the highest-ranking black judge in the state. And since Wade McCree, who was vacating the position, had a mentor-like relationship with Smith, Smith thought it was only right he receive the appointment.

In spite of the commitment Senator Hart made to Keith, many prominent members of the Democratic establishment quickly sided with Smith. They argued that the party had to look after their fallen warriors and emphasized the fact that, on paper at least, Smith did have a better résumé. And it was true.

"On paper, I could not in any way compare myself to Otis Smith," Keith would concede. "Otis was the first black to be chairman of the Public Service Commission, he was the first black to be auditor general of the State of Michigan, and he was the first black to be appointed to the Michigan Supreme Court. I was just a practicing lawyer."

Nonetheless, Senator Hart had made him a promise. And it wasn't as if Keith didn't have credentials of his own—particularly on civil rights issues, which were dotting courtrooms more and more. Keith had held his tongue when Governor Swainson passed him over for Charlie Farmer. But he remained inspired by the words of his mentor, Thurgood Marshall, reminding him of how "the white man wrote the Declaration of Independence" and that it was up to men like Keith to ensure the establishment "own up to those words." As a judge, he could do that far more effectively than as an attorney. It was his passion and his dream. He wanted this appointment. But with Smith inserting himself into the process, he realized he would have to fight.

The two men ran into each other at a social occasion.

"Otis," Keith said, "you do know that Senator Hart promised me this judgeship, don't you?"

"Well, Damon, I'd like to be a federal sitting judge. I worked very hard, and I'm coming off this election loss."

"But the senator promised it to me."

"Well, I think I deserve it."

The two men parted civilly, the issue hanging between them like a blade. Damon, who would later admit to being "heartbroken" by Smith's clear disinterest in honoring the senator's promise—or Damon's deserved recognition—went home to Rachel and looked her in the eyes.

"Here we go again," he said.

•　　•　　•

Much to the chagrin and indignation of Keith's supporters, the *Detroit Free Press* quickly picked up on the brewing controversy and jumped into the fray. The paper endorsed Smith for the position and published a series of articles and editorials questioning not only Keith's experience for the job but his intellectual heft as well. There was a very strong suspicion that Judge McCree, among others, was feeding the media that idea.

"They wrote about me failing the bar exam the first time," Judge Keith would recall. "It got vicious. I knew the publisher of the *Free Press*, and we were at an event one night when he said to me, 'Damon, what the heck does our editorial board have against you?' I looked at him and said, 'I don't know.' I wanted to say, 'You tell *me*!'"

Instead of backing down, Keith used his well-honed campaigning skills and huge network of friends to keep the pressure on Senator Hart to honor his word. In an extraordinary personal letter of support for Keith to Governor Williams, Justice Voelker weighed in again and blasted Smith for what he perceived as hubris. He wrote, in part:

> For Otis Smith to seek to be dragged across several counties and given a major Detroit appointment over a qualified and deserving (and already publicly announced) Detroit candidate simply isn't fair or politically realistic, and he shouldn't expect it.
>
> If it's a job Otis Smith wants and needs, there must be dozens of law firms and legal departments from General Motors on down or up panting to snap him up. . . .
>
> For Otis Smith to now step in and get this job in these circumstances would be almost too blatant an example of a political party "taking care" (at whatever the cost) of its political casualties and cripples.
>
> Otis Smith has, in the past, been repeatedly remembered and handsomely rewarded by his party; Damon Keith never, but instead he has taken on the chin several public rebuffs for the few modest things he has ever sought and has nevertheless still continued to work tirelessly for liberal causes and candidates.
>
> In all candor, for Otis Smith now to get this new job after all the publicity and promise and fine talk given Damon Keith would, in my mind, be a cruel and—I must be frank—unforgivable public rejection and humiliation of a very fine man and a loyal and tireless party worker—and, I may also add, do very little to attract much-needed new blood into our somewhat riddled ranks.

The letter, which was never made public, underscored the intensity of Keith's support base, but also demonstrated a growing unease over what some Democrats thought to be the unseemliness of Smith's campaign. Churning just beneath the surface was a suspicion that certain

Democratic leaders were pressuring Senator Hart to nominate Smith because of his reserved demeanor, lack of emphasis on civil rights issues, and the fact that he went to a white law school: in short, Smith was the less threatening, more socially acceptable Negro.

This led to whispers in the black community. Those whispers caught traction—especially after a series of condescending editorials and articles in local newspapers about Keith.

The *Free Press* editorialized on December 3, 1966, that "Smith is the Best Choice for a Federal Court Seat." It portrayed Keith as little more than a political party apparatchik and diminished the value of his work in civil rights, even as the country was churning in racial protest. In subsequent stories and editorials, the newspaper went on to criticize Keith as perhaps intellectually and temperamentally unfit to be a judge. At one point the media criticism became so harsh that Keith told his law partners he was going to withdraw from consideration. It was humiliating his family.

"My kids were young. They were hearing about it at school or in the neighborhood. I didn't like Rachel reading all those articles about me. I told her, 'Darling, I don't want to put you through this. The firm is doing well. I have a good practice. We don't have to endure the disappointment again. I'm ready to throw in the towel.'

"She told me, 'Darling, the decision is yours. I'm behind you whatever you choose.' But deep down, I think she wanted me to quit. It was just too much."

Later that day, Keith informed his partners that he was calling Senator Hart to withdraw. As Nate Conyers remembers, "He had the phone in his hand and was calling Washington. I said, 'No, you're not!' I literally had to jump around the table, grab his arm, and wrestle the phone out of his hand."

•　　•　　•

Stressed to see two highly regarded members of the state's black community engaged in such a contentious battle, Conyers and a group of Detroit's black leaders decided they had to do something. Arthur Johnson, Keith's closest friend from their NAACP days who was now the deputy superintendent of Detroit Public Schools, called a meeting to discuss the dilemma.

In his book *Race and Remembrance: A Memoir*, Johnson noted that the conflict put Senator Hart in a delicate situation, with mounting political pressure from both sides—Smith continued to pick up support from white institutions, while Keith had the solid backing of most black leaders in the state. Both sides let Senator Hart know, in no uncertain terms, that his selection would be watched very closely.

"We decided to meet and make sure that this decision was not ceded to white leadership and white institutions placing pressure on Senator Hart," Johnson wrote. "Our group included various leaders of Detroit's black community, including Joe Coles, Dr. D. T. Burton, Forrest Green, August Calloway, Dr. Lionel Swan, and Franklin Brown. We met in a conference room at Burton Mercy Hospital, where Dr. Burton was chief administrator."

In taking up the challenge to resolve the conflict, the group saw an opportunity to change the way political appointments for blacks were traditionally made.

"There was a prevailing belief in the African-American community at that time that when a black person was selected for a high honor in the system, the individual chosen was typically not the one that black leadership would have selected, but rather someone who was more compatible with the interests and sensibilities of white leadership," Johnson recalled. "As a result, from the perspective of the black community, blacks who moved up in the system often faced some suspicions, fairly or unfairly, about whether they were going to be . . . strong enough to say what needed to be said to the powers that be."

Johnson's group believed the controversy over Keith's appointment had little to do with being qualified for the job. Whites with similar levels of legal experience were routinely supported for judgeships. This conflict was largely driven by white power brokers being more comfortable with Smith. But while black leaders widely admired Smith and his work ethic, they felt his background was largely in state institutional work. In contrast, Keith's reputation within the community, his efforts as co-chairman of the Civil Rights Commission and president of the Detroit Housing Commission, and his brokering of African-American interests within the Democratic Party, easily made him the consensus pick of the group.

As much as the men respected Smith, the decision to support Keith was not even close. Johnson and his colleagues went to Senator Hart and explained their rationale. They asked that the senator publicly reaffirm his commitment. He agreed with their reasoning and said he was determined to stand by his word and recommend Damon Keith's nomination to the President.

Because of Arthur Johnson's personal friendship with both parties, he was asked by the group to break the news to Smith.

"I met with Otis and told him that our efforts on Damon's behalf were not intended as a fight against him and that we certainly were not implying that he was not worthy of the appointment. 'You are fully prepared for the post,' I said. 'And we know it. But we simply think it's Damon's turn to be recognized, and we ask that you understand that,'" Johnson wrote.

Not long after the meeting with Johnson, Smith withdrew his name from consideration. It was a painful episode for all involved. Smith never spoke to Keith about it. In fact, Keith learned the news in a letter that arrived at his office from the American Bar Association, stating that he had been nominated by Senator Phil Hart for appointment to U.S. District Judge.

He stared at the letter. He read it again and again. Was it really true? Had the disappointments of the past finally washed away? A seat on the bench? A chance to live up to the echoes of his teachers and legal heroes?

"I ran home and found Rachel, who was in the bedroom. I said, 'Darling, Phil has submitted my name. It's really happening.' We hugged, and she had tears in her eyes."

And for the last time, she said to him, "Darling, you'll make a good judge."

•　　•　　•

Years later, Otis Smith would describe the whole thing as "a mix-up." He would be richly rewarded—literally—by joining the Detroit legal staff of General Motors, where he would later rise to the position of vice president and general counsel.

Meanwhile, on September 25, 1967—just two months after his on-the-ground leadership during the Detroit riots—Damon J. Keith was nominated by President Lyndon B. Johnson to serve as a U.S. district court judge for the Eastern District of Michigan. He was confirmed by the Senate on October 12, 1967, and received his commission that same day.

He was, at the time, only the second black person to attain such a position in Michigan. His wife, Rachel, his fellow co-chairman of the Michigan Civil Rights Commission, John Feikens, and his friend, former justice and now-famous author John Voelker (who had written so passionately on Damon's behalf) held the Bible as he was sworn into office.

No more dreams deferred. The heavy sag had been gloriously lifted.

Years later, Senator Hart's wife said in a speech that her late husband told her nominating Damon Keith was "the best decision he ever made."

All Damon had to do now was live up to it.

15

INTO THE MAELSTROM
BUSING IN PONTIAC

There is a painting that hangs in Damon Keith's home, the image of a black man in broken chains, walking down a lonely road, heading toward sunlight and the promise of freedom. It was given to him nearly fifty years ago on the day he became a judge. It was a farewell gift from his partners at the law firm.

Keith recalls a smiling Nate Conyers telling him, "This represents the struggle that you and all of us have gone through. Good luck. We're all so happy for you."

Keith had tears in his eyes. Achieving his dream of a seat on the bench was undeniably satisfying, but his career as a practicing attorney was over. From scraping for crumbs at recorders court to the formation of his own firm to the move downtown from the Tobin Building to the Guardian Building to his heightened reputation as a rainmaker of legal business—the attorney chapter of his life was closing. He was trading his suit for a robe. He packed up his office, taking books, personal effects, and the cherished new painting, and he carried several boxes to his new workspace.

A seventh-floor chamber in the Federal Building.

"My partners were with me, and so were Rachel and my three daughters," he would recall. "The girls were running around. They jumped in the jury box; they plopped around the bench; they went in the jury room. They were saying, 'This is where Daddy is gonna do this or that.' Rachel was just quiet, taking it all in."

Damon removed two framed photographs from his boxes and placed them on his new desk. One was of his wife and children. The other was of his mother and father. He thought about his childhood. He thought about how far he had come. He thought about that painting, the promise of a sun, the nagging reminder of chains. He realized the artist was not painting a beginning or an end, but a journey.

His was about to begin.

•   •   •

Sixteen months after his appointment, Keith ran smack into national controversy—for the first but not the last time—with a case known as *Davis v. School District of City of Pontiac, Inc.* Simply put, a group of black parents was suing the Pontiac school system for racial segregation and discrimination.

But there was nothing simple about it.

As Keith read the paperwork in February of 1969, when he drew the case, he couldn't help but flash back to his own childhood. He knew what segregated schools were about. He knew the subtle and not-so-subtle ways that blacks and whites were considered differently in the education system. "It didn't make me sympathetic to one side or the other," Keith would say, "but I was sensitized to the issue. And I knew how important it was."

At the time, Detroit and its suburbs—including Pontiac, a working-class city of 83,000, less than thirty miles northwest of downtown Detroit—were still reeling emotionally from the riots of 1967. A survey taken by the *Detroit Free Press* in 1968 showed that 17 percent of Detroit whites actually favored total separation of the races (versus 1 percent of blacks) and only 24 percent of whites supported "integration" (versus 88 percent of blacks.)

The survey was a grim but accurate reflection of the profound racial polarization that had metastasized in the region. In a different world, the riots might have moved people to break down the barriers. Instead, they seemed to divide the region more, with white flight from the inner city leading to suburbs entrenched in a "leave us alone" mentality.

Against this backdrop, Judge Keith would hear arguments about educational segregation in a town, Pontiac, that had blacks living in the northern end and whites living in the south. He dug in. "Rachel, I have this very difficult case we're gonna start," he told his wife. "It could be controversial."

"Well, Darling," she said, "that's why you're a judge."

Before he heard a single argument, Keith made a tactical move to deflect potential criticism. Realizing that the NAACP was a plaintiff in the case, he called all the lawyers to a meeting in his chambers.

"Before we even get started," he said, "you should all know that while I am no longer active in the NAACP, I once was, and I remain the first vice president emeritus. I worked hard ever since I got out of law school representing the NAACP. With that in mind, do any of you have an objection to my hearing this case?"

The lawyers looked at one another. Neither side objected. Both stated clearly that they believed Keith would be fair in his rulings—a fact duly noted by a court reporter Keith had insisted on being in the room. He knew that later on, if his decision proved unpopular with one side or the other, claims of a bias might be leveled against him. With the court reporter's record of his full disclosure—and the lack of any objection—he had effectively detonated one land mine before it exploded.

There would be plenty of others.

The plaintiffs in *Davis v. School District of City of Pontiac, Inc.* claimed that the city had created a segregated school system and discriminated in the hiring and assignment of teachers. At first glance, the numbers bore these claims out. Pontiac was slightly more than twenty-five percent black. However, Pontiac schools were nearly *one hundred percent* segregated. Emerson School had 656 students, all of whom were white. Weaver, Whitfield, Wisner, Malcolm, and Willis schools were similarly all-white. Alcott School's student body, more than six hundred strong, was only slightly better; it had three black students. At most, white schools had two black teachers. Meanwhile, Whittier, for example, one of several all-black schools, had just two white teachers.

The Pontiac Board of Education argued it had no part in creating this divide. Segregated housing patterns were the primary culprit, it claimed. People chose where they wanted to live; in Pontiac, they had chosen segregated neighborhoods. Once parents made that choice, the school board had an obligation to send their kids to the neighborhood schools, right?

Similarly, the school board argued that it could not be blamed for the absence of white teachers in black schools or black teachers in white schools. Teachers voluntarily chose whether to make themselves available for transfers. If teachers weren't volunteering for such assignments, the school board could not force that decision.

The case was front-page news. Tensions ran high. Arguments were passionate. The trial itself lasted six days, with testimony from upset parents and school board officials. Keith insisted on decorum and, as would become his style, he engendered a respectful and polite tone throughout. But as he listened, he could feel the smoldering issues beneath the testimony. He also knew the proceedings were being carefully watched by judicial eyes; a similar case had been decided and ruled on by the appellate court in Cincinnati. In *Deal v. Cincinnati Board of Education,* the U.S. Court of Appeals for the Sixth Circuit had determined that courts could *not* integrate schools that were segregated due to housing patterns without any direct discrimination by a school board.

"Some of the same lawyers for that case were involved in this one," Keith recalls. "And they were saying Pontiac was the same situation. They took the same approach. They claimed I was bound by the same decision as they'd come to in Cincinnati."

In point of fact, he was bound unless he found a significant difference in the Pontiac situation.

He did.

In a strongly worded opinion, issued in February of 1970, almost exactly one year after he drew the case, Keith agreed with the plaintiffs. He ruled the school board had ultimately decided where to place its new schools and had committed a "sin of omission" by not addressing segregation when it had the capacity to do so. Instead, Keith stated, the school board had made "voluntary" choices of its own. On at least two occasions, Pontiac had built new predominantly black schools to accommodate overcrowding in existing predominately black schools, rather than send those black students to nearby predominantly white schools that had "an overwhelmingly large capacity."

Knowing he would be challenged by those following the Cincinnati decision, Keith took direct aim at the reasoning in the *Deal* case. School districts could not, he concluded, tell black families, "If you want integration, just move to another neighborhood." Such an argument was "blinded to the realities of adult life with its prejudices and opposition to integrated housing." The school board knew better, as did Keith. He privately recalled his mother's need to use a light-skinned black couple to "purchase" a house for her on a predominantly white block: "I knew it was not so easy to pick up and move into a neighborhood where you're not wanted. That shouldn't be the reason black students are denied an equal education."

Judge Keith also ruled that Pontiac had violated the Fourteenth

Amendment's equal protection and due process clauses by placing black teachers and administrators only in black schools and by hiring only enough black teachers and administrators to staff them. In the same way that the Board of Education did nothing to stop student segregation when it was in its power to do so, it did nothing to stop the accompanying faculty segregation. Noting the transfer policy, Judge Keith held that the school board did not have to limit teacher transfers to *voluntary* transfers; it had the power to assign black teachers to white schools and vice versa. It consciously chose not to, thus effectively facilitating teacher segregation. Such segregation, he ruled, was sufficient to deprive school children of their constitutional rights. Having a faculty all of one race made a school racially identifiable and tended to promote segregation.

"I thought it was a sham," he would later conclude. "It wasn't by accident all the white teachers were in one place and the blacks in another. I thought it indicated they were deliberately involved in perpetuating segregation. And I thought I could make the distinction from the Cincinnati case."

Judge Keith took particular issue with the school board's assertion that it was a passive player in the segregation:

> When the power to act is available, failure to take the necessary steps so as to negate or alleviate a situation which is harmful is as wrong as is the taking of affirmative steps to advance that situation. Sins of omission can be as serious as sins of commission.
>
> The fact that de jure segregation came slowly and surreptitiously rather than by legislative pronouncement makes the situation no less evil. The Board of Education cannot absolve itself from responsibility for this situation when it had the power, duty, and control to prevent the situation. It would be feigned modesty on the part of any Board of Education to suggest that it is controlled by a situation rather than that it can control.

> For a school board to acquiesce in a housing development pattern
> and then to disclaim liability for the eventual segregated characteristic
> that such pattern creates in the schools is for the Board to abrogate
> and ignore all power, control, and responsibility.

On the morning that Keith was to release his decision, he looked at his wife across the kitchen table.

"Darling," he said, "I've rendered my decision in the Pontiac school case. It's very controversial. And we have to be prepared for some negative publicity."

Once again, she looked at him—calmly, lovingly—and said, "Well, Damon, That's why you're a judge."

It would be the last quiet moment they would have for a while.

•　　•　　•

When the decision was announced, reaction was swift and overwhelming. The *Detroit Free Press* headline read:

"PONTIAC SCHOOLS TOLD: INTEGRATE!"

Keith's ruling, and his subsequent order for Pontiac "to integrate its school system at all levels" before the start of the next academic year, sent people scrambling to their foxholes. Weeks later, Keith approved a plan that would put nine thousand of the city's twenty-four thousand schoolchildren on buses to assorted schools, the rides averaging fifteen minutes each way.

"Busing"—a hotbed issue of the South—had come to the North.

There were howls of protest. Keith was vilified in many white communities. His ruling was predictably appealed, and the Sixth Circuit court halted the implementation of Keith's plan until after it ruled, thus plucking the 1970–71 school year out of the flames.

This calmed things temporarily. However, in May of 1971, the three-judge panel affirmed Keith's decision. It ruled his conclusions were valid, that the Pontiac case and the Cincinnati case were indeed different, and, as Keith had judged, Pontiac's decisions regarding attendance boundary lines and where to build schools, when taken together, "support the conclusion that a purposeful pattern of racial discrimination has existed in the Pontiac school system for at least fifteen years."

It marked the first time a federal appeals court held that segregation in a northern school system existed by design of the school board—and the first time busing would be used as the remedy.

That, as Keith recalls it, "was when the you-know-what hit the fan."

•   •   •

On the last day of August 1971, the Ku Klux Klan bombed ten Pontiac school buses. The ugly message was clear. With photographs of the burning bus carcasses just seven days before school began, the entire region came to a boil. Parents screamed. Pontiac was a tinderbox. School was literally about to start in smoke, and in protest, nine women chained themselves to the gates of a bus yard. A Pontiac housewife named Irene McCabe organized the National Action Group (NAG)—with L. Brooks Patterson serving as its general counsel—which vehemently opposed busing and fueled the protests. In addition to leading a thirteen-day protest, McCabe led a march to Washington to gain support for a constitutional amendment to prohibit busing.

On the morning of September 7, the first day of school, Judge Keith was in his chambers early. His spirit was disquieted: "It was so much worse than I thought it would be. I didn't know there would be such hatred. People were marching on Washington. Even President Nixon said forced busing was wrong. There were threats made against my life. The federal marshals had been driving by my house for days. Rachel noticed cars and said something about them, but I never told her they were there for our protection. I didn't want to worry her."

It didn't matter. She figured it out. As did Keith's daughters, who watched the cars through the windows.

Sitting in his office that morning, Keith began to receive multiple telegrams imploring him to send federal marshals into Pontiac "to protect our kids." He thought back to the horrific images of the burning school busses. He put his face in his hands. There had been pickets and protests and screaming crowds. The NAG group had actually closed down two General Motors facilities through picketing in an effort to get GM to use its political clout to stop busing. Would federal troops be next? Had things come to that again? Keith had seen troops on his city's streets in 1943 and in 1967. Why did the color of one's skin lead to such vitriolic reactions?

Keith recalls that first day of school in 1971 as one of the longest and most difficult of his career. Every hour there were more reports of protests and arrests and potentially explosive incidents. Keith had faith in the law but wondered if it would hold. As it turned out, it did—for that day and another and another. There was violence, yes, dozens were arrested, and many wondered why the Pontiac Police Department was not more vigilant in protecting the busing process. But slowly the protests broke up. The picketers disbanded. Arrests were made in the bus bombings; six Klansmen were charged and ultimately convicted and sent to prison.

Robert Sedler, a constitutional law expert at Wayne State University Law School, would later analyze the Pontiac case and conclude there was nothing radical about what Keith had decided—even if the reaction suggested otherwise. "The court said, 'I've looked at all your acts taken together and they add up to intentional discrimination. You can't give a neutral explanation to all the actions you took. The school board took advantage of housing patterns to maximize actual segregation. If they had followed neutral practices despite the residential segregation, you would not have had the extent of segregation that you did.'"

Keith, for his part, took solace in getting the law right: "I felt comforted when the court of appeals unanimously affirmed me and said I had made the case for distinguishing Pontiac from the Cincinnati case. It would have been easy to go the other way. If I didn't want to bite the bullet, I could have said, 'Look, I'm bound by the Circuit's decision in the Cincinnati case and this is no different.' That would have been easier and less controversial. You wouldn't have had the turmoil. Wouldn't have had the bombing of buses, the picketing of schools, the threats to my life.

"But it wouldn't have been the right thing."

It was the first of many times he would be tested that way on the federal bench. Like the man in his painting, his judicial journey was underway, and the challenge would be to ignore the chains of the past and steer himself toward the sunlight of a better future.

16.

Housing in Hamtramck and Discrimination at Detroit Edison

Some judges draw controversial cases like that of the Pontiac school system once in a career. But in the early 1970s, Damon Keith was drawing them like flies to a picnic, so much so that authorities would eventually look into the matter. They, too, found it difficult to believe that so many hotbed issues could accrue to the same court. But nothing would be found. No one was *trying* to put monumental decisions—many concerning race—in one particular docket. History, for whatever reason, was simply wrapping up difficult cases and laying them on Judge Keith's doorstep.

So it was that he drew *Garrett v. City of Hamtramck*, a case originally filed in 1968, the year after Keith took the bench.

Sarah Garrett was a black woman who lived in the Holbrook/ Joseph Campau neighborhood of Hamtramck. She was told—as were several of her black neighbors and fellow plaintiffs—that she had to move out of her home so it could be demolished for urban renewal. When she delayed, her water was turned off. This happened in other

African-American neighborhoods as well. Streets were not maintained. Sewers were allowed to back up.

The suit was filed, and in many ways, the battle lines were drawn. Battle lines that are only today—more than forty years later—being surrendered.

Hamtramck is a small city, geographically contained within the physical boundaries of Detroit. In the mid-1960s, its population was mostly Polish, drawn by work at the city's Dodge automotive plant. Black residents comprised less than fifteen percent of the city's population and were largely concentrated in three sections.

Like many urban centers, Hamtramck had become severely overcrowded, and, with no room to expand outward, the city sought to revitalize its core through various "urban renewal" projects. These projects were designed to attract and keep businesses and commerce.

Overwhelmingly, they did so by displacing blacks.

Or, as Judge Keith would later refer to it, via "Negro removal."

In 1959, Hamtramck removed more than six hundred black families from their homes in order to build a parking lot for an assembly plant. According to federal law, the city was required to provide relocation assistance to the displaced people. However, no substantial assistance was given.

That same year, construction of I-75 began and displaced approximately twelve hundred people. Seventy percent of them were black.

A few years later, something called the Wyandotte Area Project invested $3.1 million to clear land for a new civic center in an integrated Hamtramck neighborhood. Although there were both black and white citizens living there, with houses in equal condition, the city decided to demolish the houses occupied by blacks first. Not only did they not offer these blacks any relocation assistance, but the occupants were harassed to leave speedily and find other places to live.

Altogether, seventy-four percent of the people displaced by Hamtramck's urban renewal plans were black. In a half dozen years in the late 1950s and early 1960s, the city's black population was nearly cut in half. Many believed that was the idea.

•   •   •

Damon Keith was familiar with Hamtramck from his high school football and track days; Northwestern competed against high schools from that area. He knew the population was largely Polish. But he had little concept of the housing practices until the trial began. One by one, black residents told their stories of being forced out or isolated in unsanitary housing conditions. Promises to relocate them were rarely kept. The only defense from the city, Keith recalls, was that "there wasn't money for relocation." It was hardly justification, and with so many examples and such a defined pattern, his ruling came fairly easily. Because Keith had served as president of the Detroit Housing Commission for nine years (from 1958 to 1967) he was well aware of the need for decent, suitable housing for low-income communities. In addition, his knowledge of the public planning process helped him identify negative effects of urban renewal policies that might appear race-neutral to the less-experienced observer.

In the initial paragraphs of the 1971 opinion, Judge Keith used the now poignant term "Negro removal." It foretold of his eventual decision.

In finding the city guilty of intentionally discriminating against black residents, Judge Keith maintained that city officials knew it would be difficult for black residents to find similar housing once displaced. Yet it did nothing to help. He ruled that the plaintiffs had indeed been denied their rights under the Thirteenth and Fourteenth Amendments.

But he didn't stop there. He also took aim at the federal government's involvement. The nation's Housing and Urban Development Agency

(HUD) had long approved and funded Hamtramck's urban renewal programs. As early as 1959, it had reports that documented Hamtramck's intentions to eliminate massive amounts of residential housing in its black communities with no real plan to replace it. Although federal law required HUD to ensure that urban renewal programs accounted for the relocation of all displaced persons, HUD never insisted upon such assistance for the blacks who were displaced.

Judge Keith's admonishment of HUD paralleled the contempt he showed for the feigned impotency by public decision-makers in his *Pontiac* decision:

"For the Department of Housing and Urban Development to direct, fund, and foster programs that have harmed and, if unchecked, will continue to harm the Black citizens of Hamtramck, and to proceed with such activities by claiming innocence of what has been or is being done with federal funds cannot be tolerated."

As he now reasons, "It was important to bring the federal government into this case and to put some of the burden on them. They should have insisted on finding adequate replacement housing. Instead, they sat idly by."

•　　•　　•

Judge Keith issued his initial decision in the case in 1971, ordering the city and the federal government to work together with the plaintiffs to come up with a plan for relocating the displaced blacks within ninety days.

Little did he know that *four decades later* they would still be fighting to implement it.

What he did know was that the decision would bring a hailstorm of criticism. Keith was getting used to that. Not only had he found a municipality guilty of maliciously discriminating against its own residents, he'd also found that a federal agency essentially conspired with the city's discrimination.

Reaction came from many corners. Legal critics felt he was being an activist. Hamtramck residents felt he was a bully on a bench.

"Since when do we have a dictator?" read one angry letter. *"This is America, land of the free. Who are you to tell the heads of our community of Hamtramck how to run it? . . . We don't need these low housing homes here so it would be another ghetto. . . . I've seen blacks move into a nice neighborhood and in time it's like a pig sty. They just don't care."*

But hate mail would be easy compared to implementing Keith's recommendations. Four years passed between his initial decision in 1971 and his final determination of the remedy in May 1975. During the interim, he had to reorder a new development plan. The city submitted an unsuccessful appeal to the Sixth Circuit, which remanded the case for further determination of the remedy.

Finally, in May 1975, Keith issued his blueprint: the essential part required the city to replace more than five hundred homes that were wrongly demolished as part of the Negro removal program.

That should have been the end of the story. Instead, it was just the beginning of a four-decade logjam. Hamtramck may have had to accept the ruling, but it was in no hurry to do anything about it. Feet were dragged. Fingers were pointed. There was always a funding issue of some kind. The originally discriminated-against citizens grew older. Some died. It was heartbreaking to many of the former residents, who believed, as Judge Keith would state, that "justice delayed is justice denied." He felt so strongly about the case—and so desired to see its resolution—that years later, when he was elevated to the Sixth Circuit Court of Appeals, he asked for and received special permission to remain as a federal district judge by designation on the Hamtramck case. The parties continued to meet regularly over the years in Judge Keith's chambers, with Keith acting as a mediator.

It was an ongoing series of negotiations. Carlos Recio, one of Keith's law clerks at the time the case was remanded in 1974, recalls one day when the entire Hamtramck City Council came down to his chambers. "Judge put plaintiffs in one room, Hamtramck council members in another, and shuttled back and forth. The Hamtramck City Council hated the thought of low-income black residents in city-provided housing. From the glares and frowns, it was obvious that the judge had his work cut out for him. But the judge brought them around.

"He was courteous as always. You should have seen the shock on their faces when he personally served them coffee, as he often did at settlement conferences."

Keith now chuckles at the memory of the coffee—and donuts—that he offered his guests, bringing it to them as if they were sitting in his kitchen. "There was such animosity," he says. "As a judge, I always thought if we could get people talking about the issues, we might be able to resolve them."

Keith struggled with the resistance whites and blacks had to living together. His home at the time, on Outer Drive in Detroit, was in an integrated neighborhood. The house across the street belonged to whites. The house down to the left did, too. When Damon was outside working on the roses in his front garden—a favorite pastime—neighbors black and white would jog by, stop, and say, "That was a good thing you did in Hamtramck" or "That was a brave decision in Hamtramck." But the city of Hamtramck itself remained intractable for years. Only in the new millennium have efforts truly been made to compensate the parties who were harmed in the 1960s. Housing has finally been constructed and restitution delivered to most of the families. But in many cases, it is the grandchildren of those forced from their homes who are being handed the keys to new ones. On the steps of the long-awaited housing, they cry and say prayers of gratitude to their predecessors who had the courage to fight. The ceremonies are bittersweet, as is the memory of the case for Keith. The judge himself has grown old and has semi-retired waiting for the justice to be served. He can still hear the accusations against him of judicial activism and social engineering. He strongly disagrees.

"Equal justice under law. That's what the Supreme Court says. I don't select the cases that come before me as a judge. I draw them. But I am bound to make a decision as it relates to the facts. If I see inequities within the realm of the Fourteenth Amendment as it relates to discrimination and violation of the law, then I have broad authority to fashion a remedy. I don't think it's social engineering. It's giving meaning to the Constitution and the fact that all men are created equal and are endowed by their creator—not the Supreme Court or the judicial system—with certain unalienable rights."

Keith applied those principles as a young judge in deciding the *Garrett v. Hamtramck* cases. He watches today, a gray-haired man in his nineties, as decent housing is finally handed over to the descendents of the displaced black citizens.

It remains, by every account, the longest-running housing discrimination lawsuit in America's history.

•   •   •

Having ruled on discrimination within the school system and discrimination within the housing system, it seemed almost inevitable that Judge Keith would take on discrimination in the workplace. A fateful case arrived in 1971. It centered on a Detroit man named Willie Stamps, who, like Keith more than twenty years earlier, was pushing a mop when he shouldn't have been.

Stamps, an African American, grew up wanting to work for Detroit Edison. In the 1950s and 1960s, the company (now known as DTE) was one of the premier electrical utility firms in the world. Founded in 1903—the same year Henry Ford founded Ford Motor Company—DTE had a storied tradition. It powered the boom brought on by the auto industry. It powered the factories that produced much-needed tanks and vehicles during World War II. In 1956, it started construction on what was then the largest power plant in the world.

So after graduating high school, like thousands of other eager Detroiters, Willie Stamps applied for a job at Edison. Unfortunately for Stamps, Edison wasn't interested. Stamps then left Detroit for vocational training in Chicago. Determined to better himself, he enrolled in college. After graduation, Stamps came back home and re-applied to Edison. Again, Edison wasn't interested.

But that wasn't the end. Over and over Stamps tried and was denied a job—at least five times between 1955 and 1967. One time they told him that he was not properly dressed. Another time, he was told he was overweight.

Finally, in 1967, his persistence was rewarded. Willie Stamps, college graduate, was hired.

As a janitor.

His frustrations didn't end there. At least fifteen times after he was hired, Stamps was denied transfers and promotions. After a while, they told him he was *overqualified.*

Stamps wasn't alone in his frustrations. Detroit Edison, one of Michigan's largest employers outside of the auto industry, was viewed by many black Detroiters as a frustratingly hard place to gain employment. And those who managed to wiggle their way in were routinely excluded from the desirable work. College-educated black men, like Stamps, were often stuck in janitorial or stockmen positions.

Over time, Stamps and other black employees at Edison decided to do something about this. Stamps eventually got elected to an officer's position in his union, local 223 of the Utility Workers of America—the first black man to ever do so in that local—and a year later he helped form the Association for the Betterment of Black Edison Employees.

In 1969, that group rallied around an affirmative action plan for minority hiring. But little progress was made. Instead, for their advocacy, Stamps and his black colleagues were regularly harassed.

Enough was enough.

In 1971, Willie Stamps sued.

And Judge Keith drew the case.

•　　•　　•

Stamps v. Detroit Edison Co. was a private class-action lawsuit, later consolidated with a similar suit brought by the Department of Justice. Combined, the case challenged a wide range of Detroit Edison's hiring practices, claiming they were deliberately biased against blacks.

Edison and the unions fired back. They argued fiercely that they were not discriminating. They maintained that all employment decisions were made "without regard to race or color." Judge Keith, as a black Detroiter, had heard talk over the years about DTE, but he also had reason to be skeptical of the criticism: he had become friendly with the former CEO and then chairman of the board Walker Cisler. The two men had actually worked together in the black community and on NAACP efforts—a fact that Keith openly revealed before taking the case, as was his policy. "Walker was a big guy, a nice guy," Keith recalls. Inasmuch as policy spreads from the top down, it was hard for Keith to imagine his friend overseeing a discriminatory operation.

But as the trial wore on—and one witness after another took the stand—Keith felt a grim conclusion take root. "They all said the same thing: that the only blacks at Edison were washing cars, chauffeuring, cleaning the floors, running the elevators. They said, 'We have no black supervisors. No black vice presidents. No blacks in real authority.' And furthermore, they said the union was not properly representing them. They claimed it was standing idly by, allowing this discrimination to go on."

Although the company vigorously insisted it had a race-neutral operation, Keith had enough personal experience to look beneath "official policies." True, Detroit Edison's employment practices, on the surface, did not overtly reject blacks. But they consistently and disproportionately disfavored them. Promotions, for example, were contingent upon testing that had little to no relationship with adequate job performance—but resulted in favoring white candidates. Vacant positions were announced in ways that limited the spread of information mostly to white employees.

Labor unions, Keith discovered, were complicit in many of these employment practices. They misinformed black employees—telling them that there were no grievance procedures for lost job bids, for example, when in fact there were. They used various tactics to keep blacks from gaining in the unions' leadership ranks. And they supported management promotions prioritized by seniority, knowing full well this would essentially freeze the status quo— effectively blocking blacks from job promotions. If whites kept getting the senior positions, and promotions were based on seniority, how would things ever change?

And then there were the sheer numbers. In a city so densely populated by blacks, Detroit Edison managed a workforce that remained overwhelmingly white. The math just didn't add up.

As the trial went on, Judge Keith recognized a system that was clearly discriminatory—and that built racial barriers into the fabric of the operation. "I remember hearing there were black dots on every application from a black person. The lawyers asked, 'Does this black dot mean that the applicant is black?' The answer was yes. That had a real effect on me."

So did the moment when Walker Cisler took the stand.

"He was asked point-blank if he thought DTE discriminated against blacks, and he said, squarely, no, it did not. I don't know if he really believed that, but he said it as if he honestly did."

Judge Keith recognized that the perception of Edison's management ran contrary to the facts at hand. This was a major employer engaging in systematic discrimination. Unions were shirking their responsibility. "Official policy" was being held up as a paper shield against the clandestine slashing of civil rights. "I always made it a practice to never use a personal pronoun behind the bench. I always referred to myself as 'the Court.' But in my mind, as I heard all this testimony, I couldn't help but recall being around this type of discrimination much of my life."

He studied the facts and seriously mulled his decision. Once he reached a conclusion, he deliberated even longer over the proper remedy.

"I knew we had to do something significant. But what? I remembered a conversation with Judge Theodore Levin back in 1967, when I first got on the bench. We were having coffee in his chambers one morning, and he said, 'Damon, you're gonna have a lot of difficult cases here. You're a new judge, and you may become bewildered in some cases. But you will usually have a gut reaction. When in doubt, follow that gut.'

"To me, the DTE case was so egregious I had to make the remedy a sort of punishment, to ensure that such practices never occurred again. I felt that in my gut—as Judge Levin predicted. So I followed that feeling."

Keith knew the "remedy"—more than the decision itself—would be the cannon shot of his ruling. In what was becoming a family tradition, he went to Rachel the night before with a warning.

"Darling, I'm going to come down with a decision tomorrow that's going to be a little earthshaking, but I think it's the right thing to do. I want you to be prepared for any adverse publicity I might get."

She replied, "After all these years, I'm coming to think you like making difficult decisions."

Damon smiled and said, "I think you're right."

•   •   •

On October 2, 1973, Judge Keith found both Detroit Edison and the union defendants responsible for racial discrimination under Title VII of the Civil Rights Act of 1964.

"It is the conclusion of the Court," he wrote, "that the company is refusing to acknowledge the obvious."

Keith cited the slim number of black employees and miniscule number of black managers in a company whose city was, at the time, nearly fifty percent black. (By contrast, Detroit Edison's eleven-thousand-person workforce was ninety-two percent white.) He ruled that the company's discrimination had been "deliberate and by design."

His written opinion was sweeping and passionate, perhaps reflecting his own experience pushing a mop and knowing he was capable of so much more. Keith referred to the "ignoble disease of racial discrimination" and wrote, in part, citing the Declaration of Independence:

> "We hold these truths to be self-evident, that all men are created equal, that they are endowed by their Creator with certain unalienable Rights, that among these are Life, Liberty and the Pursuit of Happiness."

> To be denied an equal chance at decent employment, and an equal chance at advancement within one's employment, is to be denied that equality so nobly articulated by Jefferson. It is in this context unthinkable that a person would be denied equal employment opportunities at The Detroit Edison Company.

> Being denied a job is demeaning to a person and strips him of his dignity and assurance. A person has a right to extend his God-given working abilities to their fullest without being encumbered by artificial, irrelevant, insignificant, and superficial barriers, and reasons such as the color of his skin.

Keith also found that the word-of-mouth hiring and promotion practices at Detroit Edison created a pervasive culture of nepotism. The Sixth Circuit had previously found that such a culture, combined with discriminatory results, gave the court authority to grant relief.

Here is where Keith's decision set off a firestorm. He ordered many powerful and unprecedented remedies, including:

- Four million dollars to be paid by Detroit Edison to black employees who had been discriminated against. It was believed at the time to be the largest award ever ordered in a class-action bias case. In today's dollars, the damage award would be worth nearly $20 million.
- $250,000 to be paid by one union local to the same black employees as recoverable damages.
- Detroit Edison must bring its workforce up to thirty percent black as soon as possible.
- Detroit Edison must promote one black foreman or supervisor for every white promoted.
- Detroit Edison must stop giving intelligence or aptitude tests, as they were racially discriminatory.
- Detroit Edison must hire three blacks for every two whites in high-level technical and craftsmen jobs until twenty-five percent of workers in these categories were black.
- Detroit Edison must compensate a certain group of qualified black individuals who *did not apply for employment there* because of the perception that the company's racist hiring practices would not give them a fair shot.

•   •   •

It was tough medicine, and the judgment set off a tidal wave of reaction. In the black community, it was one of joy and relief, particularly in Detroit. For once, black citizens exclaimed, someone in the judicial system "got it." Someone truly understood on a gut level what it felt like to be denied a job merely because of skin color. Judge Keith's indignant opinion in the case, coming on the heels of the Pontiac busing case and Hamtramck fair housing case, made him something of a superhero to the black community. He received calls, letters, and telegrams expressing gratitude and admiration, from ordinary citizens and from prominent figures. He even received a congratulatory call from Otis Smith, his former rival for the judicial seat, who was then working as counsel for General Motors. And in a letter dated October 17, 1973, the legendary Clarence Mitchell, the longtime director of the Washington bureau of the NAACP, thanked Keith profusely: "Your decision points the way to getting rid of the handicaps that force so many minorities to spend their days on street corners instead of having a chance to work at gainful employment."

But it was hardly all hosannas and congratulations. The ruling outraged as many people as it inspired, and many did not hesitate to let Judge Keith know it. He received angry phone calls and insulting hate mail. One man, who signed his letter "J. B. Smith," wrote five days after the decision to express his disgust. His letter offers a peek into the often hidden racial attitudes of the time:

Dear Judge Keith:

In my opinion, that was a terrible sentence you imposed upon the Detroit Edison Company last week!! Four million dollars fine is the most ridiculous thing I have heard in many a moon.

That is all the thanks Detroit Edison gets for being so good to the Negroes over the past years. The Company has hired many more blacks than they cared to, just to give the under-privileged a chance to make good. Let's face it, if we really had our way, we employers

134

would a great deal rather employ only Caucasians because they seem to be the only ones who wish to do the work in a proper fashion. Negroes are only interested in the money, and how much they can cheat "Whitey." RIGHT???

My sympathy is 100% with the Detroit Edison organization and I believe you did a dastardly act in meting out such a huge fine. There is no reason Edison ought to be punished. They are sending out black meter readers to hundreds of all-white neighborhoods, in spite of many, many complaints from housewives who do not desire to let colored men into their basements when they are alone during the day with small children. Hundreds of husbands have gone to the expense to install outside meters. Just so their wives will no longer be afraid when a Negro meter-reader knocks on their side door. I think we whites have been inconvenienced sufficiently and punished more than enough already, without you handing down that awfully hard sentence-fine last week. Aren't you ashamed, Judge Keith? Until then, I considered you fair-minded, but not anymore!

Sincerely,
J. B. Smith

•   •   •

Not surprisingly, Detroit Edison appealed the decision. And nearly two years later, on March 11, 1975, the Sixth Circuit reversed the part of Judge Keith's ruling that Detroit Edison should pay back wages to blacks who were discouraged from applying because of its reputation for racist hiring practices. It narrowed the groups entitled to receive compensation to only individual employees denied promotions between January 1968 and March 1974 and to applicants unlawfully refused employment between June 1969 and March 1974.

It did not, however, overturn the ruling that Detroit Edison was liable.

As a result, Keith's decision in *Stamps* had immeasurable ripple effects. All over the country, companies and corporations examined their own hiring and promotion practices and quietly made adjustments—not wanting to be pummeled with their own multi-million-dollar judgment. There is no telling how many blacks were employed as a result of these preventative measures. Keith's "gut" instinct that only a powerful remedy would engender change proved wholly correct.

Years later, at the Grand Hotel on Mackinac Island, Keith ran into a former officer of Detroit Edison. He said, "Thank God for your decision, Judge Keith, because it really was vicious and intentional discrimination. And it might never have changed if you didn't give your ruling."

Keith also heard from executives around the country who confirmed their hiring practices had been adjusted as a result of the *Stamps* case.

"I didn't really think about that part when I made the decision," Keith now admits. "It was only later that I realized the effects."

And perhaps only now that he realizes the symmetry: a black man who was once told "you better keep mopping" had ensured that others would not have to.

17

Taking on the Nixon White House

The Keith Case

"Judge Keith is a courageous judge who had the courage to do what he had to do, when it was necessary to do it."

—John Dean, White House Deputy Counsel
to President Richard M. Nixon

T he sun rose brightly on June 19, 1972.

Judge Keith did not.

He stumbled into the kitchen, bleary-eyed after a mostly sleepless night. Lost in thought, he wondered what lay ahead on this historic Monday morning—for him and for the country. It was the last day of the U.S. Supreme Court's term for the year, and one way or another his world was going to change. For all the hot button cases he was or had been actively involved in—the Pontiac schools, Hamtramck, *Stamps v. Detroit Edison Co.*—a ruling was expected to come down this day that would forever define his judicial legacy. And it was out of his hands.

He had taken on the president of the United States.

The betting money was against him.

Still in his pajamas and bathrobe, the judge opened the front door, grabbed the newspaper off the front lawn, made his way back inside, and plopped himself down at the kitchen table.

"Good morning, Darling," Rachel said cheerily, entering the room already dressed for work.

"Morning," he mumbled, barely looking up. He was scanning the paper hoping for clues, a small news story, a quote, a prediction, any indication of how the day would go. But newspapers are for what happened yesterday. Today cannot be found in their pages. Today would have to be lived, endured, and dealt with. It was Damon Keith, a singular, perhaps over-achieving judge from Detroit on one side, and Richard Nixon, president of the most powerful nation on earth, on the other.

He sighed and turned to Rachel, who was preparing the eggs, oatmeal, and whole wheat toast that constituted his daily breakfast. Seeing her made him feel better.

"You all right?" she asked.

"Mmm?" he said. "Oh. Yeah. I'm all right."

Eighteen months earlier, on a January morning in 1971, Judge Keith had made a groundbreaking decision. He'd ruled that President Nixon was required to inform a Detroit-based group of anti-war activists whether his administration engaged in warrantless wiretapping of their organization—under the guise of national security.

The dramatic and unprecedented ruling, known as the *Sinclair* case, shook the nation. It was the first time a federal judge had ever challenged a sitting president's authority to pursue a particular national security strategy. Despite huge criticism leveled against Keith, the U.S. Court of Appeals for the Sixth Circuit upheld his decision on appeal.

Infuriated, the Nixon administration took a nearly unheard of step, filing a writ of mandamus against Keith. The writ meant the Nixon administration believed Keith's decision was so egregiously wrong that it personally sued him, a sitting federal judge, to stop his order from being enforced.

It was as close as you get, legally, to the president coming after you himself.

The case had gone, predictably, all the way to the Supreme Court, where Judge Keith knew the odds of affirming his ruling were low. The fact that the court had granted the writ of mandamus in the first place was already highly unusual—and deeply troubling to the legal world. Many of his colleagues on the district court had warned Judge Keith that in ruling against the Nixon administration, he was essentially substituting his judgment as a non-elected federal judge for that of a sitting president on matters of national security during a time of war.

More than a few saw this as arrogant. They felt any court should defer to the president in such matters.

"If the attorney general and the president of the United States think it's needed to defend our national security, who are you, as a judge, to tell them otherwise?" This was a common refrain. Even Judge Keith's closest legal allies—and those who admired his stance—remained skeptical that it could survive the Supreme Court.

"Damon," Rachel said as she grabbed her bag and jacket, preparing to leave. "Let the girls sleep in. The housekeeper will get them up when she arrives."

"OK," he mumbled.

His mind drifted to the arguments he'd made defending his ruling. He'd cited the Fourth Amendment and its requirement that the government show probable cause before a neutral magistrate before executing a search warrant. "They just can't unilaterally do it on their own; even if it is the president of the United States," he would tell colleagues.

But for every swing he offered, someone counter-swung. The strongest argument against him was that there was no precedent for his decision—and he knew it. Law is built on laws. He was standing on the narrow pillar of his own conviction.

Making matters worse, he had been tipped off by someone with knowledge of the Supreme Court's internal workings that Chief Justice Warren Burger had assigned a justice to write the decision who earlier in his career had suggested that the executive branch did indeed have the authority to engage in the warrantless wiretapping of citizens for the purpose of national security. Why would that justice change his tune now?

"OK, Damon, I'm going," Rachel said.

He put down the newspaper and hurried to give his wife a hug and kiss, as he had done every day of their marriage. This morning, he held on a little longer. By the time he'd see her again his legacy would be altered. He'd be a different man, professionally, for better or for worse.

Five years—five years only—he had been on the bench. He'd ruled on government forces in his city, on schools, on workplaces. But now he was in a dogfight with the U.S. attorney general and the president of the United States. Sitting back down at the kitchen table, he wondered if his grasp had outdistanced his reach.

What have I gotten myself into?"

After all, this was Richard Nixon, the most powerful man on the planet. And a man who felt it necessary to take down his enemies.

•　　•　　•

In 1971 the United States was deep into the Vietnam War. But Nixon did not see threats as confined to Southeast Asia. He saw dangers at home. He saw enemies in many corners. The power with which he viewed his office to battle such enemies was at the heart of the *Sinclair* case.

John Sinclair, Lawrence Robert "Pun" Plamondon, and John Forrest were charged with being the leaders of the White Panther Party, a group of anti-war activists and political revolutionaries who modeled themselves after the Black Panther Party. They were charged with conspiring to bomb the CIA office in Ann Arbor in 1968. The key evidence against them was based on surreptitiously obtained tapes from conversations the defendants allegedly had with employees of the Embassy of Cuba. Excerpts from records later released revealed that then FBI Director J. Edgar Hoover had personally ordered, and Attorney General John Mitchell had approved, the installation of the wiretap as part of their widespread surveillance program of liberal social activists.

White Panther Party attorneys William Kunstler and Leonard Weinglass moved to suppress the tapes, as they were obtained without a search warrant. The government did not dispute that. It admitted to taping the conversations and not having a warrant. But citing a different and unprecedented justification—a national security exemption asserted by President Nixon—the government claimed the right to wiretap any person whom it felt was a national security threat. All that was required was the president's authorization, as expressed by his attorney general.

No warrants? No judges? Even for Nixon, this was a bold declaration of power. But he had won the presidency by appealing to law and order after a year of domestic disturbances like no other in twentieth-century America. The president made direct appeals to voters who were fearful of the rapid social change taking place, a group often referred to as "the silent majority." Polls had found this group questioned not only the patriotism of anti-war activists like the White Panthers but also the loyalty of public figures who were critical of the Vietnam War.

Buoyed by such views, Nixon felt empowered—even obliged—to take action against perceived subversive or unpatriotic forces, even if they were U.S. citizens. This was witnessed in his fury at the *New York Times* and the *Washington Post* for leaking classified military documents known as the Pentagon Papers, which revealed details of America's involvement in Vietnam and how multiple administrations had misled the public. The Nixon administration obtained a federal court injunction to force the *New York Times* to cease publication of those papers, which shocked free speech advocates and ultimately led to a Supreme Court showdown.

Other presidents might have shied away from such conflicts. But Nixon's push for expansion of his power led Pulitzer Prize–winning historian Arthur M. Schlesinger Jr. to refer to his as the "Imperial Presidency."

It was against this backdrop that Judge Keith chose to take on the President over *Sinclair.*

Although, in truth, the case chose him.

• • •

Judge Talbot Smith, Judge Keith's much older, distinguished colleague on the U.S. District Court, initially drew the case in 1971; however, Smith was an Ann Arbor resident and feared for his own safety and that of his family. Therefore, he stepped aside and suggested to his colleagues that Chief Judge Ralph Freeman send the case to Cincinnati. Judge Keith, who was the newest member on the bench, was stunned. He believed that judges on the court had a responsibility to deal with hard and controversial cases, in spite of the pressures on them personally. He told this to Chief Judge Freeman, who ultimately agreed to place the case in a blind draw.

The choice would belong to fate. Whoever drew the longest straw would assume *Sinclair.*

Judge Keith won the draw. It continued the strange pattern of fate sending the toughest, most-controversial cases his way. But duty was duty, and Keith did not shy away from the process. The days were rife with protesters, finger pointing, anti-establishment slogans, and the familiar 1960s overtones of youth versus power, with Sinclair achieving high status as a cultural revolutionary.

Keith kept his eye on the ball. For him, a predominant issue was whether constitutional rights were violated. After a monthlong hearing, on January 25, 1971, he rendered his most important—and perhaps boldest—decision to date. He ordered the government to disclose to the defendants' lawyers whether their phones were tapped, despite President Nixon's contention that keeping such information confidential was necessary for national security. In a powerfully worded opinion, Judge Keith held that the Fourth Amendment prohibited the federal government from conducting electronic surveillance without a court order and flatly declared a simple but memorable sentence:

"We are a country of laws and not of men."

He also pointed out that while the Nixon administration wanted to liken the actions of the Sinclair group to those of an unfriendly foreign power, such an argument strikes at the very core of U.S. citizenship. "It is to be remembered," he wrote, "that in our democracy all men are to receive equal justice regardless of their political beliefs or persuasions."

The Nixon administration roared back. It filed the writ of mandamus against Judge Keith. The resultant lawsuit was formally called *United States v. United States District Court for the Eastern District of Michigan, et al.* Its longwinded name quickly became shortened to "the Keith case" or "the Keith decision." When it came before the Supreme Court in 1972, Keith's doubters were loud and plentiful.

To defend himself, Judge Keith had retained William T. Gossett, one of the most prominent lawyers in the country. The former general counsel for the Ford Motor Company, president of the American Bar Association, and chairman of the United Negro College Fund was a man to be reckoned with—even if Keith had to tell him up front, "Bill, I don't have the money to pay you for this." Gossett took the case anyway, a testament to how important he felt it was.

Still, the fact that a sitting judge was girding against a sitting president revealed a battle that was incomparable to anything going on in an American courtroom.

And on that last day of the Supreme Court's term in 1972, the battle would be decided.

● ● ●

When Judge Keith arrived at his chambers that morning, all the televisions were on. His law clerk, Eric L. Clay, was listening to a radio in his office. The tension was palpable. Everyone understood the magnitude of the case and what a decision might portend for the country—let alone Judge Keith. He could be elevated. He could be crushed.

Until then, however, there was nothing to do but put one foot in front of the other. So the judge, with the figurative sword of the country hanging over his head, put on his robe and sat down to hear the day's cases. Eugene Driker, then an up-and-coming young Detroit corporate attorney, was before him that morning in an unrelated case. Driker recalls that day well. Just as his opponents were finishing their arguments and he was preparing to make his, one of Judge Keith's law clerks walked hurriedly into the courtroom and whispered something into his ear.

Everyone froze.

Judge Keith smiled. He repeated the words aloud.

"The Supreme Court has upheld Keith 8-0."

It was a decision so powerful, you could almost hear it rumbling in the street. Driker remembers sitting down glumly without saying a word. "I was pretty confident the judge wasn't going to spend a lot of time reviewing a decision in a commercial case when he had just been affirmed by the Supreme Court."

Judge Keith's courage had been rewarded and his conviction sustained. In stirring and forceful language that would hold particular poignancy decades later, Justice Lewis Powell wrote for the majority: "Fourth amendment protections become the more necessary when the targets of official surveillance may be those suspected of unorthodoxy in their political beliefs. The danger to political dissent is acute where the Government attempts to act under so vague a concept as the power to protect 'domestic security.'"

As news of the decision spread, Judge Keith was heralded from coast to coast. The Keith case was seen as a triumph for civil liberties, the principle of separation of powers, and, on a broad level, constitutional rights. Because of the decision (and subsequent decisions involving defendants' rights), Keith would go on to be considered one of the nation's leading defenders of civil liberties on the bench.

In *The Benchwarmers*, Joseph Goulden described Judge Keith as "a prime example of an independent federal judge who had the courage to say 'no' in the face of a presidency which likened itself to a 'sovereign.'" "The strength of the judiciary," Goulden writes, "is rooted in just such independence as that displayed by Keith."

Bill Simpich, a prominent Oakland, California, civil liberties lawyer and author, makes an even bolder claim. He says many Washington insiders believe that the Keith case ultimately played a key role in President Nixon's resignation two years later. He notes that after the Supreme Court had reached its decision, there was a leak that the decision would be announced publicly on Monday, June 19, 1972.

"Members of the Committee to Reelect the President had previously installed bugs at offices of Democrats in the Watergate Building," Simpich writes. "The thinking goes that in view of the impending Supreme Court ruling, the White House ordered that the bugs be removed. Howard Hunt and the rest of Nixon's Plumbers came to the Watergate on Saturday night. The fallout from the break-in was what led to Nixon's resignation in 1974."

Whether or not the Keith case was the catalyst for events that eventually led to the Nixon resignation is up for debate. However, the unanimous Supreme Court decision both elevated and liberated Judge Keith. As one of the few black judges on the federal bench, the Keith Case established for him a judicial identity—not just as a strong defender of civil rights but as a man in the tradition of esteemed federal judges like the late Learned Hand and Judge Keith's mentor, Thurgood Marshall.

The decision also landed Keith in the pages of the *New York Times* the day after the decision, where he was featured in its "Man in the News" section under the headline "The Judge in the Wiretapping Case."

He shared that article with Rachel over a breakfast table noticeably less distracted than the one the morning before. He had drawn the *Sinclair* case by a straw but had wrestled it with his body and soul. He was less than five years into his career as a judge, but he had already stared down a sitting U.S. president.

And his string of high-profile cases was far from over.

Damon J. Keith as Chief Judge of the United States District Court for the Eastern District of Michigan, Detroit, 1977.

To Damon Keith

Thank you for helping me celebrate Law Day at the White House.

Law Day – Whitehouse
May 1, 1979

Jimmy Carter

ABOVE: President Jimmy Carter and Judge Damon J. Keith at Law Day at the White House, Washington, D.C., May 1, 1979.

OPPOSITE, TOP: Judge Damon J. Keith, James Baldwin, and Mayor Coleman A. Young, 1979.

OPPOSITE, BOTTOM: Rosa Parks being presented with the NAACP Spingarn Medal by Judge Damon J. Keith in Louisville, Kentucky, 1979.

Judge Damon J. Keith and Aretha Franklin at the Detroit Institute of Arts, Detroit, Michigan, June 1986.

ABOVE: Governor Bill Clinton, Judge Damon J. Keith, Hillary Rodham Clinton, Lani (Guinier) and Nolan Bowie and their daughter at the wedding of Lani and Nolan Bowie. Judge Keith performed the Martha's Vineyard ceremony, August 2, 1986.

OPPOSITE, BOTTOM: Senator Charles Robb, Prime Minister Margaret Thatcher, and Judge Damon J. Keith. The inscription reads "To the Hon. Damon J. Keith, Best Wishes, Margaret Thatcher."

ABOVE: Mayor Coleman A. Young and Judge Damon J. Keith talking at the annual Soul Food Luncheon held in Judge Keith's chambers.

OPPOSITE, TOP: Bishop Desmond Tutu, Judge Damon J. Keith, Judge Nathaniel R. Jones, and Mayor Coleman A. Young, January 1986.

OPPOSITE, BOTTOM: Judge Damon J. Keith and Anatoly Sharansky in Russia, November 1987.

Judge Damon J. Keith and General Colin L. Powell at the award reception at the One Nation Dinner in Washington D.C., May 23, 1989.

Anita Baker and Judge Damon J. Keith in his chambers at the annual Soul Food Luncheon, 1989.

Judge Damon J. Keith greets Nelson Mandela at Detroit Metropolitan Airport, Romulus, Michigan, June 28, 1990.

Arthur L. Johnson, with Charles Boyce, Bill Cosby, and Judge Damon J. Keith, Interlochen, Michigan, 1993.

Emanuel Steward with wife, Marie, and Judge Damon J. Keith in Detroit, Michigan, 1992.

In recognition of Judge Keith's service as the National Chairman of the Judicial Conference Commission on the Bicentennial of the United States Constitution, the Bill of Rights plaques commemorating this important anniversary adorning the walls of courthouses and law schools throughout the United States and Guam bear Judge Keith's name. One of these plaques hangs on the walls of the world headquarters of the Ford Motor Company in Dearborn, Michigan, the company where his father, Perry Keith, labored in the foundries to support his family upon migrating from Georgia.

The Bill of Rights

Amendment I

Congress shall make no law respecting an establishment of religion, or prohibiting the free exercise thereof; or abridging the freedom of speech, or of the press; or the right of the people peaceably to assemble, and to petition the Government for a redress of grievances.

Amendment II

A well regulated Militia, being necessary to the security of a free State, the right of the people to keep and bear Arms, shall not be infringed.

Amendment III

No Soldier shall, in time of peace be quartered in any house, without the consent of the Owner, nor in time of war, but in a manner to be prescribed by law.

Amendment IV

The right of the people to be secure in their persons, houses, papers, and effects, against unreasonable searches and seizures, shall not be violated, and no Warrants shall issue, but upon probable cause, supported by Oath or affirmation, and particularly describing the place to be searched, and the persons or things to be seized.

Amendment V

No person shall be held to answer for a capital, or otherwise infamous crime, unless on a presentment or indictment of a Grand Jury, except in cases arising in the land or naval forces, or in the Militia, when in actual service in time of War or public danger; nor shall any person be subject for the same offence to be twice put in jeopardy of life or limb; nor shall be compelled in any criminal case to be a witness against himself, nor be deprived of life, liberty, or property, without due process of law; nor shall private property be taken for public use, without just compensation.

Amendment VI

In all criminal prosecutions, the accused shall enjoy the right to a speedy and public trial, by an impartial jury of the State and district wherein the crime shall have been committed, which district shall have been previously ascertained by law, and to be informed of the nature and cause of the accusation; to be confronted with the witnesses against him; to have compulsory process for obtaining witnesses in his favor, and to have the Assistance of Counsel for his defence.

Amendment VII

In Suits at common law, where the value in controversy shall exceed twenty dollars, the right of trial by jury shall be preserved, and no fact tried by a jury, shall be otherwise re-examined in any Court of the United States, than according to the rules of the common law.

Amendment VIII

Excessive bail shall not be required, nor excessive fines imposed, nor cruel and unusual punishments inflicted.

Amendment IX

The enumeration in the Constitution, of certain rights, shall not be construed to deny or disparage others retained by the people.

Amendment X

The powers not delegated to the United States by the Constitution, nor prohibited by it to the States, are reserved to the States respectively, or to the people.

JUDICIAL CONFERENCE OF THE UNITED STATES
COMMITTEE ON THE BICENTENNIAL OF THE CONSTITUTION

Dec. 15, 1791 - Dec. 15, 1991

Judge Damon J. Keith
Chairman

ABOVE: Judge Damon J. Keith, Dr. Rachel Boone Keith, and President Bill Clinton at the opening of the Marching Toward Justice exhibit at the Thurgood Marshall Federal Judiciary Building, Washington D.C., February 3, 1999.

OPPOSITE, TOP: Judge Damon J. Keith at the memorial service for the Honorable George W. Crockett Jr., September 13, 1997.

OPPOSITE, BOTTOM: Judge Damon J. Keith, Professor John Hope Franklin, and William Halling at the Detroit Economic Club, Detroit, Michigan, October 26, 1998.

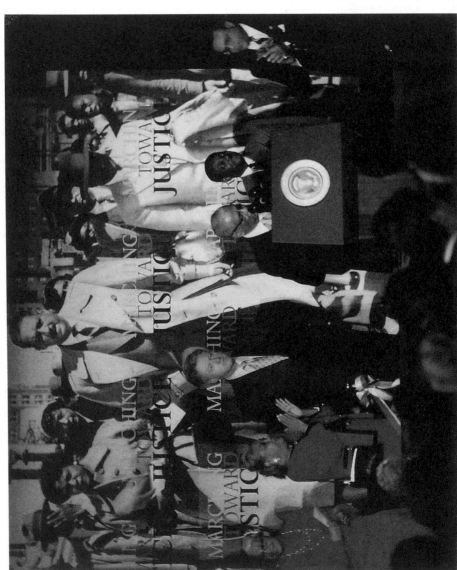

Rosa Parks, Mrs. Thurgood Marshall, President Bill Clinton, Judge Damon J. Keith, Wayne State University President Irvin Reid, and Howard University President H. Patrick Swygert at the opening of the Marching Toward Justice exhibit at the Thurgood Marshall Federal Judiciary Building, Washington D.C., February 3, 1999.

ABOVE: Judge Damon J. Keith and Charles Hamilton Houston III (Houston's grandson and Keith law clerk) standing in front of a portrait of Charles Hamilton Houston I at Harvard Law School, Cambridge, Massachusetts, April 2000.

LEFT: Judge Damon J. Keith and Dr. Rachel Boone Keith.

Former Keith law clerks Professor Lani Guinier, Judge Eric L. Clay, and Constance L. Rice with Judge Damon J. Keith at a Just the Beginning Foundation Conference, San Francisco, California, 2000.

Judge Damon J. Keith swearing in Governor Jennifer M. Granholm, Lansing, Michigan, January 1, 2003.

18

Affirmative Action in the Detroit Police Department

The mid-1970s were a tumultuous time for race relations in America. Policy changes, lawsuits, new opportunities, and accusations of bias in both directions were all part of the stew.

In the Keith household, the three daughters were now teenagers, and mother and father made a decision to get them the best education, the type of education unavailable to most blacks when Damon and Rachel were growing up. In their minds, that education was offered by the prestigious Cranbrook Schools in Bloomfield Hills, one of the wealthiest suburbs in America. Judge Keith drove his girls there each morning from their home in Detroit, traversing two worlds, letting his daughters from an ethnically mixed neighborhood immerse themselves in an almost exclusively white and wealthy environment.

"In hindsight, that may have been a mistake," Keith says now. "They were there with a lot of rich kids, and because they were very smart, we felt it was the best place education-wise. It all worked out in the end, but looking back, I'm not sure I would do it again."

Damon and Rachel, like many in the 1970s, were dealing with the delicate balance of identity and opportunity when a challenge landed on Keith's judicial bench in 1975, in the form of *Baker v. City of Detroit*, an employment-discrimination and affirmative-action case involving the Detroit Police Department. It would be a long and contentious battle. But Keith's decision greatly influenced the racial climate of metro Detroit.

And like many of the landmark decisions in his judicial career, it was partly formed by his own life experience.

•　　•　　•

Appreciating the nuances of *Baker v. City of Detroit* requires some background on the Detroit Police Department. The 1943 Detroit riots—when a twenty-year-old Damon watched helplessly as federal troops were rushed in to restore order—brought harsh light on the Motor City and its law enforcement. An NAACP report, authored by none other than Thurgood Marshall, ran in the NAACP's magazine, *The Crisis*, under the foreboding title, "The Gestapo in Detroit." It described how blacks were targeted by the nearly all-white Detroit police force:

> The police once again enforced the law with an unequal hand. They used "persuasion" rather than firm action with white rioters, while against Negroes they used the ultimate in force: night sticks, revolvers, riot guns, sub-machine guns, and deer guns. As a result, 25 of the 34 persons killed were negroes. Of the 25 Negroes killed, 17 were killed by police. . . . White persons killed by police—none.

That report recommended an immediate increase in the number of black officers and their promotion to senior positions to balance the racial composition—and, perhaps, attitudes—of the force.

The City of Detroit didn't listen.

In fact, between 1944 and 1953, annual black hires ranged from four to twenty-eight, whereas annual white hires ranged from 135 to 560. In the largely segregated force, white officers were sometimes assigned to ride with black officers as a form of punishment. The small handful of black sergeants and lieutenants were not assigned to supervise whites.

Then came the 1967 riots—in which a forty-five-year-old Damon Keith had a more active experience—and things were hardly better. In some ways, it was worse. Detroit's population was now forty percent black, yet black officers accounted for only six percent of the police force. The ugly violence—and the fact that the riots erupted in reaction to overzealous police actions—only widened the divide.

A few years later, along came a firebrand mayoral candidate named Coleman Young. A former member of the Tuskegee Airmen who loudly fought discrimination in both the military and the labor force, Young, then a state senator, made reforming the police department and its violence against blacks a central theme of his 1973 campaign. He vowed to eliminate a controversial police unit called STRESS (Stop the Robberies and Enjoy Safe Streets) that had had been accused of killing twenty-two black residents and harassing countless others in less than three years of existence. Young narrowly won the election over a white former police commissioner named John Nichols.

"He was elected largely in reaction to years of police abuse," Keith confirms. "The stop-and-frisk policies that had existed. All that. People had enough."

When Young took office as the first African-American mayor in Detroit's history, he quickly instituted an aggressive affirmative-action plan to increase the percentage of black officers from seventeen to fifty percent in three short years. Part of Young's plan also required that equal numbers of black and white officers be promoted to higher ranks. Previously, promotions were based on a numerical ranking, which incorporated factors like a written test score, educational background, performance reviews, and length of service.

Under Young's plan to diversify the force, some black officers with a lower ranking were promoted ahead of white officers.

The bypassed white officers were understandably upset. They had done everything they were told and were, in their minds, more qualified; their higher rankings proved it. All of a sudden, the playing field was turned upside down, and black officers with lower scores were leapfrogging them. Feeling that they had been illegally discriminated against, the Detroit Police Lieutenants & Sergeants Association filed a lawsuit against the city on behalf of three white sergeants who had been passed up for promotions, including an officer named Kenneth Baker.

Baker v. City of Detroit was the kind of lawsuit that would have been unimaginable when Keith first became a lawyer—whites charging discrimination in favor of blacks—yet would portend a national debate over affirmative-action policies that rages to this day.

When Keith received the case at the end of 1975, he had an unusual history with both sides. Earlier that year, he had been brought in to informally mediate conflicts between the police officers' union and the city to avoid the pain of recession-era layoffs. Keith brokered a deal that helped the union avoid layoffs of their senior officers in exchange for contractual concessions to help the mayor's budget. His diplomacy was extraordinary. Local bar associations even gave him an award for his efforts.

But once *Baker* landed on his docket, lawyers for the plaintiffs had quick and harsh reactions. Keith and Young were perceived to be friends, and the notion of a fair trial seemed, to them, impossible. Keith had sworn in Young the day he took office. He had spoken at a prayer breakfast in his honor. And Young would be part of the committee to endorse Keith for appointment to the U.S. Court of Appeals for the Sixth Circuit.

"They didn't want me hearing the case," Keith recalls. "They wanted it taken away and given to a jury. But I feel once a case has come before me, in a blind draw, it's supposed to be my baby."

On July 31, 1978, Keith ruled that he would deny the plaintiffs' demand for a jury trial in this case. Case law held that action brought for back pay and injunctive relief under Title VII of the Civil Rights Act of 1964 did not require a jury trial. He would rule on the case himself.

In a bluntly worded response, Keith addressed the concerns over his interactions with Coleman Young:

> Plaintiffs allege that extra-judicial contact between myself and Mayor Young during the pendency of this litigation is likely and thus creates an appearance of impropriety.
>
> The reality of life is that only a small number of Black persons have been elevated to positions of responsibility in our national life. It therefore is highly likely, especially in a predominately Black city like Detroit, that a Black Federal Judge would know, on a friendship basis, a Black Mayor. The mere fact that I have a personal friendship with Mayor Young, a nominal party to this action, cannot be said to support a reasonable inference of lack of impartiality.
>
> Plaintiffs do not allege that I am personally biased for or against any party to this action. In fact, plaintiffs affirmatively deny that I am biased or prejudiced, and can point to no instance in which this Court has conducted proceedings in this matter in anything but a fair and impartial manner.
>
> The conclusion is inescapable that the likely grounds upon which plaintiffs' motion is based is the fact that I am Black, that Mayor Young is Black, that this action was brought by white policemen seeking to challenge the affirmative action program in the Detroit Police Department, and that, therefore, it is reasonable to infer that I am somehow incapable of presiding over this case in a fair and impartial manner.

It was a plainly stated position that spoke in fascinating counterpoint to the case at hand, Keith saying that just because he was black, it shouldn't be concluded he couldn't do his job properly—that job being to impartially hear a suit that claimed just because they were white, it shouldn't be concluded that certain police officers were less deserving of advancement than black colleagues.

Over such a collection of draped racial wires did the case begin—with Judge Keith, not a jury, as the ultimate decision maker. The subsequent hearing would last fifty-five days, involve the introduction of 230 exhibits as evidence, and produce over 6,300 pages of transcripts. From the start, the color lines were drawn.

"I remember the police officers coming to the court and the black officers sitting on one side and the white officers sitting on another," Keith says. "It was a very hot issue."

The case, filed in 1975, would not be ruled upon until 1979. Through-out the process, Keith listened carefully to all the testimony, studied all the paperwork, and measured the issues alongside his own personal recollections of Detroit police behavior.

"I knew that for years there had never been black officers in most police positions. No black officers on horseback. No black officers on motorcycle," Keith says. "I remembered how many black citizens had been harassed or even beaten up by white police officers, and when someone asked why, they'd say, 'They were resisting arrest.' Blacks were put in jail for no reason. The police department had been infiltrated with racism, and that was one of Coleman's challenges, to change that."

Keith had to weigh that history with the legal issues regarding affirmative action. Did the city's new policy violate Title VII of the Civil Rights Act of 1964 and the Constitution? And did equal rights under the law mean the right to an absolutely colorblind process of distributing goods in society, as argued by the white police officers? Or did historical inequality and contemporary needs for diversity play a role as well, as argued by Mayor Young?

At the time of Keith's decision, two Supreme Court cases had held that affirmative-action programs were appropriate under both Title VII and the Constitution, but only under very defined and limited circumstances.

Thus when Judge Keith finally issued his opinion, on October 1, 1979—ruling for the city and upholding the affirmative-action plan—he was careful to note that the officers' complaints had "facial appeal." On the face of it, racial discrimination against whites should not be tolerated by the law any more than racial discrimination against blacks. Why should lower-ranking blacks get promotions over higher-ranking whites?

However, Keith also pointed out he saw other fundamental truths at play. First, he noted that this effort at affirmative action was a methodically created policy, a step-by-step process to diversify the police force that took months to develop and was not done so out of malice, a burden the plaintiffs needed to prove:

> An examination of the undisputed facts of this case reveals no basis for plaintiffs' assertions that the defendants acted maliciously. This affirmative action program was not imposed overnight by a reckless official.

Keith also noted a difference between discriminatory policies that were designed to keep one group of people down—like those that had existed for years in the Detroit Police Department—and policies that might have deleterious effects on one group in efforts to make amends to another:

> All affirmative action programs have some adverse effect on whites who must step aside so that blacks may be hired or promoted. The Board of Police Commissioners was well aware of this, but made the reasoned decision that promoting blacks was not unjust in the light of past discrimination since no one had a right to be promoted and since it considered the black and the white candidates to be equally

qualified. The Board concluded that the larger need of the City for Black Officers and the need to offset the effects of past discrimination mandated the affirmative action promotional model.

In addition, Keith pointed out that while the city was the target of this lawsuit, it was not the city that had actually mistreated black officers and citizens over the years. It was the plaintiffs' white colleagues:

> It was the white officers who were guilty of mistreating black citizens. It was white officers who went on a ticket strike in 1959 when the City proposed integrating squad cars. It was white officers who fiercely resisted efforts to integrate the department throughout the 1960s. This Court has no way of knowing if any of the members of the plaintiff class were guilty of such practices or of condoning such practices. The Court hopes that none were.

For Keith, context and history mattered. White officers had received preferential treatment for decades out of animus. The city's affirmative-action plan was meant to alleviate these past injustices. In Judge Keith's view, such intent was critical:

> The City's affirmative action program should not be seen as depriving white officers of any right to a promotion. Instead, it should be seen as a program conferring a bonus on blacks that have been subject to past discrimination. White officers in 1970 received an unexpected bonus when the Department decided to promote everyone on the Sergeant's eligibility list. White officers cannot reasonably complain when the Department, on a finding of past discrimination and operational need, decided to confer a "bonus" on blacks in 1974 and subsequent years.

Finally, Keith spoke to the most divisive issue regarding affirmative action—that it unfairly punishes even as it tries to heal past wrongs:

> Plaintiffs have also complained throughout the proceedings that the affirmative action plan is harsh and unjustifiable because it did not rest on individual considerations of merit. The Court feels the opposite is true. The non-retributive, class-based nature of affirmative action is perhaps its strongest asset. Affirmative action is prospective, it seeks to remedy and not destroy. When done voluntarily, it accuses no individual of wrongdoing.

A common theme that was emerging in Judge Keith's jurisprudence again appeared in his opinion in *Baker*. Unlike his more conservative colleagues, Keith wasn't afraid to let his experiences inform his reading of the law. One passage of his opinion reads like an instruction to conservative activists on the claim that affirmative-action plans are basically "reverse discrimination":

> Plaintiffs claim that this was blatant discrimination against them as whites which is illegal under the abovementioned statutes and the Constitution. A theme which they embrace is that there should be no difference between discrimination against whites and discrimination against blacks. In a perfect world, plaintiffs would be correct. The world has been far from perfect for blacks, however. It has been especially far from perfect for blacks in the Department and blacks that applied to the Department. The City did not act to favor blacks out of malice toward whites, or even capriciousness. It acted to favor blacks because, as a class, they had been subject to debilitating discrimination for years on end. The affirmative action program is unquestionably a racial preference and it unquestionably impacts against white officers. It is also an

admittedly imperfect remedy which seeks to offset past discrimination undergone by blacks, specifically black officers. Reconciling the rights of white and black officers is not easy.

Keith's decision brought affirmative action into a bright spotlight. It made huge headlines in Detroit. And, not surprisingly, his ruling was appealed by the plaintiffs. But it was broadly affirmed in an opinion authored by Judge Nathaniel Jones, a contemporary and black judge on the U.S. Court of Appeals for the Sixth Circuit. (In a subsequent proceeding, at the insistence of Judge Gilbert Merritt, that same panel determined that a voluntary affirmative-action plan should not be given the force of a court order, as Judge Keith had ruled, a minor fissure that portended much larger future disagreements over race and affirmative action between Judge Keith and Judge Merritt.)

Nevertheless, because the plan was adopted voluntarily by the city, the Sixth Circuit ruled that the city had the prerogative to proceed with it.

The affirmative action plan continued throughout Mayor Coleman Young's tenure and defined his legacy.

Carl T. Rowan, an editorial contributor to the *Detroit News*, would later write that Keith's decision in *Baker* was even more important than the Supreme Court's landmark ruling in Regents of the *University of California v. Bakke*, which established that colleges could consider diversity when making admissions decisions "because of issues like law and order, of the staffing of police and fire departments in our increasingly black cities."

To this day, Judge Keith says, "Time has not changed my opinion on this matter."

That ruling brought to a close a most remarkable decade of judicial work, from the explosive school busing issue (*Pontiac*) to housing discrimination (*Hamtramck*) to employment discrimination (*Detroit Edison*) to affirmative action (*Baker*)—all peaked by a landmark showdown with President Nixon over the Fourth Amendment.

It is almost unfathomable that one judge—let alone a new judge—should have heard and decided, in just a few years, such a myriad of crucial, high-profile cases, with issues that would cast legal shadows for decades to come. Keith himself became so concerned that at one point in the mid-1970s, he asked the chief justice of his court, Ralph Freeman, to look into whether anything untoward was going on with the supposedly blind draw of cases. "I think this blind drawer has eyes on it," he told Freeman, "because I am drawing the most difficult cases that have come out of this court."

Freeman conceded it was very unusual and even assigned an FBI agent to quietly investigate whether or not the case bay was being manipulated. Several weeks later, he called Keith and told him the investigation had turned up nothing unusual. "You just drew those," he said.

And so Damon soldiered on, delivering opinions that freshly resonate when read today, even though they were made while traversing major societal changes. By the time of his decision in the Baker case, his hair was starting to grey. All three of his daughters had graduated high school from the Cranbrook program and had landed in the University of Michigan, Princeton, and Duke—schools that were a pipe dream for Damon Keith when he was their age. He was fifty-seven years old and had gone from being a one-time victim of racially motivated police harassment to ruling that white officers had not been maliciously harmed by an affirmative-action policy favoring black colleagues.

It was a dizzying ride. Throughout the years, the ballast that Keith relied upon was his life experience, education, relationship with Rachel, and the wisdom he saw in the book of Proverbs, which he read each morning in his office. There was also the feeling in his gut that he had been advised early on not to ignore.

Had he stepped down at that point, Keith's legacy would have been weighty and secure. Yet more than two decades later, he would still be deciding cases that affected the course of the nation.

19.

"Tell Him Thurgood's on the Line"

<hr />

On Wednesday morning, November 5, 1980, Damon Keith came to
his chambers, as usual. He greeted his law clerks, as usual. Then
he sat down at his desk and quietly leafed through his Bible.

It was a unique day for reflection. The night before, the nation had
elected Ronald Reagan as its president in a landslide, representing a
decided shift away from the Democratic policies of sitting president
Jimmy Carter. Reagan didn't just defeat Carter, he trounced him, winning the popular vote by nearly ten percentage points and capturing
forty-three of the fifty states' electoral votes.

Republicans and conservatives celebrated this as a mandate to alter
the course of the country, in economic policy, in foreign policy, and in
judicial policy—including the trend of "activist" liberal judges that a
critical Reagan had made a central point of his campaign. At his desk
now, Keith—considered one of those activist judges—read from Proverbs
as he pondered what this new direction might mean, perhaps perusing

the words from chapter 16, verse 18: "Pride goeth before destruction, and an haughty spirit before a fall."

Politics will humble pride rather quickly, and it had just done so to the Democratic Party. In certain ways, Keith's boss, President Carter, had just been fired. Only three years earlier, Carter had provided Keith one of the great opportunities of his life—by elevating him to the Sixth Circuit Court of Appeals.

It happened in 1977, when the president plucked Wade McCree away from the Sixth Circuit to be the nation's solicitor general. McCree had been the first black judge to ever sit on the Sixth Circuit, and his ascension to that spot was what opened a seat on the District Court of Eastern Michigan a decade earlier—the seat filled by Judge Keith. Now the president was seeking to replace McCree on the appeals court, and once again Keith's name quickly surfaced as a replacement.

It was a huge opportunity, one that would turn most judges' heads. There are only a dozen geographic Circuit Courts of Appeals in the nation, second only in authority to the Supreme Court. And because the Supreme Court handles relatively few cases every year, the courts of appeals often have the last word on many important questions of law.

Here was Keith, just fifty-four years old at the time and being considered for a nationally prominent post where he could be an even more influential voice for justice; the Sixth Circuit heard appeals not only from the federal courts in Michigan but also those in Ohio, Kentucky, and Tennessee.

But taking the position would mean leaving the federal district court, where Keith had made so many influential decisions and achieved folk hero status in the Detroit community. Through seniority and the departure of judges before him, Keith had now ascended to chief judge of the Eastern District of Michigan, the first African American to reach that status. He operated out of what they called "the Million Dollar

Courtroom"—a stunning, historic chamber saved from demolition in the 1930s and resplendent in marble pillars and a bench made of East Indian mahogany. Keith enjoyed large, elegant judge's chambers where he regularly hosted a wide swath of movers and shakers from the community.

In short, he was entrenched. Well entrenched. Several friends and colleagues pleaded with him not to go, insisting his vision and courage were more needed at home. Relatives told him the same. Ernie Goodman, a legendary hard-fighting liberal lawyer who'd defended everyone from union workers to the Black Panthers, implored Keith to stay where he could continue making a huge social difference.

"Appeals court was a big move up," Keith recalls, "but with all these people talking to me, I was seriously considering staying put."

And then the phone rang.

•　　•　　•

Myles Lynk, now a professor of law at Arizona State University, was clerking for Judge Keith at the time. Fresh out of Harvard Law School, Lynk was the one who answered the phone that spring afternoon.

"Judge Keith, please," a gruff voice demanded.

"May I ask who's calling?"

"Tell him Thurgood's on the line."

The young clerk almost fell out of his chair. He realized he was talking to Supreme Court Justice Thurgood Marshall, the most famous black lawyer in America and the first African American on the nation's highest court. Lynk was too nervous to even transfer the call for fear of losing the connection. Instead, he bolted from his office, raced into Judge Keith's chambers, and excitedly told the judge that the big man was on the line.

Damon picked up the receiver. "Justice Marshall, how are you?"

That was as far as he got.

"Damon, what's all this silliness I hear about you deliberating over this court of appeals position? Are you out of your mind?"

Keith stammered a response, something about the importance of his role on the district bench.

"Don't be crazy. Damon, this is a great job. And if this job is offered to you, you take it, you hear me?"

And he hung up.

Keith sat at his desk, stunned. But whatever misgivings he had about the position were gone. Thurgood Marshall had been a heroic force in Keith's life since the days when Keith was a wide-eyed law student passing Marshall in the halls of Howard University. *Tell him Thurgood's on the line.* Keith had to chuckle. The decision had been made.

If Marshall said go for it, he was going for it.

Still, political appointments are never apolitical. And while many supported Keith as the best candidate, some wanted President Carter to appoint a Republican to the position, to show his objectivity and gain political capital down the line. Others felt replacing a black judge with another black judge was too overtly deliberate.

Whatever the case, when Judge Keith arrived for his interview with the search committee, he was startled by the first question.

"The chairman of the search committee starts by saying to me, 'Judge Keith, I understand that you've talked to President Carter and you told him you're happy being a trial judge and you don't want to go to the court of appeals.'

"I was flabbergasted. I said, 'Mr. Chairman, I have never spoken to President Carter. And my mother and father, who have both passed, would wonder what kind of son they'd raised if I had the opportunity to go to the second highest court in the land and turned it down.'"

Inside, Keith was fuming. He knew enough about politics to realize someone didn't want him on the court and had planted that bug in the chairman's ear. Keith had suspicions of who it might have been. It made him more determined than ever to do as Justice Marshall had advised: go full bore for the job. He answered the remaining questions intelligently and forthrightly, handling curious inquiries about his well-known cases such as Pontiac schools, *Stamps v. Detroit Edison Co.*, and the celebrated "Keith Case" involving President Nixon and wiretapping. Word later came that he had done so well, the committee was recommending him as its first choice.

Still, several months passed without a decision. "There were definitely people who didn't want me to get that job," Keith recalls. "It reached a point where somebody called Detroit mayor Coleman Young and told him President Carter was vacillating, and Damon's elevation was in jeopardy. Coleman was one of the people on the search committee. He apparently called Carter and told him that I was their number one choice, that the others agreed, and that I should get the position.

"Coleman and Carter were quite close. They'd known each other for a while. Whether that made the difference I don't know, but, subsequently, President Carter appointed me."

On October 21, 1977, nearly ten years to the day that he'd first become a judge, Damon Keith was sworn in to the second-highest court in the land.

And now, the morning after the 1980 presidential election, he pondered where that court was headed.

•　　•　　•

At the time, Keith was growing acutely aware not only of his blooming reputation as an "activist judge"—a phrase that suddenly held negative connotations—but of the perils a famous reputation can bring. Damon Keith was, in judicial circles, a celebrity. Academicians and captains of industry wanted to meet him. Black entertainers were quite familiar with him, many of them having taken part in the NAACP Freedom Fund dinners that he'd helped organize. Sammy Davis Jr. once played piano at his home, entertaining the guests after one such dinner.

But notoriety extracts a price. Jealousy was never far from the surface—despite Keith's propensity to make everyone feel at home, from the newest clerk to every janitor in the federal courthouse. And the spotlight drawn by his controversial decisions fell uncomfortably on certain people around him—including members of his own family.

"My oldest daughter, Cecile, had the hardest time with it. She was determined to do things on her own. When people would ask her, 'Are you Damon Keith's daughter?' she would get upset and answer, 'I am Cecile Keith!' She was going to make her own way.

"When we took her to college at the University of Michigan, we got her set up in the dorms, which were very diverse. But one day I asked her how she liked it, and she said she'd moved out of that dorm and into a mostly black dorm. She identified more with that. She grew a big Afro and was very into black issues.

"One time, while she was a student at Michigan, I was asked to give the commencement speech. It was a great honor. Rachel and our two other girls came. But Cecile didn't come. For whatever reason, she wouldn't come to the commencement, wouldn't come to the luncheon we had with the school president. I was actually very hurt. But Rachel said, 'Leave her be. We have to let her do what she wants to do.' Later we talked about it, and now it's OK. At the time, it bothered me. I felt my oldest daughter should be there. But Cecile was going to do things her way—away from my shadow. And it wasn't easy, I guess, being the daughter of someone who was often in the news."

As the 1980s dawned, and Cecile and the other girls were out of the house, Keith gave increasing thought to the price he'd been paying for his high-profile decisions. He had done what he could to keep a sense of normalcy within his family—driving the kids to school each morning out in the suburbs, bringing them to Rachel's family reunions in the summers and vacations down at Uncle Fred's farm in Virginia. He'd taken them skating, taken them to musicals, taken them to state fairs and to see Santa's Playland on the top floor of Hudson's department store. He'd tried to impress upon them stories about their grandparents and relatives, repeating folksy aphorisms like "Learn to listen, and listen to learn" and "Show me a batter who's never struck out, and I'll show you a batter who's never been to bat."

But, like all parents, he was coming to realize that he could not protect his children from everything, any more than he could mold them into his version of what their lives should be. When one of his daughters asked to go for a semester in Europe because "the other kids were doing it," he had to remind her that they were not rich like those other families. When one of his daughters lamented that going to college with so many white students left her no prospects for a black boyfriend, he could only listen and offer comfort. He was curious why none of his three girls gravitated to law or medicine—despite their parents' enormous accomplishments in those fields—and wondered about the recoil effect that overachieving mothers and fathers can have on their children's choices.

He was approaching sixty years of age. Neither of his parents had lived past seventy. He thought back to his mother, how he used to visit her every day in her old age, bringing her a hamburger and a pineapple milkshake from a small restaurant on Twenty-fourth Street, right up to her death in 1955. The world seemed so much smaller back then. Now that his three children had scattered to three universities in three different states, he was spending weeks at a time in Cincinnati, hearing cases in the Sixth Circuit, living in a hotel, away from Rachel, traveling home only on weekends.

On top of all this, suddenly his notion of how to do a judge's job—to adjudicate with humanity, modernity, and wisdom from life experience—was being challenged in favor of a strict constructionist approach.

He closed his Bible for the day and turned to his workload, acutely aware that, no matter how weighty the issues of the day, the world continued to change rapidly. What recourse did he have but to go along for the ride?

•   •   •

"In the early days on the appeals court, I would call Rachel every morning and tell her about the panel I would be sitting on. It was quite a change, going from a federal district judge to the appeals court, because as federal district judge, you sit alone. You try cases by yourself. In the mid-1970s, I tried [reputed mafia gangster] Tony Giacalone for *eight months.*

"But on the appeals court, it's a much different job. You're in panels of three. A blind draw. Each morning, Rachel would ask, 'Who are you sitting with?' And I'd tell her. And based on who it was, she'd say, 'Oh, you should have a good day.' And I'd chuckle and say, 'Yeah, today should be good.'"

Even now, he laughs at the recollection. But in his first few years on the Sixth Circuit, collegiality was commonplace. Admittedly, the liberal bent of the courts in those years made many decisions more palatable to Keith, but the attitude of his fellow judges was the more important factor.

"I enjoy being with people, even if I don't share all their points of view. On the court of appeals, I developed friendships with a lot of judges—Republican and Democrat. Paul Weick, who was appointed by President Eisenhower, was one of the most—if not the most—conservative judges on the Sixth Circuit. He was the one who wrote the dissent on the Keith case involving the wiretapping. He wrote that he felt the president had the inherent authority. And yet he and I got along and were very close. If I sat on a panel with him and I was concerned about the decision, I'd say, 'Paul, can you look at this again. I need another vote,' and he'd say, 'Damon, let me look at it.' Sometimes he would agree, sometimes he wouldn't. But it was always very professional and collegial."

Keith, in fact, enjoyed working with most of the judges, including George Edwards, John Peck II, and Harry Phillips, who'd been nominated by President Kennedy and was the chief judge when Keith joined the court. Phillips thought so highly of his new young colleague that he permitted him to remain involved on several important cases from Keith's federal district court workload, include the *Baker* case involving the Detroit police.

"We all got along well," Keith recalls. "We'd share meals. We'd chat walking back and forth to the courthouse. It was a pleasant experience."

But the Reagan era ushered in many changes. The nature of the court—and, at times, the very purpose of judges—seemed to shift toward conservative ideology and strict constructionism.

And clashing—not collegiality—became the norm.

Judge R. Guy Cole Jr., who would join the Sixth Circuit in 1996, said a certain type of battling common among today's judges on the Sixth Circuit had its roots during that time:

At some point over the past two decades, the communication process between colleagues broke down.

I think that to some extent judges nominated during that period were nominated not as much for their distinguished backgrounds; in fact, many had little distinction in their backgrounds but for their ideology. As those judges assumed the bench in the 1980s, they brought with them a very conservative view of the law and the rights of the individual.

So, what happened was that the collegiality that existed among the judges on the Sixth Circuit prior to the 1980s disappeared, because the new Republicans appointed came on the bench with a predetermined agenda. And that agenda included rolling back many of the liberal gains that had been realized, starting with *Brown* in 1954 and *Roe v. Wade* and the school desegregation cases of the seventies and eighties.

As the years passed, Judge Keith would find more and more conflict with his fellow judges and witness less and less interest in cooperation—particularly on hot-button topics such as abortion and affirmative action. He would sometimes need to remind himself of that very aphorism he'd repeated to his young daughters as they grew up: "Learn to listen, and listen to learn."

But he would not forget the experiences that molded him and the battles he had fought due to the color of his skin.

As he would soon be reminded, he couldn't if he wanted to.

20.

"Here, Boy, Park This Car"

<hr />

Although his chambers remained in downtown Detroit, six or seven times a year, Judge Keith traveled to Cincinnati to hear cases for the Sixth Circuit Court of Appeals. He would stay for three weeks on average, living out of the Hilton Cincinnati Netherland Plaza Hotel, close to the federal courthouse.

On one of his early trips, Keith and his then law clerk Myles Lynk were working late. They decided to have dinner at the hotel restaurant. By the time they arrived, the place was nearly empty. Nonetheless, the maitre d', a woman, sat them at a table right next to the kitchen.

"It was smelly and noisy," Keith recalls. "And we were the only ones in the place. A few minutes later, four white men came in, in motorcycle outfits. They were loud and boisterous, but she gave them the best seats in the restaurant.

"Both Myles and I noticed. It was very obvious. I looked in Myles's eyes, and I said, 'Remember this. You're a young lawyer. You finished Harvard Law School. You are clerking for a judge on the second-highest court in the United States—but you're still black. You're wearing a Brooks Brothers suit—but you're still black. I want you to remember this lesson—how the color of your skin will play a role in your life. You saw these motorcycle guys get those seats. They didn't get them on their credentials. *You* have the credentials. You've done *everything* the white world told you to do. But you—and me—we are still black."

Myles shook his head and mumbled, "Thank you."

Neither man ever forgot the sting of that moment.

Sadly, nearly fifteen years later, Keith had to relive it.

•   •   •

It was a crisp October afternoon in 1991. The event was the annual Judicial Conference of the United States, a yearly gathering of federal judges from around the country. Among those in attendance were U.S. Supreme Court justices, high-ranking federal officials, politicians, and leading legal scholars from around the world. Fittingly, the three-day conference took place in Williamsburg, Virginia, at The College of William & Mary, where John Marshall and Thomas Jefferson studied at the nation's very first law school.

But this wasn't just any judicial conference. It was the one that coincided with the two-hundredth anniversary of the Constitution and the Bill of Rights. It was the largest single gathering of federal judges in U.S. history, with more than 350 of them in attendance. The conference had created a special committee to commemorate the occasion—called the Commission on the Bicentennial of the United States Constitution. Membership was considered highly prestigious.

And Judge Damon Keith was the national chairman.

He had been appointed to the position by Chief Justice of the Supreme Court William Rehnquist. Keith, the only African American on the committee, spent four years overseeing the distinguished body. Although he already had a chamber full of awards from some of the most respected organizations in America, chairing that committee was one of the most meaningful honors of his career. Knowing his interpretation of the Constitution was frequently at odds with others on the federal bench, Keith viewed this appointment as a gesture of respect. It also meant the chief justice trusted Keith's ability to get things done in a consensus fashion. One of the committee's charges during the conference was to create a visual legacy of the Constitution that would endure in the minds of the public for years to come. But how does one do that in a lasting and meaningful way?

The committee's answer was as simple as it was enduring. The language of our forefathers would be made accessible to all Americans through stunning bronze plaques, reproducing the text of the first ten amendments to the Constitution, otherwise known as the Bill of Rights. Over three hundred of these plaques would be commissioned to grace courthouses and law schools and plazas—from New York to Guam. Plaques were also to be placed in federal buildings of prominence, among them the Thurgood Marshall Federal Judiciary Building in Washington, DC; the FBI Training Academy in Quantico, Virginia; and Detroit's own Theodore Levin United States Courthouse. Reflecting the special place it held in Judge Keith's heart, a Bill of Rights plaque was also given to the Detroit chapter of the NAACP.

It was a fine effort met with wide approval of and gratitude toward the committee. But before that committee was finished, it would bestow one final honor upon its chairman. During the last meeting, Keith's good friend and fellow committee member, Judge Frank X. Altimari, of the Second Circuit Court of Appeals, asked Keith to step outside. Confused by the request, Keith resisted.

"Frank, I'm chairing this meeting. Why should I go outside? What's going on here?"

"Damon, just leave the room, OK?"

Keith relented. He waited in the hallway. When he was summoned back a few minutes later, he entered in time to hear his friend, Judge Altimari, read a motion that had just been approved. One name would appear on these special bicentennial plaques, beneath the words of the Bill of Rights.

The one name would be that of the committee chairman—Judge Damon J. Keith.

He felt tears welling in his eyes. He looked around the room at the smiling faces and nodding heads that indicated approval of this motion—many of them the most respected judicial figures in the nation. They wanted his name to adorn these precious symbols of American history. It was a moment in which he could relish how far he had come.

And then came another moment—one that reminded him of the very words he used to caution his young law clerk in that Cincinnati hotel years ago.

You are still black.

It happened maybe a day later, during a break in the conference at William and Mary. Judge Keith and Judge Altimari were standing in front of the hotel, chatting and getting ready to attend a lunch meeting. As they stood there, a dark car pulled up, and a hotel guest stepped out. The middle-aged man in a business suit assumed the short black man he saw was a porter and he tossed Judge Keith his keys, barking, "Here boy, park this car!"

Here boy, park this car?

Judge Keith was hardly a porter and, at sixty-nine years old, hardly a "boy." But he was, as he had told Myles years earlier in that restaurant, still black.

He maintained his composure. He recalls glaring at the driver and then, without a word, turning and walking away. His colleagues, however, were mortified. Judge Altimari rushed toward the offending party, screaming at him, but he was stopped by the arm of Judge Keith, who said, "Whom the Devil would destroy, he first makes angry."

It could have been a moment for righteous indignation or a moment to holler and demand apologies. But that was never Damon Keith's way—and it wasn't that day either.

What he did instead was far better. He was scheduled to address the full judicial conference later in the afternoon, and he had prepared remarks for the occasion. But when he stepped to the podium, he began by saying, "I'm sorry I'm a little late getting here, but this is what happened to me today . . ."

And then, while his judicial colleagues listened to the ugly details of the incident, some of them with their jaws dropping, Judge Keith turned it into a moment to illuminate the reasons for his ongoing commitment to racial justice.

"Not a day goes by," he thundered, "that in some way, large or small, I am not reminded that I am an African American and that this nation is still plagued by prejudice. Not a day goes by!"

It was a bittersweet experience. At one of the most triumphant moments of his life, Judge Keith found his humanity denied by a complete stranger, due solely to the color of his skin. What happened on the curb of that hotel may have been unique to federal judges on the courts of appeals—but as Keith knew all too well, it was not unique to black Americans.

•   •   •

This partly explains why Judge Keith, even today, is loudly at odds with critics and colleagues who say that race has lost its mantle in the legal consideration of certain issues such as affirmative action. Many people shy away from the debate. Even the great Thurgood Marshall, who was at the forefront of judges acknowledging the ongoing impact of systemic racism in America, was sensitive to bringing up the topic under certain circumstances.

At the November 18, 1978, investiture of Wiley Branton as the dean of Howard University School of Law, Judge Keith introduced Justice Marshall as the keynote speaker. Judge Keith quoted a passage from Marshall's eloquent dissent in the historic affirmative action case of *Regents of the University of California v. Bakke.* The case involved a white student in California who sued after several rejections from medical school, claiming lesser candidates who were black were being given greater consideration. In his dissenting opinion, Marshall spoke of how the black experience was unlike any other group of Americans, as blacks were targeted for discrimination because of their skin color. Given this history, Marshall explained that it was unnecessary in twentieth-century America for them to have to prove that they are victims of individual discrimination, because "the racism of our society has been so pervasive that none, regardless of wealth or position, has managed to escape its impact."

Judge Keith cited this proudly in his introduction of his mentor and hero. But after the program was over and he had received warm applause, Marshall privately expressed his concern to Judge Keith that the quote might have offended Chief Justice Warren Burger—who had taken the opposing view in the case—and other bench colleagues in attendance.

"After I introduced Thurgood, he said, 'Thank you, Reverend Keith,' trying to deflect it a little, you know? Later on he told me, 'Damon, that was a little tough, with the chief justice sitting right there.'"

The incident underscores the precarious position black judges find themselves in when dealing with the thorny issue of race—no matter how high they are on the bench. But Keith has refused to shy from the topic. In personal conversations, public appearances, and official judicial records, his positions are consistent.

Take, for example, a speech he gave at the National Bar Association Judicial Council awards luncheon on July 21, 1981. He asked the audience: "Can we have colorblindness in this society as it is presently structured? Can the colorblind in any way represent the collective experience of minority groups in America?

"After fourteen years in the federal judiciary," he avowed, "I believe the answer is a resounding 'no.'"

To illustrate why, he quoted again from Justice Marshall's *Bakke* dissent, which he considers one of the greatest opinions in the history of American jurisprudence. The African-American experience "is not merely the history of slavery alone but also that a whole people were marked inferior by the law. And that mark has endured. The dream of America as the great melting pot has not been realized for the Negro; because of his skin color he never even made it in to the pot."

To find this fact irrelevant, to ignore it on purpose, even to declare oneself "colorblind" is to adopt a judicial philosophy of someone for whom race is not—and has never been—a social obstacle. Judge Keith, as a black man, could never just forget or ignore race as easily as his white colleagues. He was constantly reminded of it—from the laughs he received when he said he was studying for the bar to being mistaken for a porter and called "boy" as a sixty-nine-year-old circuit judge.

"Black judges must take every opportunity to fashion the law in a manner that reflects the three-hundred-year history of discrimination our people have suffered in this land," Keith implored the crowd at the NBA awards luncheon. "Ladies and gentlemen, those of us on the appellate benches must write opinions that provide guidance."

This would be put to the test in several notable cases Keith heard on the Sixth Circuit bench. Some he would only affect by writing the dissenting opinion to counter the majority decisions—as the courts grew less liberal and the Sixth Circuit saw Keith clashing more and more with his conservative judicial counterparts. But such dissents were critical—blueprints, perhaps, for progress later on. The strong, lone voice of today's dissent can set the template for a majority opinion in the future.

For example, consider Judge Keith's dissent in *Aiken v. City of Memphis*, which came in 1994. The case revolved around several civil rights lawsuits in the early and mid-1970s that were filed against the city of Memphis, its police department, and its fire departments, claiming discrimination and seeking remedies to "ensure that blacks and women were not placed at a disadvantage by the hiring, promotion, and transfer policies of the City, and that any disadvantage to blacks and women which may have resulted from past discrimination is remedied so that equal employment opportunities will be provided to all."

In short, these were discrimination cases that led to an affirmative action plan. But the court-ordered plan was not popular among various groups of white police and fire department employees. As the years passed, they saw their promotion percentages dwindle in favor of minority candidates. In the late 1980s, some of them sued, claiming that the program actually now discriminated against them—especially since the demographics of Memphis had changed and blacks had assumed the majority in many areas. Similar claims had been made before Judge Keith in the Detroit-based *Baker* case.

When the Memphis case found its way to the Sixth Circuit, it was ultimately ruled that although the affirmative action program had an important goal—namely, remedying past discrimination within the police and fire department ranks—Memphis's particular plan was unconstitutional. The majority opinion, written by Judge Ralph Guy, thought the plan's breadth could lead to "reverse racial discrimination" against whites.

In a separate concurring opinion, then chief Judge Merritt largely agreed with the majority's concerns over reverse racial discrimination. A Tennessee native, Merritt was appointed—along with Judge Keith—to the Sixth Circuit Appeals Court by President Jimmy Carter in 1977. But they had little else in common—especially on these issues.

In *Aiken*, Merritt's concurrence raised particular concerns about "reverse discrimination" in Memphis now that it was a "majority" black city. He wrote:

The general population and the voting population of the City of Memphis is now predominantly black, and African-Americans hold the levers of governmental power. The Mayor, the police chief, and the majority of high level administrative officials of the city are black. Accordingly, there is a substantially greater risk that the continued use of racial hiring goals which greatly exceed the qualified labor pool in question will discriminate against whites. That is what the plaintiffs claim. We may not assume in such a situation that the required employment ratio is benign. History and common sense tell us that it is possible for blacks to discriminate against whites as well as vice versa. The court has an obligation to ensure that the decree is not being used to prefer the majority race in the city, whether black or white.

From Merritt's perspective, the circumstances strongly indicated that a racial power struggle between a white minority and a black majority should be assumed:

The Equal Protection Clause does not allow the majority race in a city to use its governmental power to prefer its race over the minority race, except in the most unusual and compelling circumstances. To hold otherwise would be to reinstitute racial discrimination, the constitutional wrong that the parties and the court below were seeking to remedy when the decree was originally entered.

Judge Keith saw it quite differently. He wrote a powerful dissent, some of which was directly aimed at Judge Merritt's conclusions, which Keith found out of line.

You could almost feel angry steam rising off the page.

I write separately . . . to address the unfortunate inaccuracies and misconceptions articulated within Chief Judge Merritt's separate concurrence.

First, I must stress my displeasure and dismay with the use of a judicial opinion to politicize this legal debate. The concurrence cites no law but instead represents one Judge's personal viewpoint. It focuses on topics irrelevant to the case before us in order to present an historical view of affirmative action programs.

In this effort to denigrate affirmative action, a false picture is painted of a majority black city wielding its newly found power to wrongly deprive the white citizens of Shelby County.

There is no support for the assumption that Blacks in positions of power will discriminate against whites as their white predecessors discriminated against Blacks. It saddens me deeply to read this political button-pushing in what should be a legal opinion.

Although the population of Memphis has become "majority" African-American within the past ten years, this fact—largely a result, I assume, of white flight—does not erase the past discrimination within the City and within the fire and police departments. The consent decree was enacted to remedy this past discrimination in an attempt to put African-American officers on a realistic promotional track. Where departments historically refused to hire African-Americans until forced by court order, and where promotional requirements included a seniority factor, no realistic hiring or promotional opportunities for African-Americans exist without this remedy.

The assertion that "the Equal Protection Clause does not allow the majority race in a city to use its governmental power to prefer its race over the minority race" astounds me. This statement ignores that our legislators promulgated the Fourteenth Amendment to eradicate this Country's long history of subjugating African-Americans. Further, the Fourteenth Amendment was not intended to prohibit measures designed to remedy this Country's treatment of African-Americans.

The fact that a minority race—I assume all will concede that African-Americans are still a minority race in America—assumes a numerical "majority" within a city's limits changes nothing. The history of the discrimination against African-Americans and denials of opportunities to African-Americans within the City of Memphis ensures the "minority" white race will never be at a disadvantage there. Certainly the "minority" white population will never experience the legally segregated and underfunded education of their children, the denial of access to housing in "majority" neighborhoods, the indignity of having to use the "minority" only water fountain at a department store or the double indignity of "minority" employees having to use the back door of the Peabody Hotel in order to serve "majority" patrons.

The passion in his words is unmistakable. It would be repeated in other cases throughout his career, even as recently as 2012, in *Cleveland Firefighters for Fair Hiring Practices 93 IAFF v. City of Cleveland*, which involved, yet again, a challenge to the continued application of judicial consent decrees (mandating affirmative action plans) that sought to remedy the effects of past discrimination.

As in the Memphis cases, lawsuits were filed in the 1970s against a city—this time, Cleveland—claiming discrimination against black and Hispanic applicants by the city's fire department. To settle the matter, in 1977, the parties entered a consent decree, setting a target of one-third minority representation.

Thirty-one years later, in 2008, the city filed a motion to extend time to comply with the decree. All of the parties agreed to the extension. But the district court denied it and, on appeal, the Sixth Circuit agreed with the district court—questioning whether the consent decree was still necessary at this point, even though the target hiring limits for the fire department had not been fully realized.

Once again, Judge Keith rebuked the majority for asking the wrong question:

> Sadly, it is clear that the most salient aspect of this case to the majority and the district court is the longevity of the remedy, not whether justice has been fulfilled. The majority seems to favor expedience over effectiveness. . . . The ultimate lesson from our nation's struggle for racial equality is that justice is not always swift and convenient, but it is enduring. When pernicious forms of discrimination have infected the foundation of an institution, the remedy necessarily will take time to fulfill.
>
> It is unclear how, short of achieving the goals set forth in a consent decree, the passage of 31 years makes the racial classification less remedial. It is equally bewildering how remedying past discrimination within an institution becomes less compelling because another year has passed.
>
> Such a narrow approach would provide a safe haven for the most virulent forms of discrimination, whose effects will outlast an arbitrary number of years affixed to a remedy.

To this day, Judge Keith, now in his nineties, remains passionate—even fiery—on the subject of affirmative action and the idea that past wrongs, so piercing to the black American experience, have some sort of built-in expiration date. Those who know him best acknowledge this is a subject on which his heels are firmly planted.

This is perhaps why so many scratch their heads over his relationship with a Supreme Court justice whose conservative viewpoints run directly counter to his own—on affirmative action and other race-related issues.

Justice Clarence Thomas.

Damon Keith—who is proudly known as an "activist" and a "liberal"—frequently calls him "my good friend."

21

STRANGE BEDFELLOWS
DAMON KEITH AND CLARENCE THOMAS

"I have come here today not in anger or to anger, though my mere presence has been sufficient, obviously, to anger some, nor have I come to defend my views, but rather to assert my right to think for myself, to refuse to have my ideas assigned to me, as though I was an intellectual slave."

—Supreme Court Justice Clarence Thomas, 1998

There is a photo that hangs, among so many others, on the high walls of Judge Keith's prestigious Detroit chambers. Although so many of the framed images depict historic and heroic figures of the twentieth century, most of whom are posing appreciatively with the judge, perhaps none perplexes visitors more than the one of Keith alongside Supreme Court Justice Clarence Thomas, who signed the photograph in silver ink with the following inscription:

To Judge Damon Keith—

Thank you for your friendship and your example. I am a better person for having known you.

Clarence

Remember, Judge Keith prides himself on the Houstonian philosophy of jurisprudence established at Howard University School of Law—the belief that lawyers are social engineers and should use the law to advance social and racial justice. For more than forty years as a federal judge, Keith has stayed true to those principles. He will tell anyone without hesitation that he stands second to none in his support of civil rights for racial minorities, women, and the disenfranchised. In fact, Keith has said on many occasions that any person of color in a position of responsibility to do so who fails to do so is, in his view, unworthy of holding that position.

Given such strong feelings, even some of the judge's dearest friends remain dumbfounded (if not alarmed) by his thirty-year friendship with Clarence Thomas. Next to President Barack Obama, Thomas, the Supreme Court justice, is the single most powerful African-American public official in the nation—*and* the most controversial.

In his twenty-two years on the High Court, Thomas's well-established ultra-conservative judicial philosophy has been the polar opposite not only of the man he replaced, the late civil rights icon Thurgood Marshall, but of Judge Keith as well. Born in the small, predominantly black community of Pin Point, Georgia—a town established by former slaves—Thomas has nonetheless been a decisive fifth vote in undermining some of the most critical civil rights cases to reach the court in the past twenty years. These cases included minority voting rights; affirmative action; racial, gender, and age discrimination cases; and cases concerning school desegregation and the death penalty.

In numerous opinions and dissents over the years, Thomas has leveled insults at both civil rights lawyers and institutions that promoted affirmative action as a tool for integration. He has been characterized by some legal scholars as one of the most conservative justices of the twentieth century. Judge A. Leon Higginbotham Jr., nominated to the U.S. District Court for the Eastern District of Pennsylvania by President John F. Kennedy, and a close adviser to President Lyndon Johnson, called Thomas one of the most virulently anti-black justices to ever sit upon the Supreme Court in the twentieth century. "I can only think of one Supreme Court justice during this century who was worse than Justice Clarence Thomas," said Higginbotham—"James McReynolds, a white supremacist who referred to blacks as 'niggers.'"

Thomas also has a reputation for attending and speaking at events hosted by right-wing organizations and think tanks like the Washington, DC-based American Enterprise Institute (AEI). At a 2001 AEI gala, Thomas urged the predominantly white audience to continue pursuing what many African Americans believe to be a decidedly anti-black political agenda. "Too many show timidity today precisely when courage is demanded," Thomas asserted. He told the group that he had suffered the consequences for speaking out on "a number of sacred policies, such as affirmative action, welfare, school busing." Those "who challenge accepted wisdom should expect to be treated badly. Nonetheless, they must stand undaunted."

Given Thomas's associations and seeming contempt for many things Judge Keith represents, it is no wonder that many find the relationship between the two men curious at best and alarming at worst. Nominated to the Supreme Court by President George H. W. Bush in 1991, Thomas represents the shift to conservative and strict constructionist judges that Keith saw coming that morning in his office after Ronald Reagan's election to the White House. But he never imagined it would be personified in the second African-American man to reach the high court—and the one tapped to replace Keith's icon, Thurgood Marshall.

So how did the relationship begin? While Keith himself can no longer recall the exact details of their first meeting, during the early 1980s, Thomas was a young, new, and relatively obscure government bureaucrat, barely in his thirties, when he encountered Keith, who was already sitting on the U.S. Court of Appeals for the Sixth Circuit.

In an exclusive on-the-record interview for this book, Thomas said he first heard about Judge Keith from Lani Guinier, his Yale Law School classmate, who had gone on to clerk for Keith when she graduated from law school. However, Thomas didn't meet Keith personally until 1983, while working for the Reagan administration as chairman of the Equal Employment Opportunity Commission (EEOC).

"We were settling this big case for General Motors," Thomas says. "Well, we came up with some rather creative remedies; rather than just passing out money to people who may or may not have been discriminated against, we decided to set up scholarships and endowments to help minorities and women.

"Everything I did back then created some controversy, which made no sense. Abe Venable, who is from Detroit, also knew Judge Keith very well; he thought that he could be helpful to us and ward off some of the criticism for this program, which is still going gangbusters, by the way."

Thomas and Venable, a former high-ranking African-American executive for General Motors, met for lunch in Keith's chambers. Judge Keith told them, "If there's anything I can do to help you, you let me know." Thomas says the conversation meant a lot to him during a very tough time in his career. The EEOC and the Reagan administration were, in his words, "hated" by the media. "It was said that anything we did that was good wasn't newsworthy."

Even back then, Judge Keith, as an established member of the civil rights community, had reason to distance himself from Thomas. Instead, Thomas remembers Keith's courage in recognizing that the project itself "was good and made sense." Despite the consequences, Judge Keith saw the value of what Thomas was trying to do at the EEOC and kept an open mind.

As Keith now recalls it, "I used the same yardstick with Clarence that I use with everyone else. How can I help you? How can we make things better and eliminate inequality? Clarence remembers this better than I do, but apparently he feels that I was of some assistance. I only remember him as being warm and very cordial and very civil. There were no ideological clashes between us. And as he says, the program was a good one."

Justice Thomas recalls Keith as "more of what I thought leaders would be, and in particular what I thought black leaders would be, when I came to Washington."

Keith was one of the few black leaders, Thomas says, who was willing to take his phone calls and counsel him when he first came to Washington. Later, whenever anything was happening, "he would give you a call at home. When I was nominated to the DC Circuit, he was on the phone trying to be supportive and encouraging, and he tried to enlighten you about things. Similarly when I was nominated to the Supreme Court."

In the years that followed, their relationship continued mostly from afar. Thomas maintained his loyal appreciation of Keith as "the uncle who taught you right from wrong, who was there for you every single day.

"He's just a man of character and just the kind of leader—the quiet, the firm, resolute leader—that you would have thought would have proliferated in Washington," Thomas says. "It seems as though whenever I needed him, he was around."

To the extent that he was able, Thomas reciprocated. Judge Keith "has never asked me for so much as a nickel," Thomas quickly says, "but he will call you and ask you to help someone who needs it."

Such requests by Keith led Justice Thomas to use his influence to support the careers of black judges, ironically, even when their politics and judicial stances differed from his own. "Clarence was always responsive to me," Keith says, noting that Thomas helped to get black federal judicial nominees through the politically charged and byzantine world of the judicial confirmation process, including Judge Ann Claire Williams to the U.S. Court of Appeals for the Seventh Circuit, Judge Victoria Roberts to the U.S. District Court for the Eastern District of Michigan, and Judge Eric Clay to the U.S. Court of Appeals for the Sixth Circuit. Each of them is considered a progressive, mainstream judge, with Roberts perhaps the most liberal of all.

President Clinton nominated Roberts to the federal district court in 1997, but her nomination was held up in Congress. Judge Keith called Justice Thomas, who was able to ensure that her confirmation hearing would be delayed no longer. Judge Roberts, whose judicial philosophy is every bit the polar opposite of Justice Thomas's, readily acknowledges the critical role Thomas played in helping to facilitate the process.

Justice Thomas, for his part, sees the perceived contradiction in his support of certain black judicial nominees. He is candid in sharing that he does not agree with the liberal approach to interpreting statutes and applying law. "I don't do that," says Thomas. "But that doesn't mean it isn't *a* way to do the job."

Nonetheless, he says he concurs with Judge Keith's philosophy that, "It doesn't matter that you don't agree with me. What does matter is that you are capable, that you are a person of character, that you are conscientious, and that you will represent us as judges and as people well."

Justice Thomas also knows—firsthand—how politics can hold up many judicial appointments: "My view is that it's unacceptable. When you look around at the devastation, you see that anybody who makes it that far in this process . . . has worked hard.

"You talk to people who are getting in the middle of battles, and you want them to know that this is not going to be a delicate battle; here are some things you might want to think about."

He admits his support stems in part from his own nasty confirmation process:

> There were very few people who stood up and did that early on for me. So you wound up having to fight through all the underbrush, and I think that's unnecessary.
>
> You don't do it because you want to be recognized or you want to be thanked for it, but rather because it's right. And what you would hope is that the people for whom you do it would do it for someone else at a later time—in a sense, repeating what Judge Keith did for me.

· · ·

After fifteen years of their unusual friendship, Damon Keith and Clarence Thomas did several tangible things for each other in 1998.

And faced a hailstorm of controversy on account of it.

That year, Justice Thomas sat on the three-judge panel that awarded the Edward J. Devitt Distinguished Service to Justice Award, the highest honor given to a federal judge by his peers. The panel chose Judge Keith.

As Thomas says now of Keith, "He's a model of how you should conduct yourself, how you want to approach other people, and how you want to make this process accessible." Thomas was to present the award to Keith at Wayne State University in Detroit. However, even his involvement with giving out an award stirred controversy. Judge Higginbotham, Keith's longtime friend, Thomas's longtime critic, and himself then judge on the Third Circuit, was adamant in his opposition to Justice Thomas's involvement in the ceremony.

Higginbotham wrote a letter to the *Detroit Free Press*, stating that Justice Thomas should not be involved in Judge Keith's Devitt Award ceremony:

Because of the steady excellence of his judicial insights and impact for decades, Judge Damon Keith clearly deserves the coveted Devitt Award. However, Supreme Court Justice Clarence Thomas is not entitled to any accolade merely because he participated in a celebratory event honoring the esteemed Keith. After seven years on the Supreme Court, the tragedy is that on almost every civil rights issue involving poor people, minorities, voting rights, the criminal justice system and affirmative action, Thomas has taken positions that are the diametric opposite to the views that Keith . . . has expressed in a series of legendary judicial opinions.

Judge Higginbotham's letter, however impassioned, annoyed and embarrassed Judge Keith. More ominously, however, the fact that Higginbotham sent it to the largest newspaper in Judge Keith's hometown indicated that some prominent members of the black legal community were prepared to get confrontational with Keith over his cozy relationship with Thomas. They were equally unimpressed by Thomas's warm introductory words for their friend in connection with the Devitt Award:

> Four things belong to a judge: to hear courteously; to answer wisely; to consider soberly; and to decide impartially. I think we have our man.
>
> Your opinions have enriched the jurisprudence of our country and they have enriched our country itself. Your work and your tenure as a federal judge are enough to secure your place in history and in the hearts of all those who know your work, who know you, and who have come in contact with you.

Justice Thomas went on to further praise Judge Keith's legacy on the bench and spoke in a more personal tone—one that sheds some light on why Thomas holds the friendship so dear.

Fifteen years ago, a mutual friend of ours, Abe Venable, introduced us. You did not know me and indeed, I had begun my long tenure as quite an unpopular person. . . . You were gracious enough to meet with us, to take us to lunch, to invite us to your chambers, to offer advice, to offer wisdom, to offer assistance, to offer to receive phone calls at any time—and mean it. Judge Keith, during that time, and even now, I know that you have the capacity, as so many of us should, to transcend petty squabbles, to transcend differences, and to be larger than those who would fight and fuss and fume over things that don't really matter. You are a man, Judge Keith, recognized by the committee, through all the letters and all the recommendations, who's not only a great judge but someone who does the right things, who's a decent man, who's a good man.

Keith was touched by Thomas's remarks—no matter what the critics said. It was not because of their differences that he felt compelled to stand by Thomas when controversial winds blew; it was because of their similarities—and one similarity in particular. Each man believed strongly in the other guy having the right to his opinion—no matter how different it might be.

"I have never tried to push my views on Clarence over anything," Keith says. "We don't talk about affirmative action or a lot of civil rights issues. I admit his actions on the court are sometimes confounding to me and not aligned with my particular thoughts. Nonetheless, I respect his right to speak, and he respects mine. That may be the backbone of our friendship."

Thomas agrees. "His basic attitude was for me to just be honest—you've got the abilities, and you are entitled to have your opinions. He was very firm: 'Nobody is going to tell me what to think, so I'm not going to tell you what to think.' I thought that was right—that you are entitled to your opinion.

"I don't know how we got into this ersatz tribalism, where everybody has to think the same thing. It wasn't that way when I was a kid," Thomas says. He recalls watching *Barbershop*, the 2002 film about a black-owned barbershop on Chicago's predominantly black South Side. It reminds him of a time, he says, in which members of the black community met in black spaces like men's barbershops and hotly debated widely divergent viewpoints on the challenges facing them. Judge Keith reminds him of that time, too, when "people in black society had a lot of different opinions"—yet independence remained a core value.

In fact, Keith himself fondly recalls a night in 1997, just before Judge Eric Clay's investiture to the Sixth Circuit U.S. Court of Appeals, when Justice Thomas shared some barbershop-like laughs and cigars and fond memories with five other Yale Law School alums at the prestigious Renaissance Club in Detroit. As the men put aside their political and intellectual differences for the evening, they batted around stories from their law school days and football games. Keith watched proudly. "Six black Yale educated lawyers," he said to himself, "four of them federal judges, including a justice of the United States Supreme Court. As a young lawyer, I would have been happy to see a black judge on Detroit Recorder's Court, much less a federal court."

The night went on for hours, as Judge Keith, to this day, recalls it fondly.

Sadly, there was no such collegiality a year later, not long after the Dewitt Award, when Judge Keith agreed to introduce Thomas in Memphis before the annual convention of the National Bar Association (NBA), the national organization of black lawyers and judges.

Justice Thomas had been invited to speak by the chair of the judicial council. But once again, Judge Leon Higginbotham led a faction of dissenters. In a May 27, 1998, letter, Higginbotham expressed his concerns to Judge Bernette Johnson, the NBA judicial council's chair.

"By the very nature of your invitation, you give Thomas an imprimatur that he has never had from any responsible organization within the African-American community or any non-conservative groups of whites in America."

The plea from Higginbotham partially worked. Morris L. Overstreet, the recording secretary for the NBA at the time, sent Justice Thomas a letter stating that "the Executive Committee of the Judicial Council, National Bar Association, voted that the Chair of the Council withdraw by May 30, 1998, an invitation to you as keynote speaker for the Judicial Council luncheon. The Chair has said she will not abide by the vote of the Executive Committee. As Recording Secretary, I am notifying you of the action taken by the Executive Committee."

Even if Thomas's invitation wasn't formally rescinded, the intention was clear. He was not welcome by certain members of the organization.

Justice Thomas, however, had his supporters. Judge Keith, among others, believed that his invitation should stand. He felt the NBA was aware of Thomas's reputation when it issued the invitation; to remove him from the program now would be contrary to the principles of the First Amendment.

Judge Keith was unrelenting in his defense—and he drew rare rebukes from colleagues and friends. Judge Nathaniel Jones, Keith's colleague on the Sixth Circuit, expressed his concerns. Jones's criticism was especially pointed given the close ideological and personal relationship the two men shared. But Jones felt Thomas warranted the criticism. "All the sacrifices that were made to move civil rights," he says, ". . . then to have somebody come along and denigrate folks who laid the groundwork for his success. . . . I just didn't feel that qualified Thomas to trade on the reputation of Judge Keith. And I felt I had to share that with Judge Keith."

The controversy stressed all parties involved, and Justice Thomas finally threw in the towel. In a handwritten note to Judge Keith on June 15, 1998, he said, "This is rather silly. I altered family plans to do this. I have decided to spend my time more productively than getting embroiled in this theatre of the absurd."

Keith could have quietly nodded, accepted the sad reality, and taken the easier, less controversial route.

Instead, he fought back.

"Clarence," Keith said, "do you believe in the First Amendment?"

"Yes, I do."

"And so do I!" Keith thundered. "They invited you to this event, and we are going to attend even if it's only me and you in there!"

That moment crystallized the unique relationship between the oddly disparate men. Principle topped preference. They were united if—by nothing else—their love of unalienable rights and democratic ideals. Thomas would later characterize Keith as someone "who will stand up and tell you when you're wrong, quietly, but who will loudly stand up and tell the world that what they're doing to you is worse."

Keith successfully convinced Thomas to attend. As Tony Snow, the late conservative columnist for the *Detroit News*, wrote: "Despite the flap, the invitation stands and the justice will say his piece. Furthermore, he will enjoy at least a polite reception, thanks to a man who disagrees with him on virtually every contentious point of civil rights law, Damon Keith—a senior judge from Detroit on the Sixth U.S. Circuit Court of Appeals. Judge Keith doesn't demand that his pals pass ideological litmus tests. He has counted Thomas a friend for 15 years."

All that remained was the actual event.

• • •

On a hot July afternoon in Memphis, Judge Keith stepped to the podium and introduced his controversial friend to a packed room of an estimated forty-six hundred people. He said, in part:

On this 30th commemorative anniversary of Dr. Martin Luther King's death, the National Bar Association has for the first time the opportunity to hear first-hand the view of Justice Clarence Thomas from Justice Clarence Thomas himself. This occasion truly has the potential to be the first step in opening the lines of communication between those of differing points of view. Indeed, we finally have the opportunity, as Voltaire once stated, "To think for ourselves and let others enjoy the privilege to do so too." . . . It is my belief that the notion of coming together in the spirit of understanding suggests that we are willing to recognize that the right to express our own views is just as important as someone else's right to express theirs. It means that even if I do not agree with you, you have the right to say what you believe, and though I disapprove, we can disagree without being disagreeable. . . . Many do not know that Justice Thomas is greatly concerned about and involved in the efforts to increase the number of African-American judges in the federal judiciary. . . . In fact, throughout Justice Thomas' tenure on the bench, he has advised and encouraged numerous African-American appointees to the bench without regard to their party affiliation or judicial philosophy. . . . Whether you agree or disagree with Justice Thomas' views on the great legal issues of our time, we should all be appreciative of his willingness to join us here for the interchange and expression of philosophies. . . . Having been friends with Justice Thomas for many years, I know that he is a person of great depth, concern and sensitivity. He is also a person of great warmth and good humor, and a fierce competitor.

Judge Keith's introduction was warmly received and provided a moment of much-needed relief for the tense audience.

Unfortunately, Thomas, in the minds of some in attendance, did not pick up the ball and run with it. He delivered the sort of remarks that his critics predicted: a speech characterized by the authors Kevin

Merida and Michael A. Fletcher in their 2007 biography of Thomas as "remarks that veered from self-pitying to combative."

Justice Thomas could have used the controversy to present a thoughtful analysis of his judicial philosophy and how he believed it advanced civil rights. Instead, critics believed he used the opportunity to ridicule his doubters in a self-serving defense of his right to his own ideas.

The text of Thomas's speech reads, in part:

I've found during my almost 20 years in Washington that the tendency to personalize differences has grown to be an accepted way of doing business. One need not do the hard work of dissecting an argument. One need only attack and thus discredit the person making the argument. Though the matter being debated is not effectively resolved, the debate is reduced to unilateral pronouncements and glib but quotable clichés.

I, for one, have been singled out for particularly bilious and venomous assaults. These criticisms, as near as I can tell, and I admit that it is rare that I take notice of this calamity—have little to do with any particular opinion, though each opinion does provide one more occasion to criticize. Rather, the principle problem seems to be a deeper antecedent offense. I have no right to think the way I do because I'm black.

Though the ideas and opinions themselves are not necessarily illegitimate, they're held by non-black individuals, they and the person enunciating them are illegitimate if that person happens to be black, thus, there's a subset of criticism that must of necessity be reserved for me—even if every non-black member of the court agrees with the idea or the opinion. You see, they are exempt from this kind of criticism precisely because they are not black.

It pains me deeply—more deeply than any of you can imagine—to be perceived by so many members of my race as doing them harm, all the sacrifice, all the long hours of preparation were to help, not

194

to hurt. But what hurts more, much more, is the amount of time and attention spent on manufactured controversies and media sideshows when so many problems cry out for constructive attention.

I have come here today not in anger or to anger, though my mere presence has been sufficient, obviously, to anger some, nor have I come to defend my views, but rather to assert my right to think for myself, to refuse to have my ideas assigned to me, as though I was an intellectual slave.

Looking back on the event, Keith says he was not surprised at the speech: "Knowing Clarence as I did, I knew that he wasn't going to accommodate that audience and not state his point of view. I tried to ease the way for that in my introduction."

Just the same, the speech was hotly debated. Thomas did receive a standing ovation by most of the people in the audience—a good number of whom were non-NBA members who had purchased tickets once the NBA governing board opened the event to the general public, thus filling the room with many white and well-to-do non-lawyers.

Thomas, however, seemed extremely pleased with its reception. And most of the media gave it a positive recounting. "The appearance was a controversy," Thomas says, "but the reception was fabulous. It was wonderful, the people were wonderful, they were like Judge Keith is."

Judge Keith concedes that the night was a mixed bag. However, he remains certain it was worth the effort: "I tried to bring everyone together and at least get both sides talking to one another. That's the best I could do."

•   •   •

When you look at that photo of Keith and Thomas together, hanging on a wall, you realize how short a distance it is between fates. Asked whether Judge Keith could have been appointed to the Supreme Court under a different set of presidents, Justice Thomas says without reservation, "Absolutely, yes. I don't see how you couldn't give credit to all that he has accomplished. He has had a tremendous impact. . . . It's really a matter of timing and providence that any of us are up here. He would have been one of those that *should have* been up here. He's certainly prepared to be here. His background, preparation, and abilities certainly bespeak all the qualifications to do this job—easily."

It is the kind of road not taken—or the road not offered—that makes one wonder how the world might be different if not for this or that. And while Keith holds no deferred dreams of a Supreme Court position, there are times when he wishes he could make a difference at that level—or at least see his longtime, sometimes confounding friend do so. The June 2013 Supreme Court decision regarding the 1965 Voting Rights Act is a glaring example. With a 5–4 vote, the justices did away with a key part of the Voting Act that many feel was its heart and soul—the requirement that certain states with sad histories of voter discrimination seek federal approval before changing their election laws. Judge Keith, like his fellow civil rights champions, was mortified to see it struck down, under the majority opinion that the nation's current situation no longer warrants such precautions.

"They gutted that thing," Keith laments. "This is fundamental. We are talking about ensuring that everyone gets to vote fairly. People died for this. Especially in the South. It was very upsetting."

Keith privately wondered how Thomas, raised in a Georgia town that was founded by freed slaves, could go along with the 5–4 majority, and, numerically anyhow, be a vote that swung the decision. He cannot pretend to support the position or even necessarily to comprehend it.

But standing by your principles is a multi-pronged posture, and what sticks in Keith's craw over a particular Thomas vote is part of what holds their curious friendship together. They may not agree on each other's positions, but they fight to defend their right to hold them.

The famous Greek historian and essayist Plutarch once wrote, "I don't need a friend who changes when I change and who nods when I nod; my shadow does that much better."

Somewhere inside that is the hard kernel of their three-decade relationship, one symbolized on the walls of Keith's office. Life goes deeper than a smiling photograph. And the ways in which Clarence Thomas is "a better man for having known" Damon Keith may yet be revealed.

22

Swimming Upstream
Ideological and Political Shifts
in the Courts

Perhaps one reason Judge Keith makes elbow room for his friendship with Clarence Thomas is his affection for the man who held the Supreme Court seat before him. Justice Thurgood Marshall (always "Thurgood" to Keith) was such a towering influence during Damon's early years that even decades later, in the prime of his career, the judge was still a bit intimidated.

On the occasion of Marshall's eightieth birthday, Keith joined a planning group with Wiley Branton, the civil rights activist and former dean of Howard University School of Law, Vernon Jordan, who would become a key advisor to President Clinton, and Bill Coleman, a noted Virginia attorney. Each received a list of invitees from the famed justice himself.

"Pretty soon my phone rings, and it's Vernon Jordan," Keith recalls. "He says, 'Damon, I got this list of people Thurgood's invited, but I think he's left off some people.' I said, 'I saw it, and I think he left off *a lot* of people. Why don't you call and tell him?' Vernon says, 'Hell no, I'm not calling him! *You* call him.' I said, *'I'm* not calling him. Let's ask Wiley.' We call Wiley, and he says, 'Are you kidding? *I'm* not calling him. Try Bill Coleman. Thurgood's at his house right now.'

"So we all got on the phone, and finally we got Thurgood on the line. And one of us says, 'So, Thurgood, we have this list of invitees. Do you think maybe you overlooked anyone?'

"And he said, 'Hell, no! It's my party. I'll invite who I want!'

"And he hung up on us."

On the list and in attendance at Marshall's eightieth birthday were Justices William J. Brennan and John Paul Stevens.

Keith laughs at the memory, recalling the time years earlier when Marshall hung up after barking at Keith to take the court of appeals position because it was a "good job." This was all part of Thurgood's larger-than-life cantankerous persona that permeated birthday parties and judicial decisions. When he retired from the Supreme Court in 1991 (opening the spot that eventually went to Clarence Thomas) Judge Keith called to congratulate him on his monumental achievements.

"Yeah, well, you're a good judge, too, Damon," his mentor grumbled.

Two years later, Marshall died of heart failure.

He was eighty-four.

"There was never anybody like Thurgood," says Keith, who felt the death on several levels. Not only did it remind him of the shift taking place in America's judicial policies (Thomas was already making his very distinctive "non-Thurgood" mark on the Supreme Court), but it also marked the end of an era for Keith and highlighted the ominous passing of time. Marshall had been Keith's teacher at law school, a firebrand to whom the breathless young student looked up.

Now Thurgood was dead, and Keith was in his seventies. He and Rachel had not only welcomed their first son-in-law (Daryle Brown, who asked for Cecile's hand by sitting down to discuss it with her parents, a move that endeared him to both of them), but three years later, thanks to Daryle and Cecile, they also witnessed the birth of their first grandchild, Nia, followed five years later by a second granddaughter, Camara.

These were life passages. For many, they signal a welcome slowing down, a time to reflect, travel, relax, and retire. But there was little appetite for that in the Keith household. Rachel continued with a full workload in her medical practice, often laboring six days a week, and she was endlessly active in civil rights and civic causes, sitting on the boards of more than a dozen nonprofit organizations. She still insisted her daughters come by on Sunday evenings for dinner and a discussion of whatever sermon she heard that morning at church. And she never suggested to Damon that he retire from the bench.

"She was proud of the difference she thought I could make," he says.

This was a good thing, as that was getting harder and harder to do.

•　　•　　•

In leaving the federal district court for the court of appeals, Keith had gone from being a solitary judge trying to ensure justice for the disenfranchised to forming alliances on panels and writing dissenting opinions in an increasingly hostile Sixth Circuit. He felt, on some levels, like Sisyphus with the rock, rolling it up the hill only to see it come rolling down in majority opinions that often appeared more politically than judicially motivated.

Politics has always had a role in judicial appointments—witness the controversy between Keith and Otis Smith. But the nature of these politics had shifted dramatically over the past three decades. During his presidential campaign in 1980, Ronald Reagan railed against "liberal activist judges." If elected, he vowed one of his highest priorities would be to reshape the courts by appointing only strict constructionists who allegedly would interpret the law exactly as written, not make it.

"I don't think Reagan knew me from anybody else," Keith says now. "But my decisions were on the books. I suspect he thought I was an activist judge."

"I was cognizant of the change. I felt the shift taking place. The balance of the court was switching, and, eventually, I was doing the best I could by writing dissents."

Twenty-eight judges have been appointed to the Sixth Circuit Court of Appeals since 1980. Of those twenty-eight, seven were appointed by a Democrat and twenty-one by a Republican. (Judge Helene White, a Democrat, was nominated by Democratic president Bill Clinton, although she was eventually appointed by Republican president George W. Bush.) Only three black judges have been appointed since 1981: Judge Eric L. Clay and Judge R. Guy Cole Jr., both appointed by President Clinton, and Judge Bernice B. Donald, appointed by President Barack Obama.

Judge Cole is a former commercial litigator who also worked as a Department of Justice lawyer during the Carter administration. Before Reagan, he had viewed the Sixth Circuit as a philosophically moderate court. "You had judges appointed by Democratic and Republican presidents and a wide spectrum of ideological and philosophical viewpoints," he says. "But it became apparent to me that the judges appointed by Reagan, George H. W. Bush, and George W. Bush were far more conservative. . . . They seem to be judges that consistently voted in a conservative way in cases involving any kind of societal significance."

Some believed that President Reagan and both Bushes only nominated judges who passed a litmus test on hot-button issues like abortion, capital punishment, affirmative action, and the rights of criminal defendants.

As the Sixth Circuit wrestled with some of the most vexing social issues of the day, the ideological fissure became increasingly evident during the 1990s, when many proceedings were brought "en banc," or before the entire bench. En banc reviews are supposed to be rare, conducted usually in difficult and important cases where a majority of the judges of the circuit, who are in regular active service, feel a review of a panel's decision is warranted. Court rules provide that en banc is generally not favored unless it is "necessary to secure or maintain uniformity of the court's decisions; or . . . the proceeding involves a question of exceptional importance."

However, Judge Keith began to see the en banc option used whenever a blind draw might land two liberal judges on a three-judge panel.

"The dissenting judge in a three-judge panel could ask for en banc," he explains. "Then it would circulate amongst the other judges as to whether they thought it should happen. There would be a vote. Is this worthy of an en banc or not? If the majority said yes, then the decision of the three-judge panel was put aside and, using the en banc, the larger group voted on it."

Some argue that the en banc option might neutralize a more liberal consensus in a three-judge blind draw. The notion also exists that it could be used to squash the objection of the dissenting liberal voice if a more conservative consensus was reached.

The Sixth Circuit became so contentious that Senior Sixth Circuit Judge Harry W. Wellford and two former law clerks published an article in the *University of Memphis Law Review* to illustrate how bitterly politicized the tensions had become. One of the examples they cited involved a dispute over the 1999 case of *Memphis Planned Parenthood, Inc. v. Sundquist.*

The case involved a Tennessee law requiring minors to obtain parental consent before undergoing an abortion. The trial judge, John T. Nixon, issued an injunction preventing the state from enforcing the law—thus giving the choice to the young women. But the state appealed to the Sixth Circuit, with the case assigned to judges David A. Nelson, Alan E. Norris, and Judge Keith. Judge Norris wrote the majority opinion, which reversed the district court's injunction and allowed the state to enforce the act—inhibiting womens' right to choose.

Judge Keith dissented. Following the decision, Planned Parenthood of Memphis filed a petition for an en banc hearing. The active members of the court, however, declined in an evenly divided seven-to-seven vote. Judge Keith was so outraged he wrote a vigorous dissent.

Keith felt the court owed it to the litigants to uphold what the Supreme Court of the United States had declared—"that *every* female in this country has a fundamental right to seek an abortion guaranteed to her by the United States Constitution—and in the case of a minor, to seek the abortion without parental consent—absent undue burdens by the state."

At the outset of his dissent, Keith explained how his more conservative colleagues did not want an en banc hearing because they feared a ruling by the full court would not go their way:

> I believe that the seven-seven split among the judges vested with authority to vote on this petition is extremely significant for two reasons. First, the make-up of the sharp division among the court to rehear this case is most telling in that it reaffirms the point made throughout my original dissent—that the majority opinion's outcome-driven result is not based upon the facts or the law, but upon a proclivity towards a displeasure with the state of the law as it stands on the controversial topic of a woman's right to choose to have an abortion, and a minor girl's right to do the same without parental consent.
>
> This is the state of the law, and we as jurists have taken a solemn oath to uphold the law, not to pervert it to serve personal values or social policy preferences. However, in ignoring the monumental obstacles imposed by the State of Tennessee on minor girls seeking to obtain an abortion without parental consent—who frequently are victims of rape, incest, or abuse—the majority does violence to the state of the law and it does so for no other apparent purpose than to promote its stance on this controversial topic.

Words cannot adequately express my deep-rooted convictions regarding the seemingly careless fashion in which the majority recklessly disregards the constitutional rights afforded to minor girls, a group of people who are the least able to defend their rights.

Judge Keith's dissent was highly unusual in that it contained harsh criticism of the actions of his colleagues. And he specifically named the judges who did and did not vote to rehear the case en banc, claiming the votes cast were based on political leanings.

This was the first time such a point of view had been expressed in the Sixth Circuit.

It did not go over well.

Keith had essentially opened up the en banc playbook to the general public. "Certainly I knew they would object. But I was not going to let them hide under the covers from their decision. I thought the public was entitled to know. They didn't like it. That was OK with me."

Judge Danny Julian Boggs, a conservative voting against rehearing, was deeply offended by Judge Keith's dissent and wrote a separate statement himself. He suggested that Judge Keith violated court protocol by naming names. Boggs argued that each judge has the privilege, if he so chooses, to make known his own position by filing a separate statement, but he noted that "this happens rarely."

Judge Alice M. Batchelder, a conservative judge from Ohio appointed to the Sixth Circuit in 1991 by President George H. W. Bush, agreed with Boggs. She emphasized that disagreements between court members should never take the form of a personal attack. She asserted that collegiality and cooperation, which are essential to the proper functioning of the court, are not furthered by "publicly impugning the integrity of . . . colleagues."

Judge Keith responded that he had "not violated any rule or internal policy by making the final vote tally known." He added, "I am at a loss as to understand why any jurist would take exception to his vote being made publicly known on the controversial topic of abortion, although it appears that Judge Boggs's 'statement' was apparently spurred by his concern that his position on the abortion issue not be made known to the public."

To this day, Keith defends his decision. "What I have tried to do in life, when I believe something strongly, is to be fair to people. I thought these other judges wanted to hide under their decision, and that is absolutely incorrect for the public, which has the right to know who voted what. Maybe that's not true of every decision. But something as critical as abortion I think people should know."

It was a troubling chapter in an increasingly contentious environment. Perhaps this is why, as recently as May 2011, the Sixth Circuit was referred to in the *New York Times* as "surely the most dysfunctional federal appeals court in the nation."

Not exactly what Judge Keith envisioned when his hero, Thurgood Marshall, told him to take the job.

23

"DEMOCRACIES DIE
BEHIND CLOSED DOORS"

"You want an American hero? A real hero? I nominate Judge Damon
J. Keith of the U.S. Sixth Circuit Court of Appeals."

—Bob Herbert, *New York Times* columnist

It was the summer after the world had changed—the summer following
the 9/11 attacks on the World Trade Center and the Pentagon, events
that not only shook the nerves of the American people but also caused
ripple effects on lawmaking and justice. The Detroit weather was hot,
often humid, but there was nothing languid about the atmosphere inside
Judge Keith's chambers. He and his law clerks were working feverishly
on something they knew could have far-reaching implications.

And Judge Keith, now eighty years old, was searching for the perfect
way to say it.

It was a new millennium. There was a new American president.
Most people Keith's age were long ago retired. Yet here he was, in

his fifth decade on the bench, energized as if he had just unpacked a suitcase in his chambers. At issue was nothing less than the rights of the government versus the rights of the people.

Something Keith had experience with already.

Like nearly every American, the judge had been stunned and shaken by the terrorist attacks of September 11, 2001. He had been on the treadmill at Fitness Works, his health club, when he saw the first plane pummel into the World Trade Center. The rest of the day was a blur.

"I couldn't believe anything like that was happening in America. I rushed to the office. I was one of the few judges to have a TV in my office, and several of the other judges came down to watch with us. All courtroom business was held in abeyance. Any meetings, motions—it was all suspended. We were glued to that TV—until the federal marshals told us we had better clear the building. Then we all went home."

Nothing was the same in the weeks and months that followed. In the wake of the attacks, President George W. Bush and the U.S. government initiated widespread anti-terrorism investigations as part of the so-called war on terror. This included the United States Senate adopting the far-reaching Patriot Act by a vote of 98-1 after only one day of debate.

The corresponding wave of activity triggered a heavy scrutinizing of undocumented immigrants residing in the United States, particularly those of Arab or Muslim descent. At the time, the Department of Justice (DOJ), run by Attorney General John Ashcroft, also housed Immigration and Naturalization Services (INS), the agency administering all immigration proceedings and taking a lead role in its investigations.

On October 25, 2001, Ashcroft announced that the anti-terrorism investigations had led to the arrest or detention of nearly a thousand people, held on immigration charges, federal crimes, or material witness warrants. Hundreds had been deported, many following hearings held in secret. These hearings, which the government called "special interest cases," were closed to both the press and the public if the attorney general determined that the detainee "might have connections with, or possess information pertaining to, terrorist activities."

Under Ashcroft's authority, Chief Immigration Judge Michael Creppy issued a memorandum (later dubbed the Creppy Directive) to all immigration judges and court administrators that these cases be assigned to judges who held "at least a secret clearance" and that the hearings be held separately from all other cases on the docket.

The Creppy Directive also restricted the release of information regarding these special-interest cases and mandated that the courtroom be closed:

"No visitors, no family, and no press."

•   •   •

Like many immigrants of Arab or Muslim descent, Rabih Haddad was interrogated by the U.S. government as part of its anti-terrorism investigation. Haddad and his family had lived off and on in Ann Arbor, Michigan, since 1988. They had most recently returned to the United States on six-month tourist visas from Lebanon in 1998. Haddad became very active in the large Arab and Muslim-American communities in southeast Michigan, fundraising for various charities and even co-founding a humanitarian relief organization called Global Relief Foundation. This all came to an abrupt end when, on December 14, 2001, INS took Haddad into custody for overstaying his 1998 tourist visa and initiated deportation proceedings.

As Haddad sat in jail, the public grew disturbed. Metro Detroit has the largest Arab population outside the Middle East, and with Haddad a fairly prominent member of the community, his arrest drew outcries. A large circle of friends, local media, and even Congressman John Conyers Jr., sought to attend his deportation hearings. However, Haddad's case was designated "special interest," due to suspicions that his Global Relief Foundation was funding terrorist organizations. Without notice to Haddad or his attorney, Immigration Judge Elizabeth Hacker closed Haddad's hearings to the public.

Family, media—even a sitting U.S. congressman—were left at the door.

As a result, several newspapers (including the *Detroit Free Press*) and Congressman Conyers—along with Haddad himself—sued the government and Ashcroft in federal district court. Not only did they want Haddad's case to be open to the public, they wanted the Creppy Directive and its "special interest" designations to be declared unconstitutional.

District Court Judge Nancy Edmunds ultimately ruled in favor of the plaintiffs and granted the order. The attorney general and government appealed her decision to the Sixth Circuit, where Judge Keith was now a senior judge.

On appeal, the central legal question was whether the First Amendment allowed the government to unilaterally prevent the public from accessing deportation hearings. The government had no such unilateral right in criminal trials, but deportation hearings were considered administrative proceedings.

Still, this was more than a technical legal question. The nation was wrestling with fear versus liberty, principles versus protection. Talk radio and cable news were afire with such arguments. And they were a regular topic of discussion within the Judge's chambers, where young law clerks discussed how no one seemed to be challenging the Bush administration on the legality of these aggressive policies.

That was about to change.

•   •   •

Praveen Madhiraju, the son of Indian immigrants and a graduate of Northwestern Law School, was one of Judge Keith's law clerks at the time. A twenty-six-year-old living in a rented apartment, he was assigned to research the case and present the judge with a memo. It seemed fitting that Praveen should draw that assignment: the second day of his yearlong clerkship had been September 11, 2001. He'd spent the morning watching the terror unfold on the TV in Judge Keith's chambers—along with fellow clerks and a cluster of judges—until the building was evacuated.

Praveen, now counsel at the Washington, D.C.–based Center for American Progress, recalls that throughout the summer of 2002, there was a sense among the clerks that a huge civil liberties case was in the pipeline. Now, suddenly, it was heading their way. The clerks usually discussed briefs with the judge just before oral arguments. They could see he took a special interest in this case.

"He really engaged us on this well before oral arguments," Praveen remembers. "On this case, when I gave the judge my memo with my recommendation to affirm the district court. . . . I was nervous about it. I was a twenty-six-year-old kid telling the judge that these practices by the Bush administration, not very much questioned, were unconstitutional."

While vigorously engaging his young lawyers, Judge Keith never indicated one way or the other what his decision would be.

Then came August 6, 2002. The case was argued in Cincinnati at the main courthouse for the Sixth Circuit. It drew many members of the media; the debate over civil rights versus national security was as hot as burning coals.

Besides Judge Keith, the panel hearing the controversial case included Judge Martha Craig Daughtrey, one of Keith's colleagues on the Sixth Circuit, and James G. Carr, a federal district judge from Toledo, Ohio, who sat by designation on the court of appeals. During the oral argument, the three judges sat in black robes on the raised platform facing the lone advocates who came before them one by one at the podium. When the clerk of the court announced the start of arguments in the case of *Detroit Free Press v. Ashcroft*, the clerks noticed Judge Keith's behavior. As a senior judge, he was usually deferential to the other judges. On this case, however, he engaged the government right off the bat.

When the assistant U.S. attorney began his argument, Judge Keith interrupted him and asked, "Excuse me, are you familiar with *U.S. v. U.S. District Court for the Eastern District of Michigan*, commonly referred to as the Keith Case?"

"No," said the attorney, somewhat puzzled. "I'm not familiar with that case."

Praveen, watching the proceedings, looked at his fellow clerks knowingly. "It was the wrong answer," he recalls with a laugh. Judge Keith, usually calm and measured, seemed noticeably intense now, sitting at the edge of his seat. He went on to explain the case to the government's attorney: "In that case, the Nixon administration was attempting to unilaterally circumvent the Fourth Amendment and wiretap people without judicial approval. And the Supreme Court unanimously said that was unconstitutional. And it seems to me the same thing is happening here."

As Keith now recalls it, "I was polite to him. But I was flabbergasted that he hadn't done his homework. I was stunned. That case had gone to the Supreme Court—with almost the same issues."

The attorneys and judges had several pointed exchanges throughout the oral arguments. After the intense session, Judge Daughtrey declared, "The case is submitted." The three judges stood, left the courtroom in silence, and retired to the conference room to make their decision.

As the presiding judge, Martha Daughtrey spoke first. "I would affirm the district judge."

"I would also," said Judge Keith.

"I would affirm as well," added Judge Carr.

With all three in agreement, Judge Keith turned to Judge Daughtrey and said, "Judge Daughtrey, I would concur in your opinion affirming the district court judge." With all his years on the court, he knew it was proper to defer to the presiding judge to write the majority opinion in the most important cases; after all, an important opinion can be the defining mark of a judge's career and legacy.

So Judge Keith was surprised by Judge Daughtrey's response.

"No, Damon, I'll give you the case to write."

Judge Keith was floored. Everyone knew this was a powerful case, an important and highly scrutinized one—as evidenced by the cluster of reporters awaiting the court's ruling. That his judicial colleague respected him enough to defer her chance to be the voice of this decision, that she wanted Judge Keith to speak for the court instead, said volumes about her esteem for him.

And made him even more determined to live up to it.

•   •   •

Back in his chambers, the clerks waited in anticipation of the panel's decision. All the lawyers had presented such excellent arguments that no one was sure which way the judges would rule. Finally, the door opened, and Judge Keith strolled back into the office with a little bounce in his step.

"Well," he began, almost coyly, "we have affirmed the district court . . . and Judge Daughtrey has given *us* the opinion to write!"

The clerks jumped and screamed. The chambers were electrified. Something historic was looming, and the young clerks could almost feel it zapping in the air. Judge Keith, however, cautioned them wisely: with huge decisions came huge responsibilities. Drafting an opinion of this magnitude might very well be the most important act of their legal careers. As was his habit after hearing cases in Cincinnati, he took the clerks out for dinner; however, this time he told them to bring their legal pads.

Around the table at the elegant La Normandy restaurant in downtown Cincinnati, Judge Keith was very animated, giving direction as to what cases his clerks should review and reminding them to take a practical, commonsense approach, not to become entrenched in hard views and case law. Praveen was assigned the task of working on the proposed opinion that affirmed the district court. But he had a dilemma. His clerkship was nearly over. He had long been planning a backpacking journey around Eastern Europe—before starting his next job in the "real" world.

"Judge, my last day is in two weeks," Praveen said.

"Well," Judge Keith responded, "I guess we have to finish this in two weeks."

Before they left the restaurant that night, Praveen recalls that the young clerks were given one last edict by their boss: "We will support the Constitution and defend the First Amendment," Judge Keith said firmly.

The law clerks nodded. Their work had already begun.

The next two weeks were like a hive of activity, with clerks putting in twenty-hour days, reading every case they could find, and sending drafts of different sections to Judge Keith, who would comment and send them back for more work. Praveen's office was a monumental mess, cluttered with legal books and papers stacked all around him. Judge Keith would occasionally poke his head in on his young clerk and suggest he review cases such as the *New York Times Company v. United States* and even the late Arkansas senator J. William Fulbright's speech on dissent. Praveen recalls the irony. "With all the benefits of modern research technology—LexisNexis, Westlaw, and Google—there was still no competition for Judge Keith's mind."

Throughout the process, Judge Keith was searching for a way to say what he felt in his heart, what he knew to be the core of the issue—that even in times of fear and security concerns, the principles of the country could not be compromised.

Meanwhile, Praveen, overwhelmed with how important this was, found himself with a case of writer's block.

"I'm so sorry, Judge," he said. "I just can't get anything down."

Judge Keith offered the kind of advice that made him memorable to so many clerks. "Well, Praveen, when I get like that, I find walking on a treadmill helps me think better." Praveen nodded. He said he would try it. He didn't say that he had never used a treadmill before. On his way out, the judge reminded him of a quote from that Fulbright speech, one that had been bouncing around his head. *"In a democracy, dissent is an act of faith."* The judge was looking for something equally staunch to sum up the opinion in the Ashcroft case.

Praveen hit the gym. As he recalls, the treadmill was no dream. He was getting winded rather quickly. But somewhere around the third mile, just as Judge Keith had predicted, his thoughts loosened up. He had an idea. He ran back to the chambers, did a little more research, and finally went in to see Judge Keith, this time with writer's block behind him.

What resulted from that meeting—and all the other work in those frantic summer weeks—was a draft that everyone in Judge Keith's office felt strongly about, so much so that when it was sent over to the two other judges on the panel, there was a real concern that they would water it down. However, in less than a day, Judge Carr wrote back with his comment: "Judge Keith, I concur both as a Judge and as a citizen in this finely written opinion." Judge Daughtrey also wrote back and concurred, and the opinion was submitted.

• • •

In his now historic opinion, Judge Keith found that the First Amendment guaranteed to the public a right of access to deportation hearings. He relied heavily on the Supreme Court's decision in *Richmond Newspapers Inc. v. Virginia*, which ruled that the press and the public have a presumptive First Amendment right to access criminal hearings. Keith noted the similarities between deportation and criminal hearings and detailed how deportation hearings and similar non-criminal proceedings had traditionally been open to the public. Moreover, he reasoned that openness played an important and helpful role in the deportation process. Surveying the history of many non-criminal proceedings, he concluded that "there is a limited First Amendment right of access to certain aspects of the executive and legislative branches."

However, like in *Richmond Newspapers*, this important First Amendment right was not unqualified. Judge Keith reasoned that the government could still close individual hearings if immigration judges made case-by-case determinations that closure was necessary. Certainly the national security interests involved in anti-terrorism investigations were important, but the government had to explain why such interests were implicated in each case. For Judge Keith, the First Amendment was too important to simply rely on the government saying, "Trust us."

An excerpt of the opinion shows how powerful a piece of writing it was and is:

No one will ever forget the egregious, deplorable, and despicable terrorist attacks of September 11, 2001. These were cowardly acts. In response, our government launched an extensive investigation into the attacks, future threats, conspiracies, and attempts to come. As part of this effort, immigration laws are prosecuted with increased vigor. The issue before us today involves these efforts.

Since the end of the 19th Century, our government has enacted immigration laws banishing, or deporting, non-citizens because of their race and their beliefs. . . . While the Bill of Rights zealously protects citizens from such laws, it has never protected non-citizens facing deportation in the same way. In our democracy, based on checks and balances, neither the Bill of Rights nor the judiciary can second-guess government's choices. The only safeguard on this extraordinary governmental power is the public, deputizing the press as the guardians of their liberty. "An informed public is the most potent of all restraints upon misgovernment." "They alone can here protect the values of democratic government."

Today, the Executive Branch seeks to take this safeguard away from the public by placing its actions beyond public scrutiny. Against non-citizens, it seeks the power to secretly deport a class if it unilaterally calls them "special interest" cases. The Executive Branch seeks to uproot people's lives, outside the public eye, and behind a closed door. Democracies die behind closed doors. The First Amendment, through a free press, protects the people's right to know that their government acts fairly, lawfully, and accurately in deportation proceedings. When government begins closing doors, it selectively controls information rightfully belonging to the people. Selective information is misinformation. The framers of the First Amendment did not trust any government to separate the true from the false for us. They protected the people against secret government.

Judge Keith and his clerks were satisfied with their work. They sensed they had written an opinion for the ages and were proud to share it with the world. However, in all the excitement, Judge Keith forgot his young law clerk, Praveen, would be leaving the very next day. Because he tends to develop such close bonds with his law clerks and considers many of them members of his extended family, Keith has a rule that he doesn't want to be told when it's a clerk's last day. So when Praveen reminded him that he was leaving, Judge Keith was stunned.

"He was so brilliant, and he worked so hard," Keith recalls. "I didn't know how our office would exist without him. We were very close."

"It was kind of like the wind got knocked out of him," Praveen recalls. "He had to sit down."

Later that day, Judge Keith called Praveen into his office. They sat at the long conference table. Judge Keith couldn't speak. His eyes welled up with tears. Praveen couldn't hold back his own.

"Judge," he said, "this was the best time of my life, and I'll always do right by you and do the right thing to make you proud."

Praveen left the next day for Europe. Soon after he arrived, he received a call from fellow clerk, Olaitan Senbanjo, who told him to go to the nearest Internet café and read an American newspaper. He hurriedly got dressed, went out, and found the nearest cyber café. He was amazed; Judge Keith's opinion had made the front page of the *New York Times*. Not only that, but on the inside of the newspaper, they had his photo and a separate box of excerpts from the opinion. The *Times* usually reserves that level of coverage for precedent-setting Supreme Court cases.

The opinion was subsequently the subject of a laudatory editorial and a flattering column by then *New York Times* columnist Bob Herbert. It read in part:

> You want an American hero? A real hero?
>
> I nominate Judge Damon J. Keith of the U.S. Sixth Circuit Court of Appeals.
>
> Judge Keith wrote an opinion, handed down last Monday by a three-judge panel in Cincinnati, that clarified and reaffirmed some crucially important democratic principles that have been in danger of being discarded since the terrorist attacks last Sept. 11.
>
> The opinion was a reflection of true patriotism, a 21st-century echo of a pair of comments made by John Adams nearly two centuries ago. "Liberty," said Adams, "cannot be preserved without a general knowledge among the people."
>
> And in a letter to Thomas Jefferson in 1816, Adams said, "Power must never be trusted without a check."

However, not everyone was in agreement. A few months later, the Court of Appeals for the Third Circuit came to the exact opposite conclusion in an identical case, creating what is called a "circuit split." When two or more circuits of the U.S. Courts of Appeals reach different conclusions on the same legal question, the Supreme Court often weighs in and resolves the conflict if the losing party requests it. The Justice Department, however, decided not to appeal the *Haddad* decision. As a result, it currently argues that it has the right to close deportation hearings in all jurisdictions outside of the Sixth Circuit. In reality, it has greatly reduced the practice everywhere.

•   •   •

Despite the circuit split, Judge Keith's opinion in the *Haddad* decision has had far-reaching implications. His warning in *Detroit Free Press v. Ashcroft* that "Democracies die behind closed doors" has become a rallying call for civil libertarians and open-government advocates around the world. Senator Robert Byrd would quote it on the floor of the United States Senate to denounce President George W. Bush's heavy-handed approach to national security. Parliamentarians and advocates in Kenya, Australia, and many other countries around the world have adopted it as their rallying cry to fight for open government and liberty in their corruption-ridden and closed societies.

Timing-wise, it was particularly satisfying to Keith. Even at eighty years old—and in his fifth decade on the bench—the judge still had the passion and conviction to stand tall against an encroachment of Constitutional Rights—even if it meant going against the will of a sitting president. It was a valuable lesson in courage for his young law clerks and a grateful nation.

24.

THE KEITH LAW CLERK FAMILY

To many outsiders, the perception of young would-be lawyers is defined by the movie—and later the television series—"The Paper Chase." In it, students are terrorized by a scowling Professor Kingsfield, shaking in their boots if he even calls their names.

The perception of rookie lawyers is not much better. The stereotype is an overworked, over-caffeinated, late-night drone, scanning files and wondering when the glamour starts.

Neither cliché has much connection to the subset known as "The Damon Keith Law Clerk Family." This elite group begins its indoctrination with a common ceremony—being sworn onto the federal payroll by Judge Keith himself, followed by a warm hug and an exclamation, "Welcome to the Keith Family!"

And it often ends a year later with tears. The kind of tears that suggest, "I don't want to say goodbye."

Why is it that Keith has the most enviable clerkship program around?

Perhaps because he truly views these young minds as an asset. The *Ashcroft* case with Praveen Madhiraju is a perfect example of a judge trusting his clerks and being rewarded many times over.

But that experience was hardly unique. Every year, a small new crop joined Keith's staff. And by the end, they were hard-pressed to leave it.

Clerkships are regarded as the legal world's finishing school. They are extremely competitive and require excellent grades, law review credentials, and impressive work experience. Typically appointed for one to two years, most clerks review filings, write legal memoranda, and prepare written recommendations for the judge they serve. Some write initial drafts of opinions once the judge has decided the outcome of the case.

These posts are considered highly prestigious, as they provide an up-close and personal view of the judicial decision-making process. Some describe it as a fourth year of law school. And a clerkship with a federal judge can open many doors for future employment.

Historically, however, judicial law clerk positions have overwhelmingly gone to privileged white males.

Judge Keith has done a great deal to change that, making the mentoring of young black and minority law clerks an integral part of his legacy. He takes pride in it and always has—even when it wasn't so popular. One afternoon after having lunch with his clerks, Judge Keith stepped off the elevator to his chamber floor accompanied by them. As they walked down the corridor toward his office, they encountered another veteran judge who worked in the same building. Without so much as a hello to any of them, the judge looked at Keith and said, "Damon, I see you've got three black clerks this year."

Offended by the tone and its implication, Keith shot back, "Yes. And I see you've got three white ones."

•   •   •

In a judicial career that has spanned five decades, Damon Keith has hired more minority clerks than any federal judge in U.S. history. He has shown a commitment to diversity in race, gender, religion, and sexual orientation. "People want to know how I've been so successful finding good clerks," he says, "but I just go on instinct. I have no set questions. They are all very smart. I might look at their outside participation in things, their activities even when they are in law school.

"The fact is, these days, many of them come after having researched me. They say, 'I've read all your cases, read all the books. I want to be part of what you do.'"

It wasn't always that way. Keith's first law clerk was a young white lawyer named Irwin Deutsch, the son of Damon's friend Joe Deutsch, who owned a Detroit drug store.

"Irwin was working in the Treasury, and I called him up and said why don't you come back and work with me?" Keith recalls. "I never thought about him being white or black, any more than I think about it today. I look for character, devotion, and quality people."

Harvard Law Professor Lani Guinier, a former clerk of Judge Keith's, says, "He has respect for people with the courage of their convictions. He doesn't try to trim you down to fit into some pre-ordained, model minority. . . . He has an expansive and complex view of merit. He's looking for people who have a sense of mission and who will use the opportunity to assist during their clerkship but, more importantly, to make a difference long term."

•　　•　　•

Most of Keith's law clerks share—and have shared—a passion for equal justice. It is hard to escape that mission once you enter his chambers.

Perhaps as a result, the Keith clerkship alumni make an impressive list—one that helps feed quality candidates back through the process. For example, Judge Eric Clay was recommended as a clerk for Keith by another former Keith clerk named Karl Adkins. The following year, Clay introduced Keith to Guinier, who went on to be a stellar clerk. Keith remembers the encounter fondly.

"I was so impressed with her that I offered her the clerkship right on the spot. But then she told me she had interviewed with Judge Constance Baker Motley, who was one of the reasons she had decided to go to law school. Judge Motley told her before she accepted a clerkship to let her know."

Guinier called Judge Motley from Judge Keith's chambers to inform her that he had offered her a clerkship. Judge Motley told Lani, "Judge Keith is a good judge and a friend of mine. You should accept that offer.'"

After Guinier became very prominent, Motley would often tease Judge Keith, saying, 'Damon, you stole my law clerk!" And Keith would retort, "No, Connie, you simply took her under advisement."

Keith hired Guinier for the 1974 term. She enjoyed it so much that she extended her tenure for an additional year. As with so many of his clerks, departure from the chambers did not end the relationship.

"He became my second father," Guinier says. "He married Nolan and me, even though he had to sit in the copilot seat on the tiny airplane from Boston to the Vineyard. And this is someone who is afraid of flying."

In 1993, Judge Keith enforced that fatherly role after Guinier was unsuccessfully nominated by President Clinton for the position of assistant attorney general for the Department of Justice's Civil Rights Division. Guinier was publicly attacked for her writings by right-wing critics in a high-profile episode that was front-page news. Judge Keith, who says he was "heartbroken for Lani" remained supportive during the ordeal.

"It was really helpful to have someone like Judge Keith to talk to and to be able to maintain a sense of honor and a sense of dignity in the face of this completely unexpected, highly public piling-on by conservative commentators," Guinier says. "There are many people who might have chosen to stay out. . . . . This wasn't his fight. . . . But he provided strong faith in the work that I had done and in the honorable nature of my commitments. He gave me permission to be myself."

•   •   •

In chambers, Judge Keith expects his clerks to be both diligent and prompt. He values intellectual courage as well as strong basic skills—they must be able to read the law, explain the law, write clearly, and communicate effectively. But Keith also believes a clerkship involves life lessons beyond the legal ones. "It's about teaching, not only about the law, but about how to treat people and handle problems," he says.

Judge Edward Ewell, who clerked for Keith, fondly remembers the judge's work ethic, "arriving at his chambers before 8:00 A.M.—after he had run three miles at the YMCA. Judge Keith was also one of the last jurists to leave."

Former Keith clerk and two-term governor of Michigan, Jennifer Granholm, recalls the judge inviting his clerks to "highfalutin events," where he would then "single us out for attention." Being put in the spotlight as young lawyers at social functions gave the clerks exposure and preparation for public life.

Former clerk Spencer Overton, now a professor at George Washington University Law School, recalls Judge Keith telling him one day: "You can do anything if you're willing to give someone else the credit."

And former law clerk Carlos Recio, now an immigration attorney, recalls Keith warning him about issuing harsh statements in writing. "When in doubt, be moderate," Keith advised. "The harsh written word hits ten times harder than the harsh spoken word. Always be civil, particularly in your writing."

Guinier adds that Keith taught her to "acknowledge the humanity" of perfect strangers: "He frequently admonished me to speak to people I did not know. As someone from New York, I had been trained to avoid eye contact with people on the sidewalk, giving them plenty of space to be anonymous. Judge Keith would have none of that. I had to say hello even to perfect strangers. He told me I must always speak to someone who speaks to me, even if I don't know them. I watched him and learned from him how important it is to acknowledge the humanity of perfect strangers and my obligation to show respect to people who recognize or identify with me."

Such fatherly words of wisdom—while not strictly judicial in nature—resonate with his clerks long after they have left Keith's employ. A perfect example comes in a farewell letter to the judge, written by former clerk and now Assistant United States Attorney Muyiwa Bamiduro. In it, he listed the adages Judge Keith had shared during his year in chambers:

> You repeatedly said "do it now," "never be an ingrate," "learn to listen, and listen to learn," "you will never conquer new oceans unless you have courage to lose sight of the shore," "always do what is right and be fair," "take time to acknowledge and greet everyone you come across, even if you do not know them," "treat others with dignity and respect, even if they are not deserving," "be open-minded and not absolute in your position," "be courteous to others," "be transparent," "learn to choose your battles," "you can disagree without being disagreeable," "take no one for granted," "everyone is important," and "always take the high road."

• • •

Those who know Keith well have heard him say, "My law clerks are going to make me famous!" Few judges have had so many clerks rise to such levels of success. And a constant sentiment is that they would not be where they are without the inspiration Keith sparked in them.

The Keith clerks have excelled in a wide variety of settings and career paths—and many have gone on to become judges themselves. Eric Clay, for example, who clerked for Keith from 1972 to 1973 after graduating from Yale Law School, went on to establish one of the nation's leading black-owned private law firms—Lewis, White & Clay, now known as Lewis & Munday—and was nominated by President Clinton to the Sixth Circuit Court of Appeals—the same court on which Judge Keith currently sits. Clay has been there since 1997.

Judge Ewell is on the Third Circuit Court in Wayne County, Michigan. Judge Noceeba Southern, a former clerk, serves on the state's Thirty-Sixth District Court. Former clerk David C. Simmons is the chief administrative law judge for the District of Columbia Commission on Human Rights and an adjunct professor of law at Georgetown.

Recently, former Keith clerk Wilhelmina "Mimi" Wright was appointed to the Minnesota Supreme Court. Justice Wright, an honors graduate of Yale University and a graduate of Harvard Law, is the first African-American woman on that court. Prior to that historic appointment, she served as an assistant U.S. attorney, as a trial judge in Ramsey County, Minnesota, and as an appellate judge on the Minnesota Court of Appeals. Judge Keith has long predicted that a black woman would eventually make the leap to the Supreme Court. He would not be surprised if Justice Wright took that historic spot.

Numerous Keith clerks have served in President Obama's administration. Notably, former Keith clerk Ronald Machen was appointed by President Obama to serve as the U.S. attorney for the District of Columbia, the nation's largest U.S. attorney's office. Machen has referred to Judge Keith as "the biggest mentor of my entire career." Former Keith clerk Rashad Hussain served as deputy associate counsel to President Obama in 2009 and, in 2010, was appointed as the U.S. Special Envoy to the Organization of Islamic Cooperation. Spencer Overton, a professor of law at George Washington University Law School and leading election law scholar, was formerly the principal deputy assistant attorney general for the Office of Legal Policy at the Department of Justice. Recently, another Keith clerk, Sujeet Rao, was appointed as special assistant in the Department of Education's Office of Innovation and Improvement.

Jennifer Granholm has had a distinguished career in public service following her clerkship with Judge Keith. After clerking, she went on to serve as an assistant U.S. attorney in Detroit, was appointed to the Wayne County Corporation Counsel, served as Michigan's attorney general, and was elected as the first female governor of Michigan—serving two terms. Granholm has referred to Judge Keith as her "mentor, friend, father, and center of energy."

Other clerks have similarly gone on to work in federal and state government, including Federal Public Defenders Robin Konrad and Jerome Price and Assistant U.S. Attorneys Blanche B. Cook, Jonathan Grey, Robert Boone, and James Perez. P. Michele Ellison, also a Howard University School of Law graduate, is chief of staff to the acting chairwoman of the Federal Communications Commission. Kevin Smith is chief of staff to the emergency manager of the Detroit Public Schools.

Many of Judge Keith's former clerks have taken the path to academia. They include Jocelyn Benson, interim dean of Wayne State University Law School; Guy-Uriel Charles, professor of law at Duke University School of Law; James E. Coleman Jr., professor of law at Duke University School of Law; N. Jeremi Duru, professor of law at American University in Washington, D.C.; Bonita Reid Gardner, assistant professor of law at University of Detroit Mercy; Jasmine B. Gonzales Rose, assistant professor of law at University of Pittsburgh School of Law; Myles V. Lynk, professor of law at Arizona State University's Sandra Day O'Connor College of Law; and Constance L. Royster, director of development at Yale Divinity School.

In the nonprofit sector, Judge Keith's clerks are also well represented. Constance "Connie" L. Rice, co-founder and co-director of the

Advancement Project in Los Angeles is a former Keith clerk. Praveen Madhiraju currently serves as counsel to the Center for American Progress and a law fellow at the Public International Law & Policy Group.

In the private sector, Judge Keith's clerks have achieved similar greatness. Alex Parrish is a partner at Honigman, Miller, Schwartz, and Cohn LLP—a leading corporate firm in Michigan. Parrish is also the chairman of the board and trustee of Detroit's Music Hall Center for the Performing Arts and on the board of directors for the Detroit Institute of Arts. Claude Bailey is a partner at Venable LLP and was former legal counsel to Washington, D.C. mayor Sharon Pratt Kelly. Christopher Reynolds, group vice president and general counsel for the Legal and Corporate Responsibility Group of Toyota Motor Sales, is a former Keith clerk. Gailon McGowen, the first African-American BMW dealer in the nation, served as a Keith clerk before his transition from law to business. Peter Hurst—founder, president, and CEO of The Community's Bank (TCB)—also comes from the Keith clerk family. Former clerks have also created their own law offices, namely Carlos Recio and Charles Hamilton Houston III, grandson of Judge Keith's mentor at Howard Law.

•   •   •

This is but a sampling of the Keith clerk family. His mentorship, support, and guidance are unwavering to them.

But so is his affection. While other judges can point to impressive accomplishments of former clerks, few, if any, have a policy of not knowing about a clerk's last day—for fear of becoming too emotional at the goodbye.

"I don't want to start crying," Keith admits. "I become very close to my clerks, and it's a very emotional thing for me. We have a family here. A family. And I try to stay away from saying goodbye to family."

Hellos, on the other hand, are more than welcome. And perhaps the greatest tribute Keith can point to as a mentor is that "not a day goes by" that he doesn't get a call from a former clerk—or two or three or four calls—to see how he's doing, bring him up to date, or share some personal news.

If that's not how a family behaves, what is?

Judge Damon J. Keith and Judge A. Leon Higginbotham Jr.

Former Israeli Prime Minister Shimon Peres, Judge Damon J. Keith, and Wayne State University President Dr. Irvin Reid, May 2, 2000.

A. Alfred Taubman, Max M. Fisher (*seated*), and Judge Damon J. Keith at a luncheon honoring A. Alfred Taubman, July 23, 2003.

ABOVE: Judge Robert A. Katzmann, Judge Damon J. Keith, and Supreme Court Justice Sonia Sotomayor at the Marching Toward Justice exhibit, U.S. District Court for the Southern District of New York, New York, 2004.

OPPOSITE, TOP: Congressman Melvin L. Watt, Oprah Winfrey, Judge Damon J. Keith, Senator Debbie Stabenow, and Congressman John Conyers Jr. at Rosa Parks' memorial service in Washington, D.C., October 31, 2005.

OPPOSITE, BOTTOM: Then-Senator Barack Obama and Judge Damon J. Keith. The inscription on the photograph reads: "To Judge Keith—Thanks for your friendship and inspiration! Barack Obama." Rosa Parks's Funeral, Greater Grace Temple, Detroit, November 2, 2005.

To Judge Keith —
Thanks for your friendship and
inspiration!

Barack Obama

ABOVE: U.S. Attorney General Eric Holder and Judge Damon J. Keith at the Wade Hampton McCree Jr. Scholarship Luncheon at the Atheneum Suite Hotel, Detroit, Michigan, February 17, 2010.

OPPOSITE, TOP: Judge Damon J. Keith, Harvard University president Drew Faust, and Professor Lani Guinier when Judge Keith received an honorary degree from Harvard University, Cambridge, Massachusetts, June 5, 2008.

OPPOSITE, BOTTOM: Harry Belafonte and Judge Damon J. Keith at the Keith Biennial Lecture Series, standing in front of the Marching Toward Justice exhibit at the Damon J. Keith Center for Civil Rights, Detroit, Michigan, September 2011.

A. Alfred Taubman walking with Judge Damon J. Keith (with Judge Keith's granddaughter Camara Keith Brown behind Taubman and Keith's daughter Gilda Keith behind Keith) at the groundbreaking ceremony for the new Damon J. Keith Center for Civil Rights, May 17, 2010.

Mitch Albom and Judge Damon J. Keith at the dedication of the Damon J. Keith Center for Civil Rights, Detroit, Michigan, October 19, 2011.

Judge Keith in the lobby of the Keith Center underneath his famous quote, "Democracies Die Behind Closed Doors" at the grand opening of the Damon J. Keith Center for Civil Rights, Detroit, Michigan, October 19, 2011.

ABOVE: Judge Damon J. Keith, Edsel Ford Jr. and wife, Cynthia Ford, at the grand opening of the Damon J. Keith Center for Civil Rights, Detroit, Michigan, October 19, 2011.

OPPOSITE: The Keith family: Daryle Brown, Nia Keith Brown, Camara Keith Brown, Judge Damon J. Keith, Cecile Keith Brown, Debbie Keith, and Gilda Keith.

Judicial Group at Just the Beginning Foundation's Twentieth Anniversary Conference. (The foundation's goal is to increase racial diversity in the legal profession and on the bench). Judge Ann C. Williams chairs the JTBF's Judicial Advisory Committee. Chicago, Illinois, September 2012.

Judge Ann C. Williams.

Judge Damon J. Keith and Supreme Courty Justice Clarence Thomas at the 30th Annual Edward J. Devitt Distinguished Service to Justice Award ceremony, U.S. Supreme Courts, Washington, D.C., December 2012.

PHOTO BY MONICA MORGAN

President Barack Obama hugs Judge Damon J. Keith in Detroit, Michigan, November 2012.

FRIENDS ALONG THE WAY
FROM ROSA TO RUSSIA

S ome people make lists to chronicle their memories. Were one to compile the lists of Damon's Keith's life, his historic judicial rulings would be a long one, his awards and recognitions even longer, but the longest list by far would be of those who have called him "friend."

Evidence of this is found not only in words, but in photos, which overwhelm visitors to Keith's chambers on the second floor of the Theodore Levin United States Courthouse. Stacked almost from floor to ceiling are pictures, some grainy and faded, some fresh and highly pixilated, nearly all containing a beaming Damon Keith in the midst of a handshake or a hug with someone notable. It was Will Rogers who immortalized the saying, "I never met a man I didn't like." Scanning those chamber walls, it is hard to imagine anyone putting that more into practice than Judge Keith.

•   •   •

Some of his famous friendships over the years make both historical and ideological sense. Such is the case, for example, with Thurgood Marshall, or Arthur Johnson, or the indomitable Rosa Parks, whom Keith and most people close to the Civil Rights Movement lovingly referred to as "Mother Parks." Their friendship can be traced back more than fifty years, when Parks moved from Alabama to Detroit in the late 1950s.

It was in the midst of the modern civil rights struggle, and Rosa and her husband, Raymond, had been so badly harassed and threatened by bigots in Montgomery—following Parks's historic refusal to give up her seat on a city bus—that they were not only unable to secure stable work but also believed their lives were in danger.

They decided to move to Detroit, where they both had close relatives, and they hoped Rosa might work as a seamstress. However, upon arrival in the city, they could not find affordable housing. On October 29, 1959, while he was still a young attorney, Keith received a letter from Horace L. Sheffield, his close friend and a prominent labor activist, regarding the Parkses application to live in a Detroit housing project.

"I knew who she was, of course," Keith recalls, "and I remember thinking how courageous she must be. But I never knew our relationship would blossom into such a cherished friendship—one that began with finding her a house."

Keith, at the time, was also an official with the Detroit Housing Commission. Dismayed that a woman of Parks's stature should be scrounging for a safe place to live, he immediately made arrangements to ensure that she and her family could obtain the low-cost housing.

In the ensuing years, Keith and Parks shared many moments at ceremonies or events or civil rights commemorations. Parks worked for several decades in the office of Congressman John Conyers, who was the brother of Damon's friend and former law partner Nate Conyers. Keith sometimes saw Parks leaving work and heading for home. The two of them becamse so close that in 1979, Rosa asked Damon to be the one to present her with the coveted Spingarn Medal at the NAACP annual convention in Louisville, Kentucky.

"Mother Parks" was famously—and sometimes, to Keith, frustratingly—modest. During her life, the judge was persistent in ensuring that her struggle be remembered and honored. Sometimes he had to work harder than others—like the day he now laughingly recalls when one of the most symbolic encounters in modern civil rights history almost didn't happen—because of Parks's modesty.

It was 1990, and Mayor Coleman A. Young had asked Judge Keith to give the opening remarks during Nelson Mandela's June 28 visit to Detroit. It was to be a huge event, with historic Tiger Stadium filled with excited citizens eager to see this international icon of freedom, who, just months earlier, had been released after twenty years in South African prisons.

On the morning of the event, however, Judge Keith learned that Rosa Parks had not been invited. "I was in my office, and I called Parks's assistant, Elaine Steele, and said, 'Elaine, how are you and Mother Parks getting out to the airport when Mandela comes in today?' And she said, 'Judge Keith, we haven't been invited.' I said, 'What? This is unbelievable. You know Mayor Young loves Rosa. This must be an oversight. Something slipped through the cracks. You wait there. I'll come by and pick you and Mother Parks up, and we'll go up to the airport together.'

"So I went by and picked them up, and we drove out to the airport. Rosa was quiet and peaceful as usual. She did say, 'Judge, I'm looking forward to meeting this great man.' And I said, 'I bet he's looking forward to meeting you, too.'"

Sure enough, when Nelson and Winnie Mandela stepped off their airplane, a long line of dignitaries waited on the carpet to greet them, including the governor, the mayor, the president of the UAW, and others.

But as Mandela and his wife surveyed the crowd, Rosa's face caught their eyes. In a flash, they made a beeline straight for her.

"Rosa, Rosa, Rosa Parks," they chanted, warmly embracing the smiling civil rights icon. Nelson Mandela stated that Parks had been his inspiration during the long years he was jailed on Robben Island and that her story had inspired the South African freedom fighters. A photo of that moment—with Parks, the Mandelas, and Judge Keith all at the airport—holds a cherished space in Keith's chambers.

"And to think that almost didn't happen," he says now.

As Parks grew older, Judge Keith took on an informal role as her caretaker, supporting her personal assistant by looking out for Parks's interests. At times, this meant springing into emergency action, as he did on August 31, 1994, when Parks was robbed and physically assaulted in the bedroom of the house where she lived on Detroit's west side. A drug addict named Joseph Skipper entered her home and recognized her. "Hey, aren't you Rosa Parks?" he reportedly said. She said she was. He demanded money, and she gave him three dollars. When he demanded more, she gave him fifty dollars. Before departing, he hit Parks in the face. The incident caused international outrage and landed Skipper in prison. But Parks, then eighty-one years old, suffered anxiety at the prospect of returning to the house.

Judge Keith came to her aid. He called several of his friends in the Detroit business world, including A. Alfred Taubman, the wealthy real estate developer and philanthropist, and Mike Ilitch, the owner of Little Caesars Pizza and the Detroit Tigers and Red Wings sports franchises. Keith told them this was an emergency and that he did not want Parks returning to her old home. Ilitch and Taubman quickly secured a place at the rather exclusive—and very secure—Riverfront Apartments in downtown Detroit, where Rosa Parks would live the rest of her life.

Ilitch, in addition, began paying Parks's living expenses, including her rent at the Riverfront, and arranged for her furniture and other household needs. One of his vice presidents of development, Emmett Moten, would often deliver the checks to the Riverfront himself by hand. Ilitch continued to pay for these expenses month after month, quietly, without public knowledge, out of respect for both Parks and the judge—another unlikely Damon Keith camaraderie.

Ten years later, Judge Keith received a letter from Peter Cummings, the managing partner of Riverfront Associates, saying the Riverfront would extend the right of occupancy to Parks for the remainder of her days at no cost and that a contribution of one hundred thousand dollars would be made to the Rosa Parks Scholarship Foundation of Southeast Michigan.

The friendship between Damon and Rosa continued to the day of her death in 2005. Even then, Judge Keith flew with her body on specially arranged Southwest Airlines flights from Detroit to Montgomery and Montgomery to Washington, D.C., then back to Detroit. Both captains, as well as the flight crew, were black, and en route to Washington from Montgomery, the captain tipped the wings twice in commemoration of Mother Parks. At one point, the flight crew and then the passengers broke into a spontaneous singing of "We Shall Overcome" that brought all to tears.

On the eve of the funeral in Detroit, Parks's body was brought back to the Charles H. Wright Museum of African American History in Detroit for a final public viewing. More than seventy-five thousand admirers gathered on that cold, rainy day. Due to the commotion, a museum curator attempted to end the public viewing prematurely. Judge Keith would have none of that; he spoke to the curator privately, explained the significance of the day's events to him, and insisted that Parks's body remain as it was. Keith prevailed, and, as a result, her admirers did not wait in vain.

"Mother Parks represents everything that my legal and judicial career has stood for," Judge Keith says. "It was an honor to celebrate her life with the rest of the world."

•   •   •

Keith and Parks had a logical friendship. But many of the judge's other close-knit companions seemed, at least at first, less likely. Take his relationship with Taubman. Billionaires were not common in Keith's daily life. Yet these two men prided themselves on their long and committed friendship. They met through Rachel, who, in the 1970s, sat with Taubman on the Public Advisory Board of the University of Michigan Hospitals.

Reflecting on their four-decade friendship, Taubman says he admired and thought the world of Dr. Keith and found her husband to be equally compelling and kind. Over the years, the men got to know each other through their memberships on various civic boards and committees. Like many of Judge Keith's admirers, Taubman says what impressed him most is Keith's ability to reach across contentious lines.

"He's so well respected by such a wide cross-section of the community, because he's a good jurist, good citizen, and good human being," says Taubman. "He's a leader who came up through all ranks. He had to go through nobody."

The friendship between the two men would be tested in 2000 when an investigation into a six-year price-fixing scandal between the Taubman-owned auction house Sotheby's and rival auction house Christie's placed Taubman square in the middle of an international scandal. In a plea bargain with the government, Sotheby's CEO Diana Brooks confessed that prices had been fixed, and she implicated Taubman in the crime, which prosecutors claimed swindled customers out of an estimated one hundred million dollars. Taubman was outraged by the accusations and furiously denied any knowledge of the plot. He accused Brooks of lying to protect herself. The case went to trial in November 2001.

Judge Keith was extremely disturbed at the turn of events, but, as a sitting federal judge, was prohibited from commenting on the matter. Many of his closest friends and judicial peers were aware of his friendship with Taubman and strongly advised Keith to sever ties.

"I had several colleagues warning me to stay away from Al and not to get involved," says Keith. "But he was my friend, I had known him for close to twenty-five years, and I believed in him."

So, in one of the most controversial acts of his long career, Judge Keith agreed to be a character witness at Taubman's trial. More than a few of his judicial colleagues were appalled. No one could recall a sitting federal judge ever testifying in a criminal trial for a friend or acquaintance, especially a trial of this magnitude.

During his testimony, Judge Keith referred to his quarter-century friendship with Taubman, whom he referred to as a man of impeccable integrity and someone who had given so much to the community. Despite Keith's testimony, Taubman was ultimately convicted for anti-trust violations, fined $7.5 million, and imprisoned for ten months in 2002.

Keith's support for his friend didn't end there. During his imprisonment, Judge Keith wrote Taubman once a month with words of encouragement. When Taubman was released in 2003, Keith and another friend, the billionaire businessman Max Fisher, co-chaired a luncheon to honor Taubman and welcome him back to the community.

Fisher was another unlikely member of Judge Keith's friendship circle. An industrialist, philanthropist, and prominent Republican, Fisher was born to Russian immigrants in Ohio and developed a prosperous oil business. He later became a highly successful real-estate entrepreneur. He was a famous fundraiser for Republican politicians and shared close relationships with President Gerald Ford and President George H. W. Bush—not exactly a candidate for the front of Damon Keith's line.

Yet despite their political differences, Fisher and Keith maintained a close friendship until Fisher's death in 2005. His family asked Keith to speak at the funeral.

Similarly, Keith was very close over the years to Henry Ford II, grandson of Henry Ford and the former president of Ford Motor Company, as well as Edsel Ford II, Henry II's son. "Judge Keith has this uncanny, soft way of doing it," Edsel Ford says. "He's just been this bridge to so many communities and people of all races, classes, and backgrounds."

Industrialists. Philanthropists. Captains of Industry. Some have scoffed at such relationships as unseemly for a federal judge. They suggest that, at a minimum, they make him vulnerable to charges of being too cozy with powerful interests.

Judge Keith rejects such accusations the way he would if someone told him he couldn't hang out with his old friends from the neighborhood. He takes pride in having constructive relationships with a wide array of people—those with power as well as those denied it.

His unlikely bond with Natan Sharansky, one of the founders of the Soviet Jewish Refusenik movement in the 1970s, is a perfect example.

Keith met Sharansky in 1976, on a hastily arranged human rights mission visit to the Soviet Union with then NAACP attorney Jack Greenberg, another unlikely friend who asked Keith to go because he knew he was a bridge builder. Keith accompanied Greenberg, despite having little experience with the Soviet Union or its Jewish population, partly because the Refuseniks movement struck a chord with him. While many Jewish people were repressed in Soviet society, the Refuseniks were effectively in captivity. Requesting an exit visa was seen by the Soviets as an act of betrayal. Most requests were refused. As a black man who'd lived through blatant segregation, Keith knew what it felt like to endure second-class status. Not only did he use his connections to earn difficult travel visas for Greenberg and himself, but Rachel, equally moved by the cause, insisted on going with them.

During their two-week human rights mission, the three of them met with Soviet policymakers, administrative officials, and members of the judiciary to discuss the Refuseniks and to advocate on their behalf.

They also had a memorable meeting with Sharansky and human rights activist Dr. Andrei Sakharov, the noted nuclear scientist who won the Nobel Peace Prize in 1975 but was not allowed to leave the Soviet Union to collect it. While the KGB waited outside and watched them, the group lunched at Sakharov's home and discussed the Refuseniks' situation.

The Keiths and Sharansky instantly hit it off. Sharansky was suffering from a serious eye condition that affected his vision. Rachel Keith examined him there and treated his injured eye, causing him to marvel at her skill. Sharansky later gave Judge Keith a tan-colored hat as a keepsake of his visit—but with a caveat; he expected Keith to have that hat with him when they next met.

"When I get my freedom," he said, "I will come to the States, and I will visit you. And you must have the hat."

More than a decade later, after finally being released in exchange for a Soviet spy, Sharansky made good on his promise. He visited Keith in Detroit to thank him. "Your help and support, ever since we first met in Moscow all those years ago, has been a vital part of the campaign which has now succeeded in bringing me home," he wrote.

In a very touching moment, he asked Judge Keith whether he still had the tan-colored hat. To Sharansky's delight, Keith produced it. A photo of them together, with Judge Keith wearing that hat, hangs prominently in Keith's chambers.

Also on that wall is a photo of Keith with William T. Gossett, an unlikely friend to the judge when he desperately needed one.

This happened in the early 1970s, after the famous Keith Case put the judge on a collision course with the federal government and President Nixon himself. In appealing Keith's decision, Nixon and the government sought a writ of mandamus against Judge Keith, trying to force him to release surveillance tapes of the defendants, which Keith had impounded.

Consequently, Keith himself was now being sued.

And he needed a lawyer.

Gossett was, at first, as unlikely a legal choice as he was a friend. To use the vernacular of the time, William T. Gossett was "establishment" all the way, a well-known, high-powered corporate lawyer who grew up in Chickasha, Oklahoma. Gossett was former counsel and vice president at the Ford Motor Company—and married to Elizabeth Hughes, the daughter of Charles Evans Hughes, the former chief justice of the United States. Gossett was a long way from the Detroit streets that Keith had known as a child.

But thanks to Keith's inclination to reach across lines, he and Gossett had become friendly while serving on a Michigan civil rights commission. And in a perhaps deceptively shrewd analysis, Keith understood that someone like Gossett would eliminate any "us" versus "them" image that the government might want to paint.

He was also an awfully good lawyer.

"So I called him up and said, 'Bill, can you meet me down at the Book Cadillac for lunch?' He said OK, and we met," Keith recalls.

"I said, 'Bill you've read about this Sinclair case?' He said he had. 'Well, Bill, they're appealing my decision. And I've been mandamused. I need a lawyer to argue my case in front of the Supreme Court. Would you do it?'

"He was surprised. He said, 'Well, Judge, I don't know. I have to check with my partners. This is a very important case. It deals with national security, and it's highly unusual for a federal judge to be involved in the suit.'

"I told him, 'I know. I understand why you have to check with your partners. And you might as well know one more thing: I don't have the money to pay you for this.'"

To his credit—or perhaps to Keith's credit as a friend—Gossett ultimately agreed to defend the judge pro bono. And he won the case. "I never paid him a nickel," Keith recalls. "He just believed in my situation."

Years later, when Gossett died, his family asked Keith to speak at the funeral. "They told me of all the cases he'd tried, he considered that one the most important. 'He was so proud to represent you,' they said."

• • •

Judge Keith's uncanny ability to make people of all walks feel comfortable has made his circle of friends understandably diverse. Perhaps because of his own humble roots, he obsessively acknowledges and inquires about nearly every person he meets—from the maintenance and mail-room staff at his federal courthouse to perfect strangers that recognize him on his regular walk downtown to his favorite barbershop. He often treats a crew of friends from his gym to Detroit Lions games and his enviable midfield seats. His closest friends call him "D.K.," but many Detroiters simply and affectionately call him "the Judge," as if to say "my" judge.

Keith has managed to do what very few prominent black Americans have; he is considered a "race man," a liberal thinker who is committed to the cause of civil rights yet does not alienate members of the white community or sacrifice friendships with conservatives or Republicans.

His personal bonds are rivaled only by the one he has with his hometown. Having endured two calamitous riots, Keith has had lifetime seats to the deep-seated racial divide in metropolitan Detroit. He has dedicated himself to closing the gap. His rise to the bench was, in part, marked by his exemplary service to the community. And he could not imagine sitting idly by as the same old toxic brew of racism, poverty, alienation, and police brutality combined to keep the region paralyzed with anger and fear.

Once he became a federal judge, his ability to participate in certain civic organizations was constrained. But Judge Keith felt he had to do something to help heal the racial tensions that smoldered beneath the surface. It was not in his DNA to make rulings on people's lives then sit back in his chambers and let the chips fall as they may. He figured a very basic way to make an outreach effort was to literally break bread with people.

●　　●　　●

For years, Judge Keith and his closest friends, Joe Coles, Oliver Broome, and Aubrey McCutcheon, had a tradition during the holidays. They would take turns holding dinners at their homes. Damon and Rachel, for example, would host the group for Thanksgiving.

Following the turmoil of the 1967 riots, and especially after the divisive 1974 election of Mayor Coleman A. Young, the Keiths decided to open that dinner to a wide array of leaders from the community. The idea was to encourage dialogue during the holiday. Thanksgiving at the Keiths' soon became a tradition among some of the most powerful and well known leaders in the metro Detroit region.

"We didn't have any agenda," says Judge Keith. "We just wanted to show that people of power could talk together: Jew and gentile, white and black, male and female. It was a non-partisan affair."

Some of the distinguished attendees included Mayor Young, *Detroit Free Press* publisher David Lawrence Jr. and his family; former Wayne State University and Temple University president David Adamany; Chacona and Dr. Arthur Johnson of the NAACP; Congressman Charles Diggs; federal judge Anna Diggs Taylor; Congressman John Conyers Jr.; Michigan Secretary of State Richard Austin; Longworth Quinn, publisher of the *Michigan Chronicle;* Oscar Feldman, general counsel of the Detroit Pistons; businessman Max Pincus and his wife, Lois; GM Vice President Roy Roberts; the late educator Dr. Cornelius Golightly, and many others.

The discussions were off the record, with an emphasis on respectful and thoughtful listening. The event also demonstrated Judge Keith's ability to recognize future talent. When he first began inviting some of these individuals to his home, many of them had not reached the ranks of prestige that they later achieved. He was able to see them for who they would become.

Gilda Keith, the Keiths' youngest daughter, recalls Rachel immersing herself in the planning of the dinner. "My mother was a gracious hostess. It just came naturally to her. The three of us girls helped do the cleaning and put the elbow grease to the dinner. We washed the silverware, china, set up tables."

Not that the event ever lapsed into formality. Friendship and family were still at its core. One year, Judge Keith tried to get a few of his friends to talk his eldest daughter, Cecile, out of wearing her hair in an Afro, which he felt was unbecoming and too militant looking. Cecile was an undergraduate at the University of Michigan at the time.

"Over the course of the day, I think it was three different people who came over to me and told me my father didn't like my Afro and thought I'd look nicer without it," she remembers with a laugh. "I still kept my Afro, though."

The most dramatic moment would be when Mayor Young arrived. The boisterous Young would usually come in the evening, often wearing his trademark Stetson hat. He was in the prime of his life, as well as his political prime, and his larger-than-life personality would animate the entire event.

He also stayed late. Very late.

"Sometimes he'd still be there talking with my dad and others," Cecile recalls, "and my mother would just wish them all a good night and go to bed."

Those Thanksgiving dinners also became the impetus for another famous meal, courtesy of Judge Keith.

•　　•　　•

The Soul Food Luncheon started in 1987 as a small gathering of individuals interested in celebrating black history month. Judge Keith and Judge Marcia Cooke, the first black female federal district court judge in Florida and a previous magistrate judge in the Eastern District of Michigan, decided they would gather annually to honor one black person who they felt strengthened the community.

They decided to hold the luncheon in Detroit's federal courthouse. This was no small feat. An event like the Soul Food Luncheon could be construed as being exclusionary and controversial—a tough sell in a public facility. But Judges Keith and Cooke managed to obtain the necessary permissions, and the event blossomed into one of Detroit's premier fêtes.

The Soul Food Luncheon now spills from Judge Keith's chambers to the adjacent courtroom of Judge Denise Page Hood and sometimes into yet another courtroom across the hall. Several hundred people join the festivities each year.

Throughout the event, Judge Keith plays host to past and present Michigan governors, Detroit mayors, judges, and politicians from near and far. Regular guests have included governors Jennifer Granholm and Rick Snyder and Senator Carl Levin. Media members are frequent attendees, including local TV and radio hosts and newspaper personnel. Paul Anger, editor and publisher of the *Detroit Free Press*, and his wife, Vickie Dahlman-Anger, are regulars. Even former house majority leader Nancy Pelosi has participated.

Because the event is invitation-only, it's not uncommon for people to call Judge Keith's chambers several months in advance, claiming their invitation is "lost" in the mail. Many arrive an hour early to make sure they don't miss out on the fare, which usually includes ribs, black-eyed peas, fried corn, collard greens, peach cobbler, and other southern foods.

The primary purpose of the Soul Food Luncheon is to celebrate black achievement and to renew a commitment to the community each year. The highlight of the event is the presentation of the Soul and Spirit Humanitarian Award, which is given to acknowledge one black individual's outstanding contributions to the Detroit community. Many prominent figures have received the honor, including Rosa Parks, Dr. Arthur Johnson, Willie Horton, John Conyers, Sam Logan, Aretha Franklin, Detroit mayors Dave Bing, Dennis Archer, and Coleman Young, former Detroit Piston Joe Dumars, Carol Goss, president and CEO of the Skillman Foundation, and Faye Nelson, president and CEO of the Detroit RiverFront Conservancy.

Unlike at the Thanksgiving dinners, political conversations are discouraged at the Soul Food Luncheon. The day is purely about fellowship. In that way, it is a pure reflection of its creator.

"I Don't Work on Your Plantation!"

Speaking Out, Standing Strong

D amon Keith is a bridge builder, a consensus maker, an open-minded judge, civic leader, and grandfather—but he still has his limits. It would be unfair and inaccurate not to relate certain moments when his temper heated up.

There was a time, for example, in the mid-1980s when he was already a member of the Sixth Circuit, hearing cases in Cincinnati. He was staying, as was custom, at the Westin Hotel; and as a guest on a premier floor, he was entitled to a continental breakfast in the VIP lounge. Before he headed to the courthouse, he got himself some coffee and fruit and wandered over to an open seat, next to two white men dressed in business suits. They had briefcases and breakfast plates between them. Both appeared to be in their mid-forties. As Keith went to sit in a nearby chair, they glared at him.

"Do you mind?" one of them snapped. "Can't you see we're busy?"

Keith had heard that tone enough times in his life. "Excuse me, I'm sorry," he said and headed for another corner.

"Here I was, a judge on the court of appeals," he recalls, "and I couldn't even sit down and have a cup of coffee. Like I told Myles that night in the restaurant—I was still black."

But this incident had an unusual twist. An hour later, Keith donned the robe and approached the bench.

"Hear ye, hear ye!" the clerk's voice bellowed. "The United States Court of Appeals for the Sixth Circuit is in session, the Honorable Damon J. Keith presiding!"

Keith sat down.

"Would you call the first case, Mr. Clerk?"

The clerk did. And who should step up? The two men from the lounge. They were the appellants' lawyers.

They saw Judge Keith. And their faces dropped.

"You could tell a mile away," Keith recalls, with a chuckle. "They were dumbstruck. These same guys who didn't want me sitting near them now had to plead their case in front of me. And I was the presiding judge on the panel."

For a moment, nobody spoke. It was Keith's turn to stare. He could have said something. He felt his anger simmering. But he was above the boil.

"Counsel, you may proceed," was all that came from his mouth.

•   •   •

A few years later, Keith would be more vocal. The recipient of his comments would not be a lawyer, but rather a judge—a fellow judge on the Sixth Circuit, to be exact.

His name was James Ryan.

Ryan came out of the navy and had been a military judge in the naval reserve. He was appointed to the Michigan bench by Republican governor William Milliken and was nominated to the Sixth Circuit by President Ronald Reagan in 1985—during a time when the Reagan administration seemed bent on elevating certain types of conservative adjudicators.

Three years later, on November 8, 1988, the day of the presidential election between George H. W. Bush and Michael Dukakis, an issue arose at sixteen polling places in the city of Southfield in Oakland County, Michigan. There were reports that these polling places did not have sufficient "devices" for voting and thus long lines ensued and many voters grew impatient and left.

A lawsuit was hastily filed, around 5 P.M., by lawyers for the Democratic Party in Michigan, seeking to keep the affected polling sites open until 11 P.M. to make up for the delays. A judge in district court approved. But the decision was quickly appealed—not surprisingly —by lawyers for the Republican Party. Judge Keith was contacted and asked if he would hear the emergency appeal. He agreed. He affirmed the district court decision, and the polls remained open the extra hours.

The media hurriedly reported on the story (on election night, any story will be hurriedly reported) and in the weeks that followed, Judge Ryan took an interest in addressing what happened. In February 1989, three months after the event, he asked for a meeting of the active judges on the Appeals Court. He circulated a memo to all of them spelling out what took place and indirectly criticizing the process, suggesting a better method should be in place for such emergency election issues—"for those who, like me, are disinclined to 'fix' that which is not 'broke.'"

Keith could sense the veiled criticism behind the memo. "Judge Ryan was basically saying I didn't have the authority to do what I did, when, as an article III judge, I most certainly did. There was no need for him to send a memo to everybody and call a meeting. If you have an issue, come talk directly to me about it."

Keith was clearly bothered by Ryan's approach. When Ryan began to bring the matter up at the meeting, Keith stopped him in his tracks.

"Jim, you have a plantation mentality," he barked. "And I don't work on your plantation!"

Such exchanges—in the buttoned-down, procedural world of high-level federal courts—are not common. Ryan could tell he had overstepped and began to backtrack. He asked that the record not reflect Judge Keith's comments. But Keith was adamant the other way. "I wanted every word in there," he says now. "He knew exactly what he was doing, and I knew exactly what he was saying.

"The next day, he came to see me, and he was almost in tears. He apologized and asked again for my comments to be removed from the official record. I told him I accepted his apology and I understood. But I said, I'm sorry, Jim, but what happened, happened, and the record needs to reflect that."

•　　•　　•

Judge Keith does not deny his sensitive nature. The same emotions that allow him to cry easily also leave him hurt at slights or insults. Following the old proverb he occasionally paraphrases—"Whom the Devil will destroy, he will first make angry"—he attempts to maintain civil discourse at all times.

But he also realizes that his power, history, and celebrity do not sit well with everyone. He confronted this once in a most unlikely place—his own church.

"I had a very unpleasant experience there," he relates. "It was after our reverend had passed away."

Rev. Frederick Sampson had been a beloved force at Tabernacle Missionary Baptist Church, known by many as "a pastor's pastor." His death in late 2001 left a hole in the congregation. And Judge Keith, as a deacon, was in on the meetings to discuss a replacement.

At one point, he thought about a clergyman he knew from a congregation in Chicago. Damon believed this man might be a good fit for his church. "I'm going to bring his name up at the deacons' meeting," he told Rachel one night.

She gave him a look.

"Don't," she said.

"Why not?"

"Just please don't go, Darling."

"I have to go. I'm a deacon. Anyhow, I think he'd be a good fit. There's no reason for me not to go."

Rachel bit her lip. She knew when a disagreement with her husband was pointless. But even as he drove to the church, Damon wondered about her reticence over such a simple thing.

He went to the deacons' meeting—as he had done countless times before. And at one point, he brought up the name of the reverend he knew out of Chicago, suggesting perhaps he could come in one Sunday and preach.

"As soon as I did that, one of the deacons turned to me and said angrily, 'Who do you think you are? We're not in your courtroom now!'"

"I was stunned. Do you know to this day, that scar is still on me. I couldn't believe it. I had been going to that church for fifty years. I pay my tithings there every year. I serve as a deacon there. But as soon as I suggested something, I got 'Who do you think you are? We're not in your courtroom now!'"

When he went home to Rachel, she saw the crestfallen look on his face. He told her what happened. She looked down and shook her head.

"I had a feeling that would happen," she said, softly. "I figured there'd be resentment because you're a judge."

Keith had experienced resentment before—resistance, jealousy, it was not uncommon. But he never expected it from his fellow deacons whom he sat with every Sunday.

It forever changed his view of his church. To this day, he still makes his tithings and other contributions to that institution but he attends services elsewhere and rarely visits his old church. "I hardly go at all. That really hurt me."

•   •   •

Still, nothing in his professional or civic life has disappointed Damon J. Keith as much as the current direction of his beloved Detroit branch of the NAACP, under the reigns of Rev. Wendell Anthony, a man Keith has said he neither trusts nor condones.

The operations of Detroit's NAACP under Anthony are heartbreaking for the man who helped bring the chapter to prominence when he was a young, ambitious lawyer more than sixty years before.

To understand the deep roots of the judge's feelings, first picture a warm spring evening on Sunday, April 28, 1974. Cobo Hall, Detroit's premiere convention center, jam-packed with people at the elegant Detroit NAACP Fight for Freedom Fund Dinner—commonly referred to as the Freedom Fund Dinner—a tradition Keith helped start with his dear friend Dr. Arthur Johnson nearly twenty years earlier in a hotel ballroom a fraction of Cobo's size.

Judge Keith sat on the main dais along with Mayor Coleman A. Young, Governor William Milliken, Congressman John Conyers, and other dignitaries. Bishop Stephen Spottswood, chairman of the national NAACP's Board of Directors, stood up to give his speech. First, however, he needed to make a brief announcement.

Looking over the audience of thousands of men and women, of all races and ethnicities, he happily declared that federal judge Damon J. Keith had been named the winner of the fifty-ninth NAACP Spingarn Medal—perhaps the highest honor an African American devoted to civil rights could hope to achieve. It would be presented on July 2 at the sixty-fifth annual convention of the NAACP in New Orleans.

"Congratulations, Judge," he said.

The audience jumped to its feet, clapping and roaring with pride. At fifty-one years old, Keith was one of the youngest recipients of the distinctive award. He was so taken aback he began to cry.

Who could blame him? This grandson of slaves and child of a Ford foundry worker was now officially in the company of the most revered African Americans in the nation's history. J. E. Spingarn initiated the gold medal in 1914, to be awarded to a black American for distinguished achievement. It had grown into the NAACP's highest honor. Previous recipients included W. E. B. Du Bois, George Washington Carver, Richard Wright, Dr. Martin Luther King Jr., Paul Robeson, Jackie Robinson, Langston Hughes, Medgar Evers, and two of Keith's personal heroes, Thurgood Marshall and Charles Hamilton Houston.

As he sat there, soaking in the goose-bumping applause, Keith was especially struck—even amused—by the fact that while working his way through college, he used to chauffeur around campus some of the luminaries he would now be identified with in perpetuity.

"Not bad for a poor boy from the west side of Detroit," he thought.

His mind naturally ran back to his early NAACP memories and his first affiliation with the branch in 1950 as a very green lawyer just one year out of law school. At that time, the chapter was too financially strapped to sustain itself. It relied on weekly contributions by a good-hearted numbers runner. Yet working with Art Johnson late at night in that second-floor office of the storefront building on Vernor and St. Antoine reminded Keith of the potent power that sweat and dreams create.

By 1960, ten years after young Damon got involved, the Detroit NAACP had more lifetime members than any branch in the nation. In a few short years, he, Johnson, and others had turned the once struggling chapter into perhaps the most influential in America.

Now jump ahead several decades, from that joyous night at Cobo Hall to April 1993, when the NAACP National Board of Directors selected

Dr. Benjamin Chavis as its new leader. Chavis, a former director of the United Church of Christ's Commission for Racial Justice, was the second youngest person to head the NAACP.

Not long after he took the position, however, Chavis, a Pan-Africanist, began to depart radically from the organization's traditional, middle-of-the-road positions. He met with members of street gangs in Los Angeles, Chicago, and Kansas City and defended rappers like the late Tupac Shakur, whose lyrics had been heavily criticized by many prominent civil rights advocates as misogynistic and misanthropic. He also attempted to develop closer relationships with the more militant elements of the black community as well as the Nation of Islam, which was under the leadership of Minister Louis Farrakhan.

Those actions were alarming to Judge Keith and other older, more traditional members of the NAACP. Chavis argued that he was revitalizing the organization, which his supporters criticized as stodgy and out of touch with black youth. His actions stirred debate. The association with Farrakhan angered important Jewish allies and numerous corporate donors. In addition, it perplexed many national board members, who for years had been the target of much of Farrakhan's hyperbolic criticism.

Chavis's ultimate undoing, however, was his failure to reduce the organization's mounting debt and scandal. Under his watch, the NAACP's debt ballooned to more than three million dollars. A year after taking the reins, it was revealed that in an out-of-court settlement, Chavis had agreed to pay former employee Mary E. Stansel some $332,400 from NAACP coffers without the knowledge or approval of its board. The settlement was to avoid a sexual harassment and sex discrimination lawsuit.

Then, while the board prepared to meet with Chavis on that issue, another woman claimed in a memo to the NAACP board that she, too, was preparing a sexual harassment case against him.

After only eighteen months in office, Chavis was dismissed by the board on August 20, 1994, "for actions inimical to the best interests of the civil rights organization."

From his chambers in Detroit, Judge Keith kept a close watch on the entire episode. It disturbed him greatly. Such national difficulties only underscored his deep reservations about the new leader at the helm of the Detroit branch of the NAACP—a close ally of Chavis's.

The Reverend Wendell Anthony.

Over a two-year period, Anthony repeatedly declined to be interviewed for this book.

·   ·   ·

Anthony shared Chavis's view that the NAACP was out of touch with young people and, in the case of the Detroit branch, the working class and poor, too.

Although officially inactive due to his position as a federal judge, Keith had been alarmed by Anthony's late 1992 bid for the presidency of the Detroit branch, fearing that the wrong person at the helm could spell disaster. Like Keith, many older Detroit members were disturbed that they did not know Anthony and that he had not been previously involved in the branch. A divorced father of two known for his fiery sermons and powerful organizing of boycotts and protests, Anthony was perceived as a stranger kicking in the doors of the branch and declaring that he was about to take over.

There was a very real sense among the older members that Anthony was a loose cannon and that his campaign was fundamentally disrespectful to those who built the branch over decades. "To just come in and try to take over an organization that so many people put so much blood, sweat, and tears into? What kind of message does that send to all those volunteers who worked their behinds off for the NAACP?" Keith ponders.

But Anthony had some powerful supporters, including Ernie Lofton, vice president of the United Auto Workers (UAW), a longtime active member of the Detroit NAACP, and a brilliant and influential tactician. Lofton's backing of Anthony further exacerbated the divisions. Besides his lack of previous involvement, Anthony's proclivity toward confrontation struck the older NAACP members as counterproductive. There was a general feeling that it would scare off white businesspeople and leaders in the nonprofit and political communities throughout the region with whom the branch had worked assiduously to develop good relationships.

Anthony did not shy away from his characterization as a "militant." He had become pastor of Fellowship Chapel five years earlier, following the death of the legendary Reverend James E. Wadsworth Jr., himself once a Detroit NAACP branch president. After ascending to the pastor position, Anthony put Detroit's religious community on notice that he was a different generation of preacher, one who emerged from community activism and whose preaching style was not only imbued with the traditional African liberation theology but also was firmly rooted in the Pan-African perspective.

He aggressively pushed young people to become members of his church and often traveled to Africa, establishing close ties with various Christian and cultural communities there.

Anthony came into prominence after leading a 1990 boycott against the *Detroit Free Press* for what he and his supporters argued was racist and misleading coverage of the city. He also earned substantial attention for his very public and aggressive defense of the city following media coverage of "Devil's Night" on Halloween Eve, a night typically marked in Detroit with the burning of abandoned buildings. Anthony helped organize a trip to New York City to confront ABC News executives over their sensationalistic coverage in a special edition of *Nightline*.

Lofton made that trip as well. He came away impressed by Anthony's tenacity. "I suggested he think about running for president of the Detroit NAACP."

Anthony was hesitant but agreed to seriously consider it only if he was unopposed and had the backing of the unions. Lofton says, "I told him I couldn't prevent any opposition, but I could ensure that we could get the UAW behind him."

During his campaign, Anthony persistently criticized the branch's close ties to the corporate community—which he claimed compromised its ability to challenge discriminatory business practices. He also promised, if elected, to immediately de-emphasize the Freedom Fund Dinner—which sold tickets of up to ten thousand dollars a table—in favor of a much smaller, community-focused dinner for five dollars a plate.

What Anthony did not discuss was that the existing dinner also served a larger purpose. More than eighty percent of the branch's annual operating budget came from corporate donors like GM, Ford, Detroit Edison, and other national foundations, and the bulk of that support came through their sponsorship of the Freedom Fund Dinner. Equally important, the dinner was a marquee event for the chapter and regularly garnered national media attention.

Judge Keith, Dr. Johnson, and others viewed Anthony's plan as not only naive, but reckless. They knew it could almost immediately bankrupt the branch. Keith saw the driving force behind Anthony's campaign as nothing more than raw, hungry opportunism.

His opponent was Charles Boyce, who, in contrast to Anthony, was a longtime branch member, a former chairman of the Freedom Fund Dinner, and a prominent executive for Michigan Bell. His experience in the chapter earned him the backing of both Keith and Dr. Johnson.

Boyce was the safer bet, with a familiar profile and a record of accomplishment that many assumed would be enough to earn a victory.

But the undercurrent of restlessness among some members was real. Lofton and Anthony identified themselves as the "Freedom Caucus" seeking to challenge the "old guard." They suggested experience, longevity of service, and contributions to the local branch were irrelevant. This election was about energy, grassroots appeal, a new dynamic—and new blood.

Stepping down after serving as branch president for three consecutive terms, Dr. Johnson was alarmed at the turn the campaign was taking. He understood the need for new faces. He also knew the dire need to maintain strong and respectful working relationships with the veteran members. This was becoming a showdown of old guard versus new—with the power of the UAW backing the latter. The media became interested and hyped the battle.

The vote was conducted on a cold January day in 1993. So strongly did Judge Keith feel about the ramifications that he went to the election site to observe.

After a ten-week campaign marred by tense rhetoric, Anthony prevailed by a vote of 1,023 to 931.

Even the final tally, however, was not without controversy. Bernice Smith, a lifetime member of the Detroit branch and an original supporter of Anthony's Freedom Caucus, says on the evening of the vote, busloads of people unknown to active members were brought in to vote. "Ernie had brought in busloads of white union members from a Cadillac Local at Livernois and Warren to vote for Anthony," she remembers. "I was quite surprised, and I figured there was some underhanded stuff going on."

Smith, who later became an outspoken critic of Anthony, says she was fine with bringing in new members but became concerned at the blatant way the vote seemed to be manipulated by the process. "We never saw them again after the election. They never came to any meetings. Never. They came for the purpose of electing Wendell Anthony because Ernie was a staunch supporter."

•   •   •

Immediately after winning the election, Anthony called for unity and extended an olive branch by inviting Boyce to sit on his executive board. Boyce accepted, but Dr. Johnson and Judge Keith were much more circumspect. Both men were disturbed by what they, too, saw as the manipulation of the voting process and what they believed was a campaign of insults against the most loyal members of the branch. Because he was a sitting judge, Keith could only privately fume among friends and family. Johnson, however, spoke for Keith and many other older NAACP members when he told the *Detroit Free Press* two days after the vote that the election was the most bitter and divisive one he had seen in his more than forty-year involvement with the branch.

"The election had the unfortunate result, in my view, of insulting a large body of the most faithful and consistent members of this branch," Johnson said.

No sooner did Anthony take office than he began to move longtime NAACP employees and volunteers out of the main office and replace them with his church members, who were faithful only to him. Then he sued senior officials of the national NAACP for defamation of character after they told the *Detroit Free Press* that the Detroit branch had not contributed its fair share to the national board's deficit reduction campaign.

The suit left many longtime NAACP members aghast. Few could remember a local branch suing the national organization for anything, let alone for holding branches accountable. But the message was clear. Anthony had kicked in the door. He was the new sheriff in town—and he would do things his way.

•   •   •

Today, after eight consecutive terms as president of the Detroit branch, Anthony has consolidated his power base and, since 1994, has run for reelection every two years virtually unchallenged. At the same time, Anthony's critics have continued to grow. During the summer of 2010, he was summoned before a federal grand jury to testify in a Detroit corruption case involving kickbacks for city contracts granted while he sat on the Detroit General Retirement System Pension Fund Board. The sight of the president of the Detroit NAACP being hauled before a grand jury and loaded up with lawyers was as appalling as it was unthinkable to longtime NAACP supporters like Keith.

Even as his appearance before the Detroit grand jury set tongues wagging, few were prepared for the bombshell dropped later that fall when the *Detroit Free Press* revealed that the national office of the NAACP had declared the Detroit branch "inactive" and "noncompliant" due to its failure to pay its annual assessment. Inactive status meant that the branch's delegates were prevented from voting on more than one hundred resolutions at the 2010 national convention. Shortly thereafter, the *Detroit News* reported that the branch's new headquarters were in foreclosure status because of its failure to pay approximately forty-seven thousand dollars in back property taxes. Anthony attributed the financial crisis to an overall bad economy and its impact on fundraising. (By January 2011, however, the branch had paid the national office the more than 250,000 dollars it owed in back dues, fees, expenses, and contributions.)

Still, the news of the financial difficulties exploded in Detroit and led some of Anthony's closest allies to distance themselves. Even Lofton expressed his disappointment at how things turned out. "I was initially happy with the choice, but I haven't been involved with the NAACP for the last four years," said Lofton in 2010. "Anthony made me man of the year, trying to get me to come back. But I said no, because I started seeing things that I didn't like."

The ongoing controversies have only served to raise Judge Keith's ire. This was particularly true after Keith learned that the branch had received a one-million-dollar grant for programming activities from the Ford Foundation in 2008 that it did not announce to the public. The grant was the largest single donation ever made to one branch of the

NAACP. And it was awarded around the same time Reverend Anthony was claiming difficulties in fundraising, which only furthered Judge Keith's belief that he was not being honest about branch finances.

Keith asks why they didn't publicize the awarding of such a tremendous amount. "My God—Art and I would have been honored to receive such a grant and would have called a press conference to announce it. Yet you haven't heard a word about it from the branch."

Many question the appropriateness of another organization set up by Anthony called the Freedom Institute, of which Anthony is chairman. Until the spring of 2011, the Freedom Institute, which is not formally affiliated with either the NAACP or the Freedom Fund Dinner, held a series of activities including workshops, speeches, a hip-hop summit, and other political, educational, and cultural events leading up to the Freedom Fund Dinner, including a major event the day before the dinner.

Anthony's critics believed he was unethically using the lure of the Freedom Fund Dinner to attract donors to the Freedom Institute, thus conflating the two and siphoning money away from the NAACP to his personal organization. Why else, Keith asks, schedule the two so close together?

•   •   •

Under Wendell Anthony, the leadership of the Detroit branch has tried to rewrite its history in ways that expunge the contributions of people like Dr. Johnson and Judge Keith. Conspicuously, their names appear nowhere on the organization's website, including the page dedicated to "Branch History" that includes the names of the founders of the Freedom Fund Dinner. Three names are given credit for organizing the inaugural dinner in 1956. But Johnson and Keith—who did everything from sell tickets to pick up the speaker, Thurgood Marshall, at the airport—are nowhere to be found.

In the early 1990s, Judge Keith made sure that the Detroit NAACP was one of the privileged sites to receive a copy of the bronze bicentennial "Bill of Rights" plaque that bears his name. The five-hundred-pound monument was a great source of pride for Keith and a symbolic connection between his early NAACP years and his laudable judicial career.

Sadly, however, the plaque can no longer be found in the halls of the Detroit NAACP. When Judge Keith inquired as to why the plaque was removed, Reverend Anthony told him it was "stolen."

•　　•　　•

It takes a great deal to get Judge Keith angry. Yet he remains convinced that Reverend Anthony has not only abused the authority he wields as president of the Detroit NAACP, but has also ruthlessly tried to thwart the ambitions of anyone who does not accommodate him.

One egregious example came in Anthony's treatment of Eric Clay, Judge Keith's former law clerk and now a fellow judge for the Sixth Circuit Court of Appeals. At the time of his nomination in 1996, Clay had a stellar civil rights record.

Yet Clay claims Anthony threatened to sabotage his appointment because he did not come seeking Anthony's approval. Never mind that at the time his nomination was under consideration, Clay had the support of Judge Keith, Senator Carl Levin, Senator Spencer Abraham, Detroit mayor Dennis Archer, and a host of prominent, well-connected, and distinguished citizens. Equally important, Clay, a Yale Law graduate and classmate of President Clinton, had been a member of the Executive Committee of the Clinton/Gore Finance Committee for Michigan during Clinton's 1992 presidential campaign.

After Clay's original nomination to the bench languished in the Senate for a year, President Clinton nominated him again in January 1997. While the Republican Senate held up the nomination process, Clay and his supporters quietly worked through back channels, reaching out to Justice Clarence Thomas and Utah senator Orrin Hatch, chairman of the Senate Judiciary Committee, to break the impasse.

Finally, just when everyone thought the delay was over, a friend told Clay that he needed to go speak with Reverend Anthony because Anthony was upset that Clay had not come to him to request his support for the nomination.

"He tells me I might have a problem with Reverend Anthony because he doesn't want my appointment to go through and he's going to start calling the White House and complain about it in his capacity as president of the local NAACP," a still-incredulous Clay says.

A lifetime member of the NAACP whose law firm had long done pro bono work for the Detroit branch, Clay could not figure out the problem.

Judge Keith, meanwhile, was enraged by Reverend Anthony's brashness. "I was just flabbergasted. The ABA had given Judge Clay its best rating, he finished Phi Beta Kappa at the University of North Carolina, finished Yale Law School, and the Michigan Bar and *Michigan Chronicle* both supported him."

But the combative Anthony continued to escalate the tension and initiate a public spectacle in Washington during Clay's hearings— "threatening to picket against me in public," Clay remembers.

Finally, after many deliberations and consultations, Clay decided "to go and have a word with Reverend Anthony, since that's what he was demanding." After a nearly three-hour meeting, the tension was eased, and Reverend Anthony withdrew his threat to picket the hearing. Clay, however, was stunned when Anthony blamed Judge Keith as the reason Clay did not seek Anthony's support.

"He knows that I'm close to Judge Keith, so he thinks that he was being snubbed on account of the judge," Clay remembers with a laugh. "Of course, I had not thought about Reverend Anthony one way or the other."

Sadly, little surprises Keith about Wendell Anthony's behavior—particularly when it reflects a desire for power or a taste for confrontation. Keith had witnessed it a few years earlier when Myrlie Evers-Williams, wife of civil rights icon and martyr Medgar Evers, ran for the office of chairwoman of the National Board of Directors of the NAACP.

Evers-Williams was a reluctant challenger to incumbent William Gibson, whose leadership was under attack after the disastrous selection of Chavis, a strong ally and protégé of Gibson's.

The organization was hurting. Its image was taking a beating. Many traditional members saw Evers-Williams as a candidate who had the history, moral authority, temperament, and reputation to restore much-needed integrity to the NAACP.

Anthony, however, didn't see it that way. He was strongly opposed to Evers-Williams's nomination. After a very bitter election, Evers-Williams prevailed by one vote, and Judge Keith arranged for three black federal trial court judges and three black federal appellate court judges to swear her in to office. *Washington Post* columnist Colbert King wrote of the event: "The arrival of Myrlie Evers-Williams is supposed to signal an end to the turmoil and the inauguration of a new day."

But even after all that, Evers-Williams says, her troubles were not over. Reverend Anthony was among a group of dissenters who were disruptive at her first convention as chairperson in Minneapolis that July. As she recalls it, he was not only vocally obnoxious, but also personally rude and disrespectful.

"He and some of his supporters were bent and determined to destroy my first convention in Minneapolis, and they threatened to shut it down," she says.

At eighty years old, Myrlie Evers-Williams says life has taught her that the best way to judge character is to look deep into a person's eyes. She says about Anthony, "When I looked deep into his eyes, all I saw was evil."

Now retired after serving three terms as chairwoman, Evers-Williams says to this day she regards Anthony as nothing more than a "troublemaker."

"Who will stand up to him? It's like everybody was afraid of this man."

Keith—at ninety-one and perhaps no longer worried about mincing words—echoes her sentiment. "Everybody is afraid of the guy. Nobody says anything about all the things he does. But I will not sit quiet. I don't want to see him get away with it."

In Keith's mind, "he's a bully, he's a thug, and a two-bit hustler who has used the presidency of the Detroit branch of the NAACP for his own financial and political gain."

Keith knows that organizations live on long after its shapers are gone. In 2012 the Detroit branch of the NAACP celebrated its one-hundred-year anniversary, the same year that Judge Keith celebrated his ninetieth birthday. He cherishes its history and yearns for a better future. He knows the city of Detroit—his city—is facing challenges today as great, if not greater, than in any period in its history. The population has fallen rapidly, residents are becoming increasingly isolated from prosperous suburbs, schools are in crisis, and, in 2013, the city officially declared bankruptcy and fell under the control of an emergency manager appointed by the governor. All of these problems implicate issues of civil rights and racial justice, which an active, engaged, and revitalized NAACP chapter can address.

Unfortunately, in Keith's view, the present leadership is not up to the task.

Less than nine years from his one hundredth birthday, Damon Keith, who says he has felt the winds of change blow enough times, prays to feel them blow again.

CRUSADER FOR JUSTICE
INTO THE SUNSET

E lie Wiesel once said this about shadows: "Most people think that shadows follow, precede or surround beings or objects; the truth is that they also surround words, ideas, desires, deeds, impulses and memories."

Wiesel spent his adult life chasing the justice he was denied as a child—in his case, as a victim of Nazi concentration camps.

Damon Keith spent his adult life chasing the justice he was denied as a child—in his case, as a victim of racism and prejudicial hate.

Now, like Wiesel, Keith sees shadows wherever he looks. He sees shadows of his grandfather, a slave in this country; he sees shadows of his father and mother, who died at home, aged before their time. He sees shadows of southern trains divided by black and white, shadows of a war, shadows of corpses he buried.

But he also sees shadows of positive influence, of mentors named Davis and Houston and Marshall, of Cousin Ethel who cradled him in kindness, of an Uncle Fred who told him to pursue his dream, of countless citizens he has helped on their American journey, of a bench from which he made the world a little more fair for all of them.

He sees shadows of his children playing, of his grandchildren playing.

Above all else, he sees shadows of his wife.

Even now, he finds it hard to believe that six years have passed without Rachel by his side. He still gets as animated as a schoolkid when recounting his first look at her in her lab coat at the hospital.

"She's the one," he said then.

He still says it today.

They were married for more than half a century. Although neither had wanted to slow their work lives, Damon sensed Rachel was struggling in the final months of 2006. She was fatigued. Her energy lagged. When his daughters wanted to take her on a trip, Keith would protectively refuse, saying, "It's just the two of us here. I don't want anything to happen to your mother. I can't lose her."

Dr. Rachel Keith might have preferred to go on for years, quietly practicing her brilliance in medicine, offering free services for indigent patients, and feverishly supporting civil rights causes. But as the old Emily Dickinson poem suggests, if you cannot stop for death, it will kindly stop for you.

The truth was, Rachel had been battling kidney issues for months. According to Judge Keith, she kept it mostly quiet but went to regular dialysis appointments during the last year of her life. She was scheduled for another one on the morning of Thursday, January 4, 2007.

Three days earlier, in a cold drizzle on the steps of the state capitol, Judge Keith had sworn in Jennifer Granholm, one of his former law clerks, for her second term as governor of Michigan. Rachel, as usual, had been by his side, proud of both her husband and the history the moment signified. The Keiths had been together fifty-four years—long before Michigan had a female governor or a black judge who would conduct her swearing-in ceremony.

They hooked each other's arms.

Neither knew it would be their last public event together.

"Darling, why don't you go down to Washington a day early?" Rachel suggested on the ride home. Damon was scheduled to swear in the Congressional Black Caucus on Thursday morning. "If you go in early, you can get some rest, maybe visit with some people."

"All right, Darling," he said. "That's a good idea."

Before he left, he implored his daughters to make sure they didn't leave their mother alone. When he got down to Washington, he met with friends and ate dinner at his and Rachel's favorite restaurant, the Oceanaire Seafood Room on F Street. After dinner, he hurried back to his hotel room to call his wife and see how she was doing. Her habit was always to brush aside concerns over health issues—"I'm fine," she would say, or "Don't worry, I'm not going anywhere"—but Keith, for some reason, felt a pang of concern.

"Darling, how are you?" he asked over the phone.

"Oh, Gilda just brought me the nicest dinner," Rachel said. "We've been sitting here watching the coverage of the burial services for President Ford. It was a beautiful ceremony. So sad."

Keith nodded to himself. He'd known Ford, who'd died a week earlier at the age of ninety-three. The two men had been honored together at Michigan State University. The judge, too, had watched some of the ceremonies.

"Guess what?" Keith said, lightening the mood. "I ate at our place, the Oceanaire. I had the salmon again."

"And the baked Alaska?"

"Yep. The baked Alaska. I wished you could have been here with me, Darling."

"Me, too. Don't make too long a speech tomorrow."

"I won't."

"Good."

"I love you, Darling."

"I love you, too."

"Let me speak to Gilda and thank her for taking such good care of you. See you when I get home."

That would be their final conversation. The next morning, as Keith prepared for his very public duties, Rachel drove herself to her dialysis appointment.

She never made it.

•　　•　　•

The official record shows that her car stopped near the Detroit Police Department's Western District station, by 7 Mile and Woodward, around 9:50 A.M. Rachel was found outside the station, collapsed, by officers who called the paramedics.

"Apparently, she was driving, and she had a heart attack," Keith recalls. "I think she knew what was happening. That's why she pulled to the station."

At the time, five hundred miles away, Keith was in the midst of the Congressional Black Caucus ceremonies. He was introduced by the scholar Dr. Michael Eric Dyson, a longtime family friend from Detroit—now a professor at Georgetown University—who called upon Judge Keith to give the oath of office.

"Before I did, I shared one of my favorite verses of Martin Luther King," Keith recalls. "Cowardice asks the question 'Is it safe?' Expediency asks the question 'Is it politic?' Vanity asks the question 'Is it popular?' But conscience asks the question, 'Is it right?' And there comes a time when one must take a position that is neither safe, nor politic, nor popular, but one must take it because one's conscience tells you it's right."

"Then I administered the oath to them, saying, 'This is what I want you to do: Do what is right.' And then I sat down. I probably talked too long, as Rachel warned me. But that's what I said."

As soon as he took his seat, someone rushed up to Keith and told him to call his office immediately, that his wife had been hospitalized. Jasmine Gonzales Rose, a Harvard Law School graduate who was clerking for Judge Keith at the time, answered the phone when he called.

"Jasmine, this is Judge," he said. "I hear my wife is in the hospital. How is she doing?"

Jasmine hesitated. She felt the tears falling. Unbeknownst to Keith, his chambers had been notified fifteen minutes earlier that Rachel had passed away. Jasmine didn't know what to do but be direct.

"I told him just straight out, 'I'm so sorry, but Dr. Keith passed away about fifteen minutes ago.' And there was just silence on the line."

Jasmine began to sob. She said she was so sorry, that they didn't have much information other than that Dr. Keith had collapsed and was taken to the hospital.

And that she was gone.

"Thank you, Jasmine," Judge Keith whispered.

•   •   •

Although he had certainly suffered loss before, there was nothing to prepare Damon Keith for this. By his own recollection, "I was empty. Stunned. Here is the most important person in my life having passed—and I just talked to her the night before."

Tellingly, Keith's first act was to fall to his knees—not in grief, but in gratitude. "As soon as I reached my hotel room, I got down and prayed and thanked God for us having all those years together, fifty-four years, all the love and happiness she gave me.

"Then I took a cab to the airport. On the plane, somehow the captain knew, and the flight attendant knew. They came up and said, 'Judge, our condolences. Is there anything we can do?' I said thank you, but I just want to be left alone."

It was the longest trip he would ever take. On the ground, word quickly spread. Dyson mentioned Dr. Keith's passing while being interviewed on C-SPAN. That resulted in a nonstop flood of telephone calls into Keith's chambers that nearly overwhelmed the office. The clerks and staff tried to deal with the tragedy, the confusion over what exactly had happened, and endless inquiries from friends and media.

When Judge Keith landed, he briefly thought about going home. "Then I realized it would just be an empty house. It was just the two of us. But she was gone. I couldn't handle being there by myself."

Instead, he went to his chambers, where about a dozen of his friends and colleagues were waiting, along with his daughters, all of them in shock and shared sadness. Judge Eric Clay and Dr. Arthur Johnson were amongst the consolers. "We all cried together," Keith says. "Debbie and Gilda were there. Debbie said, 'Dad, I went and saw Mom. Would you like to go see her? Her body is still at the hospital. But I said, 'No, I don't want to go.' I didn't want to see her dead. I still couldn't believe she was gone."

He spoke to Cecile, who was in Chicago and was racing home. But for the most part, the man who prided himself on his open and welcoming manner was, for once, too heartbroken for company. "He looked so pale and was hunched over and crying nonstop," Gonzales Rose recalls. He stayed in his office for a long while. Then he came out to comfort his crying clerk, who was three months pregnant at the time.

"He looked at me and held my hand, and he said, 'Jasmine, are you okay? Are you feeling alright?' It touched me so deeply. . . . His capacity for empathy is really amazing."

After things settled down a bit, family and friends began making funeral arrangements and contacting people all over the country. "I remember then senator Obama called the Judge more than once, and Colin Powell wrote multiple letters of support," says Gonzales Rose. "I also remember Judge Keith writing personal letters of thank you back to persons who had heard or read about it. Several months later, we counted nearly a thousand personal letters which he'd sent out."

In a special tribute Judge Keith wrote for the *Michigan Chronicle*, he referred to Rachel as his "darling Valentine whom I continue to treasure, as though she lives."

"You know, they say in a good marriage, over time, you become one," Keith now recalls. "I'd heard people say that and I never believed it. But I tell you, it's true. And it is a wonderful thing. To know each other's idiosyncrasies. To depend on each other. To root for each other. To be such a part of each other. You really do become one."

Their first date was a football game. Their wedding was on a farm. They said goodbye over a telephone. And they parted company for this life in a Baptist church and at a Detroit cemetery. Rachel Hannah Celestine Boone, born in Monrovia, Liberia, died at age eighty-two, having never reached five-feet tall. But through her pioneering medical work, her tireless activism, and her fierce, quiet dignity in raising and standing by her family, she cast a giant shadow that dances before her husband today in all his quiet, reflective moments. It looks achingly familiar.

Because it is part of him.

•   •   •

Perhaps in movie scripts, the story ends here, with the grieving husband leaving this world to follow the truest love he'd ever known. But life is not a gyroscope; it rarely holds in perfect balance. Judge Keith was left to endure solitary years as a widower. He has made the most of it. He continues to work. He still hears cases down in Cincinnati with the Sixth Circuit. He still gives the occasional interview. Although no balm could salve the wound in his heart from Rachel's passing, he can enjoy the many tributes and awards and accolades for his accomplishments—all of which continue to this day.

In 2010, three years after saying farewell to his wife, Keith witnessed with bittersweet tears the groundbreaking of the first legal institute named after a black federal judge. On May 17 of that year, a crowd of nearly a thousand people gathered on the northwest corner of the Wayne State University Law School to officially commence construction on the Damon J. Keith Center for Civil Rights, dedicated to the advocacy and study of civil rights and civil liberties. During the ceremony, Judge Keith, white-haired, slightly stooped, sat quietly on a small stage under a canopy, as U.S. Attorney General Eric Holder related his deep respect and admiration for the man.

Holder spoke eloquently about Keith's fealty to the law, his commitment to civil rights and liberties, and his courage in standing up to two U.S. presidents—in wartime—by demanding that they adhere to the rules of the Constitution, as the citizenry is expected to do. Perhaps most significant, and certainly the most moving, was the attorney general's tribute to Judge Keith for paving the way for African-American lawyers to move into the highest echelons of government and the law by being the fiercest advocate in the nation for the efficacy and importance of the black lawyer.

Turning from the podium to look straight into the eyes of the man he was there to celebrate, the nation's first black attorney general, appointed by the nation's first black president, paused and said softly but firmly:

"Without him, there would be no me."

Three years later, on a cool September morning, Keith would board an airplane and head to West Virginia State University, for the groundbreaking of a residential hall named in his honor—the Judge Damon J. Keith Scholars Hall. In the shadow of a 1939 train that forced him to disembark from the back, in the shadow of his cousin Ethel handing him a sweater, in the shadow of a place where a naive young Detroit teenager would first begin to realize his potential, Damon J. Keith, more than seventy years later, would see his name honored by a new building, and the shadow of his remarkable legacy grow even longer.

•　　•　　•

As Judge Keith now approaches what Nelson Mandela calls "the end of the long walk," the power in Holder's simple, declarative statement, "Without him, there would be no me," succinctly captures a lifetime of effort to achieve racial justice and equality and the willingness to reach back so that he might help another person along.

It is a value first instilled in Keith by his parents, Perry and Annie Keith, and later fortified at Howard University School of Law. It is a value nourished by legal pioneers like Spottswood Robinson III, Oliver Hill, William Hastie, Constance Baker Motley, and, of course, Charles Hamilton Houston and Thurgood Marshall. It is a value that is passed along to every anxious young law school graduate who gets a hug on the first day of a yearlong clerkship and hears a short, white-haired, smiling judge exclaim, "Welcome to the Keith family!"

Damon Keith lived through a time when hatred of black Americans was so pervasive, the U.S. Senate would not even pass an anti-lynching law. In his second year of law school, a South Carolina senator named Strom Thurmond ran a campaign for president redolent with themes of genocidal hatred toward blacks—and swept most of the South.

Keith endured racial insults, police harassment, military inequity, and professional prejudice. He and his generation of black lawyers took these lessons to heart. They did not hesitate to tell America how wrong it was to live under such injustice. They were willing to fight for their freedom and rights. And they consistently honored the struggles of those before them.

So on that majestic May day in Detroit, and that stirring September afternoon in West Virginia, Judge Keith, having become one of the most celebrated judges in U.S. history, knew those praising his lifetime of achievement were also praising the wisdom and foresight of his mentors.

Without them, there would be no Damon Keith.

"We all stand on the shoulders of those who came before us," he says.

•　　•　　•

This book began with a dream deferred, a fiery young law school grad coiled tightly behind a mop bucket in a Detroit bathroom. So perhaps it would be fitting to end it with the long, thunderous, ovations he received in Detroit or West Virginia or at countless other events honoring his accomplishments.

But it will not end there, because as powerful as those moments were, they were more about taking—applause, accolades, affection. And a final scene, to truly befit Judge Damon J. Keith, would be more about giving.

So instead, let the final spotlight fall on a warm Atlanta afternoon in May 2013, when a ninety-year-old Keith walked in the sunshine alongside his granddaughter, Nia Keith Brown, at her graduation ceremony from Emory Law School. As the other graduates and their families looked on, a voice announced over the microphone, "Nia will be hooded by her grandfather, the Honorable Damon Keith, Howard, 1949." And to small applause, he stepped behind his smiling granddaughter and draped the hood over her head as she wiped away tears.

He remembered sitting outside the delivery room the day she was born. He remembered the day, twenty-two years later, when she surprised him by bounding up and saying, "Grandpa, I've decided to go to law school." He remembered saying, "Nia, your grandpa's very happy." And now, hugging her as a photographer snapped a picture, he whispered, "I wish your grandmother could be here. You've made us very proud."

From that moment forward, there was a second lawyer in the Keith family, an extended shadow of the first. And the legal inspiration he had shared with the world was never closer to his heart.

For all the glowing accomplishments in life, the judge's most consistent act is his morning meditation with the Bible. One of his favorite passages, from the book of Micah, reads this way:

"He has showed you, O man, what is good. And what does the LORD require of you? To act justly, to love mercy, and to walk humbly with your God."

Damon Jerome Keith continues to make that walk. And the shadow that follows him—yesterday, today, and forever—is that of a crusader for justice. He casts it long and true.

A NOTE ON SOURCES

INTERVIEWS

Many people gave generously of their time for interviews. Their insights have helped make this biography possible. Interviews were conducted with David Adamany, Cecile Keith Brown, Eric L. Clay, R. Guy Cole Jr., James Coleman, John Conyers, Nathan Conyers, John Dean, Eugene Driker, Harry Edwards, Myrlie Evers-Williams, Edward Ewell, Richard Fields, Edsel Ford II, Jasmine Rose Gonzales, Carol Goss, Jack Greenberg, Lani Guinier, Willie Horton, Joseph L. Hudson, Arthur L. Johnson, Gilda Keith, David Lawrence, Ernie Lofton, Myles Lynk, Praveen Madhiraju, Boyce Martin, Gil Merritt, Mary Mohr, Charles Ogletree, Spencer Overton, Laura Harris Hood Parks, John Payton, William Pickard, Carlos Recio, Don Riegle, Victoria Roberts, Gerald Rosen, Robert Sedler, Bill Simpich, Noceeba Southern, Bernice Smith, Marc Stepp, Alfred Taubman, JuJuan Taylor, Clarence Thomas, Reginald Turner, and Judi Walker-Miles.

PRIMARY SOURCES

This biography has drawn extensively from notes, letters, correspondence, photos, inscriptions, and historic newspaper clippings in the private files of Judge Damon J. Keith. References to primary materials can be found in the main text.

GENERAL REFERENCES

The grandson of former slaves, Damon J. Keith embodies the struggle of African Americans for justice in the wake of failed reconstruction, Jim Crow segregation, and entrenched racial discrimination. His life traces the history of Detroit—wild prosperity in the midst of racial segregation, civil unrest, and the economic struggles of a declining industrial base. Those interested in learning more about Detroit in the 1920s can read Kevin Boyle, *Arc of Justice: A Saga of Race, Civil Rights, and Murder in the Jazz Age* (New York: Henry Holt, 2004); Forrester B. *Washington, The Negro in Detroit: A Survey of Conditions of a Negro Group in a Northern Industrial Center during the War Prosperity Period (Detroit: Research Bureau, Associated Charities of Detroit,* 1920); and Clarence Hooker, *Life in the Shadows of the Crystal Palace 1910–1927: Ford Workers in the Model T Era* (Bowling Green, OH: Popular Press, Bowling Green State University Press, 1997). The American Experience ("Detroit Race Riots 1943," www.pbs.org/wgbh/americanexperience/features/general-article/eleanor-riots) provides a detailed account of the turmoil Damon Keith faced upon his return home from West Virginia State College immediately following the untimely death of his father. Readers interested in the history of Detroit in the postwar years can consult Elaine Latzman Moon, *Untold Tales, Unsung Heroes* (Detroit: Wayne State University Press, 1994) and Thomas J. Sugrue,

The Origins of The Urban Crisis: Race and Inequality in Postwar Detroit (Princeton: Princeton University Press, 2005). Sidney Fine, *Violence in the Model City: The Cavanagh Administration, Race Relations, and the Detroit Riot of 1967* (Ann Arbor: University of Michigan Press, 1989) and National Advisory Commission on Civil Disorders, *Report of the National Advisory Commission on Civil Disorders*, Executive Order 11365 (U.S. Govt. Printing Office, 1968) (commonly referred to as the Kerner Commission Report) provide useful accounts of the 1967 riots.

Judge Keith's life also tracks the arc of the legal fight for civil rights and social justice, running from Charles Hamilton Houston to Thurgood Marshall and into the present. Cynthia Neverdon-Morton, "African Americans and World II: A Pictorial Essay," *Negro History Bulletin* 51, nos. 1–12 (1993), examines the experience of black soldiers in World War II. For excellent treatments of the lives and work of Charles Hamilton Houston and Thurgood Marshall see Genna Rae McNeil, *Groundwork: Charles Hamilton Houston and the Struggle for Civil Rights* (University of Pennsylvania Press, 1984); Rawn James Jr., *Root and Branch: Charles Hamilton Houston, Thurgood Marshall, and the Struggle to End Segregation* (New York: Bloomsbury Press, 2010); and Juan Williams, *Thurgood Marshall: American Revolutionary* (New York: Random House, 1999). Readers interested in thoughtful treatments of the Civil Rights Movement more generally can consult John Egerton, *Speak Now Against the Day: The Generation Before the Civil Rights Movement in the South* (New York: Knopf, 1994); Michael Jay Friedman, *Free at Last: The U.S. Civil Rights Movement* (U.S. Department of State, 2008); *Thomas* Sugrue, *Sweet Land of Liberty: The Forgotten Struggle for Civil Rights in the North* (New York: Random House, 2008); Richard Kluger, *Simple Justice: The History of Brown v. Board of Education and Black America's Struggle for Equality* (New York: First Vintage, 1976); and Harry S. Ashmore, *Hearts and Minds: The Anatomy of Racism from Roosevelt to Reagan* (New York: McGraw-Hill, 1982).

On the bench, Judge Keith handed down landmark ruling after landmark ruling. The principle cases discussed in this biography include *Davis v. Sch. Dist. of City of Pontiac*, 309 F. Supp. 734 (E.D. Mich. 1970) (the Pontiac bussing case); *Garrett v. City of Hamtramck*, 335 F. Supp. 16 (E.D. Mich. 1971) (Hamtramck housing discrimination case); *United States v. Sinclair*, 321 F. Supp. 1074 (1971) (the Keith Case); *United States v. United States District Court for the Eastern District of Michigan*, 407 U.S. 297 (1972) (the Keith Case), *Stamps v. Detroit Edison Co.*, 365 F. Supp. 87 (E.D. Mich. 1973) (employment discrimination case); *Baker v. City of Detroit*, 483 F. Supp. 930, 1002–03 (E.D. Mich. 1979) (police affirmative action case); and *Detroit Free Press v. Ashcroft*, 303 F.3d 681 (6th Cir. 2002) (containing the famous quote "democracies die behind closed doors."). The highly conflicting views of Judge Keith (dissenting) and Judge Merritt over affirmative action can be found in *Aiken v. City of Memphis*, 37 F.3d 1155 (6th Cir. 2004). Judge Keith's recent siring dissent in *Cleveland Firefighters for Fair Hiring Practices v. City of Cleveland*, 669 F.3d 737 (6th Cir. 2012) continues to defend the ongoing importance affirmative action programs.

Judge Keith has made a number of important speeches. Some of these include Damon J. Keith, "Introduction of Associate Justice Thurgood Marshall at the Investiture of Wiley Branton as the Dean of the School of Law" (Howard University School of Law, Washington, DC, November 18, 1978, in the private collection of Damon J. Keith) and Damon J. Keith, "Should Colorblindness and Representativeness Be a Part of American Justice?" (National Bar Association Judicial Council Awards Luncheon, Detroit, MI, July 21, 1981, a transcript of which can be found in box 7, no. 6, Damon J. Keith Law Collection of African-American Legal History, Wayne State University Library, Detroit, MI). In addition, Keith has written about his encounters with President Kennedy and reflected upon his civil rights work in the early 1960s. See, for example, Damon J. Keith, "Anatomy of Racism": Review of Harry Ashmore, *Hearts and Minds: The Anatomy of Racism from Roosevelt to Reagan* (New York:

McGraw-Hill, 1982) in the *Michigan Law Review* 81 (March 1983): 1040. Readers interested in further discussions about the life and jurisprudence of Judge Keith can see Edward J. Littlejohn, "Tribute: Damon Jerome Keith—Lawyer—Judge—Humanitarian," *Wayne Law Review* 42, no. 2A (1996): 321 and Blanche Cook, "A Paradigm for Equality: The Honorable Damon J. Keith" *Wayne Law Review* 47 (Winter 2001/Spring 2002): 1196.

Those caught up in the drama of Judge Keith's life would also be interested in learning more about his close friend and colleague Arthur L. Johnson in Johnson's *Race and Remembrance: A Memoir* (Detroit: Wayne State University Press, 2008).

CHAPTER-SPECIFIC REFERENCES

CHAPTER 1: For information about the work environment for black employees at automobile plants and for more on population and employment numbers, see Clarence Hooker, *Life in the Shadows of the Crystal Palace 1910–1927: Ford Workers in the Model T Era* (Bowling Green, OH: Popular Press, Bowling Green State University Press, 1997), 93–97; "Ebony Salutes Ford Motor Company and Black America," *Ebony*, June 2003, 44; the 1930 Bureau of the Census for Detroit; and Elaine Latzman Moon, *Untold Tales, Unsung Heroes* (Detroit: Wayne State University Press, 1994), 109.

CHAPTER 7: For more on Damon Keith's early years, see "Damon J. Keith: A Guiding Light for Equal Justice Under Law," in *Voices of Historical and Contemporary Black American Pioneers*, ed. Vernon L. Farmer and Evelyn Shepard-Wynn (Santa Barbara, CA: ABC-Clio, 2012).

CHAPTER 13: For more on the participation of Damon Keith, Arthur L. Johnson, and John Conyers in the 1967 Detroit riot described, see Arthur

L. Johnson, *Race and Remembrance: A Memoir* (Detroit: Wayne State University Press, 2008), especially pages 103 and 104. For a discussion of oppressive police practices in Detroit at the time, see Burton Levy's "Cops in the Ghetto: A Problem of the Police System," published in *American Behavioral Scientist* 11:31 (1968). For general information about the effect of the riot in Detroit, including population figures, see Sidney Fine, *Violence in the Model City: The Cavanagh Administration, Race Relations, and the Detroit Riot of 1967* (Ann Arbor: University of Michigan Press, 1989).

CHAPTER 14: For a copy of the *Detroit Free Press* editorial favoring Otis Smith, see "Smith Is the Best Choice for a Federal Court Seat," *Detroit Free Press*, Dec. 3, 1966. The encounter between the group led by Arthur Johnson and Senator Hart is detailed in Arthur L. Johnson's *Race and Remembrance: A Memoir* (Detroit: Wayne State University Press, 2008), especially 145–58.

CHAPTER 15: For quotes regarding Judge Keith's decision to desegregate the schools in Pontiac and to read the opinion, see *Davis v. Sch. Dist. of City of Pontiac*, 309 F. Supp. 734 (E.D. Mich. 1970). The Sixth Circuit's opinion in *Deal*, can be found at *Deal v. Cincinnati Board of Education* 419 F.2d 1387 (6th Cir. 1969). The results of the *Detroit Free Press* survey contrasting black and white attitudes toward separation are reported in Sidney Fine's *Violence in the Model City: The Cavanagh Administration, Race Relations, and the Detroit Riot of 1967* (Ann Arbor: University of Michigan Press, 1989), 370.

CHAPTER 16: For quotes from Judge Keith's initial opinion in the Hamtramck housing discrimination case, see *Garrett v. City of Hamtramck*, 335 F. Supp. 16 (E.D. Mich. 1971). The parameters of Judge Keith's final remedy are outlined in *Garrett v. City of Hamtramck*, 394 F. Supp.

1151 (E.D. Mich. 1975). For coverage of the descendants of the original plaintiffs receiving housing, see Cecil Angel, "Old Wrong Is Made Right in Hamtramck Neighborhood," *Detroit Free Press*, Jan. 18, 2010; "Ed White." Readers can find Keith's landmark employment discrimination case against Detroit Edison at *Stamps v. Detroit Edison Co.*, 365 F. Supp. 87 (E.D. Mich. 1973).

CHAPTER 17: Judge Keith's initial decision can be found at *United States v. Sinclair*, 321 F. Supp. 1074 (1971). For the Supreme Court decision in the Keith Case, see *United States v. United States District Court for the Eastern District of Michigan*, 407 U.S. 297 (1972). For Goulden's assessment of the significance of Judge Keith's role in the "Keith Case" in terms of judicial independence, see Joseph Goulden, *The Benchwarmers* (New York: Ballantine, 1974), 351. For Bill Simpich's assessment of the possible connection between Judge Keith's opinion and the Nixon Watergate scandal, see Bill Simpich, "Wiretapping in America: The Moment of Decision Is Near," *Truthout* (August 24, 2006), *accessed* January 10, 2013, http://archive.truthout.org/article/bill-simpich-wiretapping-america-the-moment-decision.

CHAPTER 18: For Marshall's assessment of Detroit police practices at the time of the 1943 race riots, see Thurgood Marshall, "The Gestapo in Detroit," *The Crisis*, August 1943. For a copy of Judge Keith's ruling that plaintiff police officers were not entitled to a jury trial on their employment discrimination claims for back pay and his response to plaintiffs' concerns over his relationship with Mayor Coleman Young, see *Baker v. City of Detroit*, 458 F. Supp. 379 (E.D. Mich. 1978). For Keith's opinion rejecting the white police officer's claims of reverse discrimination, see *Baker v. City of Detroit*, 483 F. Supp. 930 (E.D. Mich. 1979). On appeal, Judge Gilbert Merritt filed a separate opinion, objecting to Judge Keith giving the city's voluntary affirmative action plan the force of a court order, as seen in *Bratton v. City of Detroit*, 704 F.2d 878 (6th Cir. 1983). The Sixth Circuit order was subsequently modified on rehearing in light of Judge Merritt's objection, as seen in *Bratton v. City of Detroit*, 712 F.2d 222 (6th Cir. 1983). For Carl Rowan's assessment of the significance of the *Baker* decision, see Carl T. Rowan, "Keith Ruling on Police More Vital than *Bakke*," *Detroit News*, Oct. 15, 1979.

CHAPTER 20: For a description of the 1991 Judicial Conference at the College of William and Mary celebrating the two-hundredth anniversary of the Constitution and the Bill of Rights, see "Historic Conference Celebrates Bill of Rights," *The Third Branch*, November 1991. For the College of William and Mary law professor Rodney Smolla's independent recounting of the racist incident in front of the hotel and Judge Keith's response, see Rodney A. Smolla, letter to Edward J. Littlejohn, reprinted in "Tribute Letters of Congratulations," *Wayne Law Review* 42, no. 2A (1996). For Judge Keith's remarks introducing Justice Marshal at the investiture of Howard Dean Wiley Branton, see Damon J. Keith, "Introduction of Associate Justice Thurgood Marshall at the Investiture of Wiley Branton as the Dean of Howard School of Law" (Howard University School of Law, Washington, DC, November 18, 1978, in the private collection of Damon J. Keith), in which he quotes *Regents of Univ. of California v. Bakke*, 438 U.S. 265 (1978) (Marshall, J., dissenting). For Judge Keith's speech on colorblindness, see Damon J. Keith, "Should Colorblindness and Representativeness Be a Part of American Justice?" (National Bar Association Judicial Council Awards Luncheon, Detroit, MI, July 21, 1981, in box 7, no. 6, Damon J. Keith Law Collection of African-American Legal History, Wayne State University Library, Detroit, MI). The widely different opinions over race and affirmative action between Judge Keith and Judge Merritt can be found in *Aiken v. City of Memphis*, 37 F.3d 1155 (6th Cir. 2004). Judge Keith's strong dissent advocating for the continuing need for affirmative action and race consciousness can be found in *Cleveland Firefighters for Fair Hiring Practices v. City of Cleveland*, 669 F.3d 737 (6th Cir. 2012).

CHAPTER 21: Justice Clarence Thomas gave an exclusive interview for this biography, conducted by Rochelle Riley (July 17, 2008). For coverage of Justice Thomas's 2001 remarks before the American Enterprise Institute, see Jeffrey Toobin, "Unforgiven: Why Is Clarence Thomas So Angry?" *New Yorker*, Nov. 12, 2007. Thomas's speech awarding Judge Keith with the Devitt Award can be found at Justice Clarence Thomas, remarks at the 16th Annual Edward J. Devitt Distinguished Service to Justice Award (Wayne State University, Detroit, MI, June 5, 1998), box 40, no. 14, Damon J. Keith Law Collection of African-American Legal History, Wayne State University Library. Judge Leon Higginbotham's letter concerning Justice Thomas's role in presenting Judge Keith with the Devitt Award can be found in A. Leon Higginbotham, "Thomas Must Stand on His Record, Not on His Attendance," *Detroit Free Press*, June 5, 1998. For Judge Higginbotham's statement "I can only think of one Supreme Court justice during this century who was worse than Justice Clarence Thomas," see Kevin Merida and Michael Fletcher, *Supreme Discomfort: The Divided Soul of Clarence Thomas* (New York: Doubleday, 2007). For a general discussion of the controversy surrounding Justice Thomas's invitation to speak at the National Bar Association (NBA) event, see Joan Biskupic, "Clarence Thomas, Another Invitation and Another Flap," *Washington Post*, June 18, 1998. For Judge Keith's introductory remarks at the NBA Memphis Luncheon, see Damon J. Keith, Introduction of United States Supreme Court Justice Clarence Thomas, National Bar Association Judicial Council Luncheon, Memphis, TN, July 29, 1998 (private collection of Damon J. Keith). For a transcript of Justice Thomas's remarks from the National Bar Association Judicial Council Luncheon, National Bar Association, Memphis, TN, July 29, 1998, see PBS NewsHour, www.pbs.org/newshour/bb/law/july-dec98/thomas_7-29.

html?print. The quote from Tony Snow's *Detroit News* article comes from an undated news clipping in Judge Keith's private collection.

CHAPTER 22: For a discussion of the increasing divisions on the Sixth Circuit U.S. Court of Appeals, particularly as they pertain to en banc proceedings, see Harry Wellford, Anna M. Vescovo, and Lundy L. Boyd, "Sixth Circuit En Banc Procedures and Recent Sharp Splits," *University of Memphis Law Review* 30 (Spring 2000): 479. One of the most contentious examples of this arose in the controversial case of *Memphis Planned Parenthood*. Judge Keith's dissent from denial of the en banc petition, as well as the separate statements from Judge Danny Boggs and Judge Alice M. Batchelder can be found in *Memphis Planned Parenthood, Inc. v. Sundquist*, 184 F.3d 600 (6th Cir. 1999). The description of the Sixth Circuit as "the most dysfunctional federal court of appeals in the nation" can be found in Adam Liptak, "Weighing the Place of a Judge in a Club of 600 White Men," *New York Times*, May 17, 2011.

CHAPTER 23: For general background on President George W. Bush's policies concerning closed deportation hearings in "special interest" cases, including specific quotes in the text, see Karen Anderson, "The First Amendment Right of Access Challenged on the Homefront: *Detroit Free Press v. Ashcroft* and *North Jersey Media v. Ashcroft*," *Temple International and Comparative Law Journal* 17 (2003): 545. Judge Keith's opinion in the case can be found at *Detroit Free Press v. Ashcroft*, 303 F.3d 681 (6th Cir. 2002). For Bob Herbert's assessment of the significance of the case and the role of Judge Keith, see Bob Herbert, "Secrecy Is Our Enemy," *New York Times*, Sept. 2, 2002. Illustrations of the cry "Democracies Die Behind Closed Doors" being invoked by others around the globe can be found in 148 Cong. Rec. S8646 (daily ed. Sept. 17, 2002) (statement of Sen. Byrd); The Kenyan Section of the International Commission of Jurists, *Ending Graft as We Know It: The Role of Freedom of Information*

(May 2006), accessed Jan. 7, 2013, www.icj-kenya.org/dmdocuments/
policybriefs/policy_brief3.pdf; Rob Stokes, MP (Australia), *A New
Planning Act for NSW*, accessed Jan. 7, 2013, www.planning.org.au/
documents/item/1907.

CHAPTER 24: For a general discussion of Judge Keith's law clerk family,
including quotes from Governor Jennifer Granholm, see Robert Ankeny,
"Judge of character: From Guinier to Granholm, Keith's Clerks Have Gone
Far," *Crain's Detroit Business*, June 28, 2004. For Governor Granholm's
reference to Judge Keith as her "mentor, friend, father, and center of
energy," see Michael T. Hodges, "Center a Tribute to Judge's Lifetime
Pursuit of Civil Rights," *Detroit News*, May 13, 2010. Information on the
background and accomplishments of former Keith clerk Ronald Machen,
President Obama's appointee to serve as the U.S. attorney for the District
of Columbia, can be found in Marisa M. Kashino, "US Attorney Ronald
Machen: Vince Gray's Worst Nightmare," *Washingtonian*, Oct. 2, 2012.

CHAPTER 25: For a description of the elaborate memorial services prepared
for Rosa Parks, see Kevin Chappell and Scotty Ballard, "Nation Mourns
Civil Rights Legend Rosa Parks," *Jet*, Nov. 21, 2005. Coverage of Judge
Keith's testimony in Mr. Taubman's legal proceedings can be found in
Ralph Blumenthal and Carol Vogel, "Sotheby's Trial Witnesses Attest
to Chief's Integrity," *New York Times*, Nov. 27, 2001.

CHAPTER 26: For background on the shared political beliefs of Benjamin
Chavis and Wendell Anthony, see Jerry Thomas, "Under Chavis, NAACP
Embraces All-except Critics," *Chicago Tribune*, July 11, 1994. For a
discussion of the NAACP Board's dismissal of Chavis as executive
director of the NAACP "for actions 'inimical' to the best interests of
the civil rights organization," see Steven A. Holmes, "N.A.A.C.P. Board
Dismisses Group's Executive Director," *New York Times*, Aug. 21, 1994.

For coverage of the election results putting Reverend Wendell Anthony at the head of the Detroit NAACP, see Brenda J. Gilchrist, "Anthony will Lead Detroit NAACP, Pastor Defeats Longtime Official in Close Vote," *Detroit Free Press*, Jan. 18, 1993. Coverage of Reverend Anthony's summer 2010 federal grand jury testimony concerning kickbacks for city contracts granted while he sat on the Detroit General Retirement System Pension Fund Board can be found in Tresa Baldas, "Grand Jury Hears Wendell Anthony," *Detroit Free Press*, Sept. 30, 2010. Problems associated with the Detroit chapter being placed on inactive status for failure to pay its annual assessment are detailed in David Ashenfelter and Jennifer Dixon, "NAACP Leadership Questioned," *Detroit Free Press*, Nov. 13, 2010. For discussion of the Detroit NAACP being placed in foreclosure status for failure to pay back property taxes, see Leonard Fleming, "Detroit NAACP May Lose Building," *Detroit News*, Dec. 18, 2010. Coverage of Myrlie Evers-Williams being sworn in as executive director of the national NAACP by Judge Keith and other black federal judges can be found in Colbert I. King, "New Day for the NAACP," *Washington Post*, May 13, 1995.

CHAPTER 27: Judge Keith's moving Valentine's Day tribute to his wife, Rachel, can be found in Damon J. Keith, "Valentine's Day Homegoing Tribute," *Michigan Chronicle*, Feb. 21–27, 2007. For coverage of U.S. Attorney General Eric Holder's remarks at the groundbreaking ceremony for the Damon J. Keith Center for Civil Rights at Wayne State University Law School, see Bankole Thompson, "Attorney General Holder Launches Keith Center at Wayne," *Michigan Chronicle*, May 19, 2010.

INDEX